T0367865

A Shadow of Good Things to Come

THE TESTIMONY OF CHRIST THROUGH
THE OLD AND NEW TESTAMENTS

BOOK 1 OF A TWO-PART SERIES

LOUISE A. FUGATE

WESTBOW
PRESS
A DIVISION OF THOMAS NELSON
& ZONDERVAN

WestBow Press books may be ordered through booksellers or by contacting:

WestBow Press
A Division of Thomas Nelson & Zondervan
1663 Liberty Drive
Bloomington, IN 47403
www.westbowpress.com
1 (866) 928-1240

ISBN: 978-1-4908-5127-3 (sc)
ISBN: 978-1-4908-5126-6 (hc)
ISBN: 978-1-4908-5128-0 (e)

Library of Congress Control Number: 2014916164

Printed in the United States of America.

WestBow Press rev. date: 11/14/2014

Copyrights

DEDICATIONS

I dedicate this book to the beautiful family God has given me.
Nothing has given me more earthly pleasure and joy than
knowing and loving my family. My relationship with them
has cultivated a greater understanding of my relationship
with my Father in Heaven. There is no greater legacy I
can pass down to them than my faith in Jesus Christ,
for without Him, we are nothing.

My Husband, Dale
My Mother-in-law, Cordelia Klinger

My Sons and their families:
Randy and Sonya
Daughters, Maren and Nicole

Carey
Daughter, Taylor

Christopher
Sons, Tylor and Michael

I also dedicate this book to all who desire to
learn more about the character of God
and His love and pursuit of mankind.

ACKNOWLEDGMENTS

I thank God for giving me the desire to research and retell the story of how God implemented His plan of salvation through Jesus Christ. It has been an incredible experience, which has only broadened my own trust in my faithful God. I pray that this book will truly glorify His Name!

I thank my husband, Dale, for the patience he has extended to me for over four years, as I have studied and written these pages. It was truly a test for both of us.

I thank Pastor Roger Bodenstab for reading the "very first" rough drafts of the first five chapters, and for his kind words that encouraged me to keep going.

I thank Roy Holloway, who spent countless hours proofreading every chapter, more than once. His comments and suggestions were valued and appreciated. Meeting with Roy and his wife, Pam (my long-time and dearest friend), to review Roy's questions, comments, and ideas sometimes brought us tears of laughter as we reviewed my grammar and language. It was Roy who sent me home to develop study questions at the end of every chapter and gave me the subtitle for this book. Time after time, feelings of frustration would come over me when I would realize I still had a long road ahead of me, and Roy would remind me, "You've come too far to quit now." I knew he was right. "Thank you, Roy for your honesty, expertise, friendship, and your sacrifice of time."

Finally, I thank my mother, Irene June Brown, who went to be with Jesus during the writing of this book. She always believed in me and stood by me, my woman of faith and my encourager, teaching me to say, "Jesus, help me," in times of trouble.

CONTENTS

PREFACE

As a child, I heard many of the Bible stories of the Old Testament and sang many songs about them, but to me, they were random stories about people of faith from long ago. I believed they were true, but I did not understand that the stories were connected in any particular way to each other and were actually telling the story of God's plan to bring salvation to everyone in the world. In fact, for much of my adult life, I thought the Old Testament was more of a history book and that the New Testament was for Christians today. I would even encourage new Christians to stay in the New Testament and especially read Jesus' words written in red. Yet, as strange as it may seem, God used the Old Testament stories about Moses and David to call me back to Him and build my faith.

I had beautiful Christian parents who would have answered my questions, if I had known that there were questions to ask. It was not until I was in my mid-twenties that I listened to an evangelist talk about Jesus being God, the Son, coming down from heaven to be born of the virgin, Mary. I remember being blown away when I realized that Jesus had pre-existed in heaven before He came to earth.

Not too many years ago, I was studying at Life Pacific College. God began to open my eyes to the fact that there was something very important going on in the Old Testament besides a history lesson. I became enthralled when I learned that God's plan of salvation was actually written about in the pages of the Old Testament. The prophets had spoken very profoundly about His coming. I also learned that the Bible stories weren't random at all, but part of a complete picture, which pointed to Christ and the cross.

I became very hungry for God's Word of Truth. The more I learned, the more I found myself wanting to share what I was learning. I thought if I had missed these things that are so relevant to my salvation, there were probably other people who had missed them, too. I was right. As I talked with various women, some of them indicated that they had never heard about some of the things I was telling them. As time went on, I had the opportunity to lead a women's Bible study to share some of the basic things I was learning about. The women related to me that their favorite part was reading the scriptures, allowing God's Word to speak to them as we walked through the Old Testament, story by story.

About three months after my class was finished, I woke up one morning knowing I needed to write a book in much the same way as I had taught my class—allowing the Bible to tell the story of why and how Christ came to save mankind. I believe God laid it on my heart and mind to write this book for someone, even if it was just for me.

It has taken over four years of intense study to write this two-part series. I have been brought to my knees with many tears of frustration as I have cried out to God for direction and knowledge for the "next step." I quoted Philippians 4:13 many times: "I can do all things through Christ which strengtheneth me," knowing that without His help, I would not be able to finish the task I felt He had given me. Two years ago, during "one" of several times when I thought I was finished writing, my family made a "Book" cake for me with Philippians 4:13 on it. They had no idea that it had been my survival scripture for two years.

I hope you will be as inspired in reading this as I have been in writing it, and I hope you will have a few "ah-hah" moments by realizing something you had not realized before. Remember, this is my own personal study, so I encourage you to do further study on areas you feel might be uncertain to you. As I have studied the Scriptures, I have experienced many moments of joy, peace, conviction, revelation, and faith building as God has guided me along the way. It has been through the study of the Jewish nation, that I see my own sinful state of humanity and my need for a Savior. I believe that now, more than ever, we need to know what we believe and why we believe it. God wants us to know Him, and through His Scriptures, He will reveal His truth about Himself to our hearts.

INTRODUCTION

People flock to the theaters to see science fiction movies about aliens, monsters, witchcraft, and super-heroes. We want to believe there is something more than what we can now see. We are desperately searching for the answers to life, looking for hope, trying to make some kind of sense out of the chaos in the world system in which we belong. Through reading the Bible, we find that there really is a God Who is mysterious, supernatural, powerful, and romantic; and He is the supreme "super-hero" of all time. He is full of love and compassion for us, and He has a purpose and plan that does give us hope and a future.

Join me now as we embark on a journey from ancient times to the life of king David to learn more about God's eternal plan for us, and God, the Ancient of Days, will be our guide.

CHAPTER 1

IN THE BEGINNING

What In the World Is Going On?

It seems that almost every time we turn on the television, check the Internet, or read newspapers and magazines, we are inundated with news of political corruption, family breakdown, immorality, human degredation, and violence. Some of us only hear about it, but most of us have been personally affected by it in one way or another. These things are not new. In fact, they have been going on since before the beginning of time. Today, however, we seem to be witnessing the "flowering" of a darker age. It is as if people have lost their way and have no hope or direction. Evil and darkness surround us, and the world's downward spiral seems to be picking up speed. Why is this happening, and when and how will this craziness come to an end?

Do you want to believe there is more to life and the future than what we are seeing right now? Do you want to believe that each one of us has a purpose and a plan for our lives? Would you like to know that someone is watching and is actually in control of this chaotic world in which we live? You can! Believe it or not, the Bible holds the sacred writings of the ancients and tells us where we came from, why we are here, and where we are going.

You might be asking, "How can we be sure that the Bible is true?" The Bible is evidenced by history and science, but there remains many scriptures that must be accepted by faith. Faith is not about reasoning—it is about "believing." Listen to the Bible's own definition of what faith is:

> *"Faith is being sure of what we hope for. It is being certain of what we do not see"* (Hebrews 11:1, NIrV®).

> *"And without faith it is impossible to please God, because anyone who comes to him must believe that he exists and that he rewards those who earnestly seek him"* (Hebrews 11:6, NIV®).

Even though mere men recorded the words that are written in the Bible, the Bible says God inspired them and gave them the words to write:

> *"All scripture is given by inspiration of God, and is profitable for doctrine, for reproof, for correction, for instruction in righteousness: That the man of God may be perfect, thoroughly furnished unto all good works"* (2 Timothy 3:16-17).

Who Is God?

The Bible speaks of eternity. It is hard to try to wrap our minds around the thought that there was no beginning, and that there is no end. In fact, it is mindboggling! One thing we do know for sure is that we are here on this beautiful planet with all its majesty—mountains, rivers, oceans, deserts, plants and trees, and people. We can look up into the sky and see the heavens, the sun, moon, stars, and the universe; and we can study the earth and the depths of the sea. Scientifically, everything has a pattern and design—our solar system, cells, molecules, even our own DNA. We are wonderfully made and have been well provided for. Something did happen to bring this about. God has given us glimpses of that "something" throughout various scriptures in the Holy Bible. The Bible does not give us all the answers or all the details; but it gives us enough to believe in God, if we choose to. Many scientists believe in endless time, not eternity; but the Bible proclaims that God's time is eternity, and that He is the eternal God. The Bible is full of mysteries, and to our surprise, we find that it says that Jesus Christ, Who came to earth over 2,000 years ago, is eternal. His earthly birth was not the beginning of His existence. Listen to what Jesus declares about Himself in the Book of Revelation of the New Testament: *"I am Alpha and Omega, the beginning and the ending..."* (Revelation 1:8).

The Bible says, *"In the beginning <u>God</u> created the heaven and the earth"* (Genesis 1:1). In this verse, the Hebrew word translated *God* is "ĕlôhîym,"[1] which is the plural form of "ĕlôwahh." The meaning of the word "ĕlôwahh" is "...a deity or the Deity...God, god...."[2] Here *God* is referred to as the <u>Deity in plural form</u>.

1 John 5:7 says it this way:

> *"...For there are three that bear record in Heaven, the <u>Father</u>, the <u>Word</u>, and the <u>Holy Ghost</u>: and these three are one."*

The Bible also declares that Jesus created all things, and that He existed before He was the Creator. It is important to note that Jesus is often referred to as the <u>Word</u> in the New Testament. John, inspired by the Holy Spirit, makes a bold statement when he agrees with Jesus' statement in Revelation above, adding that Jesus was the Creator.

> *"In the beginning was the Word* (Jesus), *and the Word* (Jesus) *was with God, and the Word* (Jesus) *was God. The same* (Jesus) *was in the beginning with God. All things were made by him; and without him was not any thing made that was made"* (John 1:1-3).

God, Himself, proclaimed that Jesus was in the beginning, and that He was the Creator. After Jesus came to earth, God, Jesus' Father, told Him this:

> *"And, Thou, Lord, in the beginning hast laid the foundation of the earth; and the heavens are the works of thine hands"* (Hebrews 1:10).

After Jesus' death on the cross, the Apostle Paul said this about Jesus:

> *"For by him* (speaking of Jesus) *were all things created, that are in heaven, and that are in earth, visible and invisible, whether they be thrones, or dominions, or principalities, or powers: all things were created by him, and for him: And he is before all things, and by him all things consist"* (Colossians 1:16-17).

So, according to the Bible, the historical Jesus, Who died on the cross to save us from our sins—the baby boy Who was born to the virgin, Mary, existed in the beginning in the *"...form of God..."* (Philippians 2:6).

As humans, we want to believe that there is a purpose for our lives—we want to believe that we matter. The Bible gives us enough information to know that someone has a purpose and a plan for us—and that things did not just happen by accident. As we study the scriptures about creation, we find out something far deeper than could ever be imagined or hoped for—God had a plan for all people, each of us, before the beginning of time as we know it, and He is still in control of that plan.

Creation

To find out where we came from, and what our purpose really is, we are going to take a journey way back into the past. We are going to visit the period of time we will call "our" beginning. The Bible says that God created the heaven and the earth and everything on the earth, but how did He do it? The following scriptures say that God breathed and spoke creation into existence:

> *"By the word of the LORD were the heavens made; and all the host of them by the breath of his mouth"* (Psalm 33:6). *"For he spake it, and it was done; he commanded, and it stood fast"* (Psalm 33:9).

To some, this may sound like a science fiction story, because it is so unbelievable, yet we find no trouble in accepting these kinds of things when our super heroes do them in the movies. We know we're here, and that something started all of this, so why don't we give the Bible's theory a try. What have we got to lose?

God made His creation for His own pleasure, and we are part of that creation. Why would He do that? He wanted to be near us and love us forever. Have you ever designed or created something just for pure pleasure and satisfaction, or longed to be with someone you loved? Do you remember how you felt? That is how God is. It was God's pleasure to design and create us!

> *"Thou art worthy, O Lord, to receive glory and honor and power: for thou hast created all things, and for thy pleasure they are and were created"* (Revelation 4:11).

The Greek word translated *pleasure* is "thĕlēma." The meaning of the word is "…a determination…choice…purpose…desire…will."[3] God desired to create us; He chose to create us. It was His pleasure!

The Account of Creation

> *"In the beginning God created the heaven and the earth. And the earth was without form, and void; and darkness was upon the face of the deep. And the Spirit of God moved upon the face of the waters"* (Genesis 1:1-2).

The account of creation is recorded in Genesis 1:3-31. The words, *"And God said, Let there be…,"* are repeated at the beginning of each new day that He created. He literally breathed and spoke everything into existence. Remember, we are taking a step of faith—we cannot explain or understand everything about this. The Bible is specific about what God created each day:

Day 1: God created day and night.

Day 2: God separated the heavens, forming the sky.

Day 3: God separated the land and seas, and vegetation.

Day 4: God made the sun, moon, stars.
Day 5: God made sea creatures and birds.
Day 6: God made land animals and man.
Day 7: God Rested.

> *"And on the seventh day God ended his work which he had made; and he rested on the seventh day from all his work which he had made. And God blessed the seventh day and <u>sanctified</u> it because that in it he had rested from all his work which God created and made"* (Genesis 2:2-3).

The Hebrew word translated *sanctified* is "qâdâsh´." The meaning of the word is "…make, pronounce or observe as clean (ceremonially or morally)…consecrate, dedicate…(be, keep) holy…."[4]

Adam, the First Man

Mankind was the highlight of God's creation, and mankind is the only part of creation that was created in God's image! God intended for man to be the caretaker of the earth and all that was within the earth that He had given him.

> *"…the <u>LORD</u> God had not caused it to rain upon the earth, and there was not a man to till the ground. But there went up a mist from the earth, and watered the whole face of the ground. And the LORD God formed man of the dust of the ground, and breathed into his nostrils the breath of life; and man became a living soul. And the LORD God planted a garden eastward in Eden; and there he put the man whom he had formed. And out of the ground made the LORD God to grow every tree that is pleasant to the sight, and good for food; the tree of life also in the midst of the garden, and the tree of knowledge of good and evil"* (Genesis 2:5-9).

God gave man the responsibility *"…to dress it and to keep it"* (Genesis 2:15).

The Hebrew word above translated *LORD* is "Y^{e}hôvâh." The meaning of the word is "(the) self-existent or eternal…Jewish national name of God…."[5]

The Garden of Eden

There are theories that the Garden of Eden was located in ancient "southern Mesopotamia."[6] Mesopotamia was located in the area we now call "eastern Syria and northern Iraq"[7]:

> *"A river watering the garden flowed from Eden; from there it was separated into four headwaters. The name of the first is Pishon; it winds through the entire land of Havilah, where there is gold. (The gold of that land is good; aromatic resin and onyx are also there.) The name of the second river is the Gihon; it winds through the entire land of Cush. The name of the third river is the Tigris; it runs along the east side of Ashur. And the fourth river is the Euphrates"* (Genesis 2:10-14, NIV®).

Cush was "…a place in Mesopotamia." [8]

God called the man He had made, Adam. The Hebrew word translated *Adam* is "'âdâm." The meaning of the word is "…the name of the first man…."[9] God placed the man in the garden in Eden, which He had planted, so that the man could take care of it.

God's law, the Ten Commandments, and other laws He would establish later, did not exist at that time, but God did speak law to Adam. He gave Adam this one rule: *"But of the tree of the knowledge of good and evil, thou shalt not eat of it: for in the day that thou eatest thereof thou shalt surely die"* (Genesis 2:17).

To some it may have seemed like a cruel thing to do—to give Adam a tree that would bear fruit and then tell him not to eat it. We have to remember that God made people with souls and free wills to choose between good and evil—to choose to love and obey Him or reject Him. These choices were, and still are, times of testing and growth in faith, or times of self-destruction and death. We have to choose life or death, because with God, there is no in-between; and there is nothing we can do to change God.

God brought all the animals to Adam so he could give them names, but God understood that Adam still needed a companion for himself, so He created a woman for Adam.

God Creates a Woman

God gave Adam surgery:

> *"And the LORD God caused a deep sleep to fall upon Adam, and he slept: and he took one of his ribs, and closed up the flesh instead thereof; And the rib, which the LORD God had taken from man, made he a woman, and brought her unto the man. And Adam said, This is now bone of my bones, and flesh of my flesh: she shall be called Woman, because she was taken out of Man. Therefore shall a man leave his father and his mother, and shall cleave unto his wife, and shall be one flesh: And they were both naked, the man and his wife, and were not ashamed"* (Genesis 2:21-25).

God showed His love toward Adam by giving him a wife. He wanted Adam to have someone to help him and to share his life with—someone to have children with. He united them together and gave them a gift of sexual intimacy to share that would continually bring them together as one. God gave man, including all living creatures the ability to reproduce offspring after themselves—in their own likeness. He even gave the plants and trees the ability to reproduce. This is evidence of His great love for all He created! God created the earth and its inhabitants for His pleasure, with the hope and desire that men would seek Him and find Him. He desires a relationship with us.

> *"The God who made the world and everything in it is the Lord of heaven and earth and does not live in temples built by hands.*

And he is not served by human hands, as if he needed anything. Rather, he, himself, gives everyone life and breath and everything else. From one man (Adam) *he made all the nations, that they should inhabit the whole earth; and he marked out their appointed times in history and the boundaries of their lands. God did this so that they would seek him and perhaps reach out for him and find him, though he is not far from any one of us. 'For in him, we live and have our being.' As some of your own poets have said, 'We are his offspring'"* (Acts 17:24-28, NIV®).

"To him that by wisdom made the heavens: for his mercy endureth for ever. To him that stretched out the earth above the waters: for his mercy endureth for ever. To him that made great lights: for his mercy endureth for ever: the sun to rule by day: for his mercy endureth for ever: the moon and stars to rule by night: for his mercy endureth for ever" (Psalm 136:5-9).

John Calvin has said, "Creation is entirely dependent on his power for its continued existence," and is "...the theatre of his glory."[10]

In Conclusion

The Bible says that God is made up of three distinct persons, the Father, the Son, and the Holy Spirit (the Trinity); and they live in an eternal realm. In the beginning, Jesus was with God, and He was God. He is the beginning and the ending, and the Father declares that He was the Creator. He created everything for His pleasure by breathing and speaking it into existence. Included in His creation were a man and a woman, made to be together, and they were created in the image of God. 1 Corinthians 11:12 says, *"For as the woman is of the man, even so is the man also by the woman; but all things of God."*

God gave the man and his wife, and all living creatures, the ability to procreate. He placed them in a beautiful garden where they were free and had no need of clothing; and they were not ashamed or embarrassed. He gave them the responsibility of caring for the earth and everything in it. They lacked nothing, and they lived in a paradise, enjoying the very presence of the living God. They were only given one command, and that was to not eat of the fruit from the tree of knowledge of good and evil. It was a simple command, but would they be able to obey it?

Deeper Insights:

1. The Bible says that God is a triune God—the Father, the Son, and the Holy Spirit. Read 1 John 5:7.

   Read the following scriptures that verify the Trinity of God: Galatians 4:4-6; Matthew 3:16-17; Colossians 2:6-10; and 2 Corinthians 13:14.

   Sometimes when God is speaking, He refers to *"Us,"* for example, *"Let us make man in our image"* (Genesis 1:26). After reading the scriptures above, who do you think God is talking about?

2. Jesus says He is the *"beginning and the ending"* (Revelation 1:8). Genesis 1:1 says, *"In the beginning God created the heaven and the earth."* God, the Father, also states that Jesus is the Creator: *"And, Thou, Lord, in the beginning hast laid the foundation of the earth; and the heavens are the works of thine hands"* (Hebrews 1:10).

   Read Isaiah 40:28, which declares that God and the Creator are one in the same.

   Jesus is God, the Son. Read Isaiah 9:6; Matthew 1:23, 28:17-20; John 1:1-2, 15, 17:5; Hebrews 1:3, 6-8; and Philippians 2:10-11.

3. The Bible says that it was God's will and pleasure to create us. Having been created in God's image and His likeness, what do you think it means? Read Genesis 9:6; 1 Corinthians 11:7; 2 Corinthians 3:18; and Colossians 3:7-11.

4. God designed marriage to be between a man and his wife in order to procreate, love, and be in relationship with God. A man is to love his wife, and a woman is to respect her husband. Read Ephesians 5:21-33 and 1 Corinthians 11:8-12.

5. God rested on the seventh day after He was done creating. Read Exodus 20:9-11. Why did He set that day aside for rest?

6. Man cannot prove everything that is written in the Bible. After reading Hebrews 11, how do you think God expects us to believe the Bible?

7. Creation depends on God's sustaining power.

   Read Hebrews 1:10-12 and Colossians 1:16-17. Can you think of some possible things or events that might occur if God were to withdraw His sustaining power?

CHAPTER 2

From Paradise To Paradise Lost

The *Fall* of Man

God had created a beautiful paradise for Adam and Eve to live in, and they were in an intimate relationship with Him, talking and walking with Him. As we look closer, though, we see that there was also a serpent in that paradise (see Genesis 3:1-5). As it turns out, this particular serpent had been a beautiful angel that God had created, who turned bad through pride and rebellion. His name was Lucifer. God had banned Lucifer, and the angels who had rebelled with him, from heaven and cast Lucifer down to the earth. Isaiah 14:12-15 gives us a clue when he prophesize against the king of Babylon:

> *"How art thou fallen from heaven, O Lucifer, son of the morning! how art thou cut down to the ground, which didst weaken the nations! For thou hast said in thine heart, I will ascend into heaven, I will exalt my throne above the stars of God: I will sit also upon the mount of the congregation, in the sides of the north: I will ascend above the heights of the clouds; I will be like the most High. Yet thou shalt be brought down to hell, to the sides of the pit."*

Because of the devil's pride and self-exaltation, God banned the devil and his angels from His presence forever:

*"And there was war in heaven: Michael and his angels fought
against the dragon; and the dragon fought and his angels. And
prevailed not* (they lost the war); *neither was their place found
any more in heaven. And the great dragon was cast out, that old
serpent, called the Devil, and Satan, which deceiveth the whole
world: he was cast out into the earth, and his angels were cast out
with him"* (Revelation 12:7-9).

The angels had gone to a place of confinement and are still there
to this day: *"And the angels who did not keep their positions of authority but
abandoned their proper dwelling—these he has kept in darkness, bound with
everlasting chains for judgment on the great Day"* (Jude 6, NIV®).

*"...God spared not the angels that sinned, but cast them down
to hell, and delivered them into chains of darkness, to be reserved
unto judgment..."* (2 Peter 2:4).

In Ezekiel 26-28, we find an interesting prophecy, in which the
prophet Ezekiel wrote about king Tyrus in a future time, which would
take place after the fall of Jerusalem. It has been included here to
further show the reason for the downfall of Lucifer. King Tyrus, who
was heavily involved in trade with other nations, was ruler over an
extremely wealthy nation; and he was happy about the downfall of
Jerusalem at that time.

*"Son of man, because that Ty´-rus hath said against Jerusalem,
Aha, she is broken that was the gates of the people: she is turned
unto me: I shall be replenished, now she is laid waste: Therefore
thus saith the Lord GOD; Behold, I am against thee, O Ty´-rus,
and will cause many nations to come up against thee, as the sea
causeth his waves to come up"* (Ezekiel 26:2-3).

The Lord continued, *"Now, thou son of man, take up a
lamentation for Ty´-rus, O thou that art situate at the entry of
the sea, which art a merchant of the people for many isles, Thus*

saith the Lord GOD; O Ty´-rus, thou hast said, I am of perfect beauty" (Ezekiel 27:2-3).

This is where the prophecy takes a twist and reveals the true identity of evil behind king Tyrus. Ezekiel could be speaking to no one but Satan, himself. Could king Tyrus have been an evil spirit set up by Satan to rule over the city of Tyrus, or at the very least, a king who was demon possessed?

> *"Thou hast been in Eden the garden of God; every precious stone was thy covering, the sardius, topaz, and the diamond, the beryl, the onyx, and the jasper, the sapphire, the emerald, and the carbuncle, and gold: the workmanship of thy tabrets and of thy pipes was prepared in thee in the day that thou wast created. Thou art the anointed cherub that covereth; and I have set thee so: thou wast upon the holy mountain of God; thou hast walked up and down in the midst of the stones of fire. Thou was perfect in thy ways from the day that thou wast created, till iniquity was found in thee. By the multitude of thy merchandise they have filled the midst of thee with violence, and thou hast sinned: therefore I will cast thee as profane out of the mountain of God: and I will destroy thee, O covering cherub, from the midst of the stones of fire. Thine heart was lifted up because of thy beauty, thou hast corrupted thy wisdom by reason of thy brightness: I will cast thee to the ground, I will lay thee before kings, that they may behold thee"* (Ezekiel 28:13-17).

Jesus would later make a comment to His disciples about Satan's downfall: *"I beheld Satan as lightning fall from heaven"* (Luke 10:18).

The Bible has many names for Lucifer: *"...angel of the bottomless pit..."* (Revelation 9:11); *"...Be-el´-ze-bub, the prince of the devils"* (Matthew 12:24); *"...prince of this world..."* (John 14:30); and *"...angel of light"* (2 Corinthians 11:14), to name a few. Lucifer was filled with pride. His desire to be like God was his downfall. He was a created being and was not equal with God. God, Who is holy, would not tolerate his evil heart. The serpent, which had been thrown down from heaven, along with the angels in his charge who had rebelled with him, was filled with a cesspool of hatred, rebellion and anger against God. The Bible says he was cast down to the earth and he is the "...*god* (small "g") *of this world...*" (2 Corinthians 4:4). When he saw God's beautiful creation of Adam and Eve, he must have seen what he thought was an opportunity to destroy the work of God's hands. He took that opportunity to seduce the woman and fill her heart with pride. He must have thought that if he could deceive her, he could ruin God's plan and everything that God had created. He must have rejoiced in the thought of hurting God! The Bible says in Matthew 13:19 that he is the "...*wicked one....*" He disguised himself as a serpent and came to deceive Eve in the garden.

> *"Now the serpent was more subtil than any beast of the field which the LORD God had made. And he said unto the woman, Yea, hath God said, Ye shall not eat of every tree of the garden? And the woman said unto the serpent, We may eat of the fruit of the trees of the garden: But of the fruit of the tree which is in the midst of the garden, God hath said, Ye shall not eat of it, neither shall ye touch it, lest ye die. And the serpent said unto the woman, Ye shall not surely die: For God doth know that in the day ye eat thereof, then your eyes shall be opened, and ye shall be as gods, knowing good and evil"* (Genesis 3:1-5).

The serpent had called God a liar and had introduced doubt and unbelief about God to the woman. She had never had any reason to mistrust God; but as she listened to the serpent and dialogued with him, she began to question why God would lie to her and why He would want to keep something good from her (the delicious fruit and wisdom). The serpent convinced her that God had not been completely honest with her, and she chose to believe the "creature" rather than her Creator.

The serpent also introduced pride to the woman. Pride says, "I have a right, and I deserve to be happy and have what I want." She must have felt a pull, a powerful temptation to take what she felt God was keeping from her. She no longer felt content and grateful for what God had provided for her and went out from under God's protective covering, choosing to sin against God. She could not have realized that her one act of rebellion would change the course of humanity and the world forever. She may have told herself that God would surely understand that it was important to her. After all, He loved her and wanted her to be happy. Eve talked herself into ignoring what God had said by justifying what she knew was wrong.

> *"And when the woman saw that the tree was good for food and that it was pleasant to the eyes, and a tree to be desired to make one wise, she took of the fruit thereof, and did eat, and gave also unto her husband with her: and he did eat. And the eyes of them both were opened, and they knew they were naked; and they sewed fig leaves together, and made themselves aprons"* (Genesis 3:6-7).

It didn't matter what they wore, they could not hide or take away their disobedience to God—they had fallen into sin.

Adam and Eve Change

For the first time, Adam and Eve hid from God because they felt guilt and shame and did not want Him to see them, because they were aware of their nakedness. Adam's wife had been deceived by the serpent and had given in to his lies and deception, which allowed her heart to be filled with pride and rebellion. Adam simply made a choice to sin. Adam and his wife had gone their own way, choosing to disobey their God—they sinned against God. They had risked everything for a moment of pleasure and false satisfaction. God knew that they had disobeyed Him. One day, God was walking in the garden, which apparently was a common thing for Him to do, but this time Adam and and his wife did something different:

> *"And they heard the voice of the LORD God walking in the garden in the cool of the day: and Adam and his wife hid*

themselves from the presence of the LORD God amongst the trees of the garden. And the LORD God called unto Adam, and said unto him, Where art thou? And he said, I heard Thy voice in the garden, and I was afraid, because I was naked; and I hid myself" (Genesis 3:8-10).

Adam and his wife knew they had done something wrong, because their conscience had become alive—they now knew the difference between good and evil, just as the serpent had told Eve. Adam did not want to take responsibility for his actions of doing wrong, so he cast the blame on his wife and God. When God asked him if he had eaten the fruit and disobeyed Him, Adam said, *"...The woman whom thou gavest to be with me, she gave me of the tree, and I did eat"* (Genesis 3:12).

"And the LORD God said to unto the woman, What is this thou hast done?" And the woman cast blame on the serpent: "The serpent beguiled me, and I did eat" (Genesis 3:13).

The Hebrew word translated *beguiled* is "nâshâ'." The meaning of the word is "...lead astray... to delude...seduce...deceive...."[1]

God Curses His Creation

God didn't even bother to ask the serpent why he had lied and deceived the woman. God knew who he was—He had dealt with him before—and He immediately cursed the serpent and passed judgment upon him:

"...Because thou hast done this, thou art cursed above all cattle, and above every beast of the field; upon thy belly shalt thou go, and dust shalt thou eat all the days of thy life: and I will put enmity between thee and the woman, and between thy seed and her seed; it shall bruise thy head, and thou shalt bruise His heel" (Genesis 3:14-15).

The Hebrew word translated *seed is* "zera'."[2] The meaning of the word is "posterity...child...." The Hebrew word translated *posterity* is "sh^{e}êrîyth." The meaning of the word is "...surviving...remnant...."[3]

In this Scripture, God had prophesied of the coming of His Son, Jesus Christ. "...Commencing with Genesis 3:15, the word 'seed' is regularly used as a collective noun in the singular (never plural)... This technical term is an important aspect of the promise doctrine, for Hebrew never uses the plural of this root to refer to 'posterity' or 'offspring'...Precisely so in Gen 3:15. One such seed is the line of the woman as contrasted with the opposing seed, which is the line of Satan's followers. And then surprisingly the text announces a male descendant who will ultimately win a crushing victory over Satan himself."[4]

This would take place in the future when Jesus would sacrifice His life for us, and the Spirit of God would raise Him from the dead, taking the power away from Satan. In the end, Jesus will become the Victor when He throws Satan into the lake of fire and takes away the last enemy of death (see Revelation 20:10, 14).

God passed judgment of pain and hardship on the woman:

> *"Unto the woman He said, I will greatly multiply thy sorrow and conception; in sorrow thou shalt bring forth children; and thy desire shall be to thy husband, and he shall rule over thee"* (Genesis 3:16).

Up until this point, the man and the woman were equal in their positions. God now made the woman to be in a submissive position to the man. Sin changes things.

God passed judgment on Adam and cursed the ground:

> *"And unto Adam He said, Because thou hast hearkened unto the voice of thy wife, and hast eaten of the tree, of which I commanded thee, saying, Thou shalt not eat of it: cursed is the ground for thy sake; in sorrow shalt thou eat of it all the days of thy life; thorns also and thistles shall it bring forth to thee; and thou shalt eat the herb of the field: in the sweat of thy face shalt thou eat bread, till thou return unto the ground; for out of it wast thou taken: for dust*

thou art, and unto dust shalt thou return. And Adam called his wife's name Eve; because she was the mother of all living. Unto Adam also and to his wife did the LORD God make coats of skins, and clothed them" (Genesis 3:17-21).

Even though they had sinned against their holy God, and sin now stood between God and them, God still loved them and was merciful to them. Sin caused the first spiritual death, and it also caused the first physical death—God killed an innocent animal. God made the first blood sacrifice to cover Adam and Eve with coats made from the skins of animals. The skin coats covered their bodies, but they would still have to deal with the consequences of their sin. Sin would never end for humanity until the end of time, as we now know it. God covered His beloved children, even though they had went their own way. Later He would cover His children again by implementing a temporary sacrificial system of atonement that would be given through Moses. These were really foreshadows of a time that would be coming when Jesus Christ, God's seed, would sacrifice His life, shedding His own blood, to forgive us and cover our sins for eternity.

> *"And the LORD God said, Behold, the man is become as one of us, to know good and evil: and now, lest he put forth his hand, and take also of the tree of life, and eat, and live for ever: Therefore the LORD God sent him forth from the garden of Eden, to till the ground from whence he was taken. So he drove out the man; and he placed at the east of the garden of Eden cheru'-u-bim, and a flaming sword which turned every way, to keep the way of the tree of life"* (Genesis 3:22-24).

Sin had separated them from God and it had separated them from the *"tree of life."* If they had eaten from the *"tree of life,"* they would have lived forever. The *"tree of life"* on earth was guarded and never to be found again, but it is not gone. The Bible says that the *"tree of life"* is in heaven:

"And he showed me a pure river of water of life, clear as crystal, proceeding out of the throne of God and of the Lamb. In the midst of the street of it, and on either side of the river, was there the tree of life, which bare twelve manner of fruits, and yielded her fruit every month: and the leaves of the tree were for the healing of the nations. And there shall be no more curse: but the throne of God and of the Lamb shall be in it; and his servants shall serve him: And they shall see his face; and his name shall be in their foreheads. And there shall be no night there; and they need no candle, neither light of the sun; for the Lord God giveth them light: and they shall reign for ever and ever" (Revelation 22:1-5).

We inherited our sin nature from Adam and Eve. Sin also separates us from God until we come to Jesus, Who is our Tree of Life. 1 John 5:20 says this about Christ:

"And we know that the Son of God is come, and hath given us an understanding, that we may know him that is true, and we are in him that is true, even in his Son Jesus Christ. This is the true God, and eternal life."

When we confess our sins to Him and ask Him to forgive us, He gives us eternal life.

"Who hath saved us, and called us with a holy calling, not according to our works, but according to his own purpose and grace, which was give us in Christ Jesus before the world began, But is now made manifest by the appearing of our Savior Jesus Christ, who hath abolished death, and hath brought life and immortality to light through the gospel...." (2 Timothy 1:9-10).

God is love, but He is also just. In His mercy, He drove Adam and Eve from the garden in Eden and the *"tree of life"* so that they would not live forever in their sinful condition. Suffering over their losses and experiencing hard times might help them realize what they had in their relationship with their Father. Then they might accept responsibility for what they had done. God would wait for them; but for now, they would be spiritually alienated from Him, and all of God's creation would now be cursed. Romans 5:12 gives a description of the condition of mankind: *"Wherefore, as by one man* (Adam) *sin entered into the world, and death by sin; and so death passed upon all men, for that all have sinned."*

As they were leaving the garden, they must have looked back and seen the angels guarding the entrance, knowing they could never return. How sad for them! Their sin had caused a spiritual separation between God and themselves, and a physical separation from their home. Their sin would also be the cause of their death. They were now thrust into an unknown place and an unknown future. They must have been thinking, "If only I had not listened to that serpent and disobeyed God." They must have been overwhelmed with feelings of guilt, failure and fear. What a sense of shame, loss and isolationism! They were experiencing spiritual death.

In Conclusion

Lucifer, because of his pride, had been banned from God's presence and thrown to the earth where he became the god of the earth. God imprisoned the angels who had rebelled and fell with him. In his hatred for God, he had lied to Eve, causing her to doubt God and sin, and in turn, she enticed her husband to do the same. Everything had changed from that moment on—mankind, animals, and the earth, were now in a state of deterioration. Everything would now suffer, toil, and die. Hostility had entered into the world God had created for man, and it would affect the animals, plants, and all future people. Even the relationship between husband and wife had changed. Sin had placed Adam and Eve under the curse of sin, which is death. No, they didn't die right away while they were in the garden, but they had died spiritually and eventually they did die physically, returning to the dust of the ground, as God had said. From that time forward, all mankind would inherit death, physically and spiritually. God never intended it to be that way, but He knew before He created it that it would be.

It appeared as though the serpent had ruined God's plan for man and everything He had created; but God's plan of eternity with His creation would not be stifled. He was not surprised or shocked at what happened with Adam and Eve, and He knew what He was going to do to redeem mankind back to Him for eternity, and He even prophesied it to the devil. It would only be a matter of time until His plan of redemption would be fulfilled, but many things would have to happen before that could take place. For now, God would begin to select people who would have faith in Him, and who would pass that faith on to their descendants. He would establish a line of people, from whose lineage, His Son, Jesus, would come to earth and be born.

Deeper Insights:

1. Read Ezekiel 28:13-15 and Colossians 1:14-17. Based on these two scriptures, do you believe that Jesus created Lucifer?

2. Lucifer was banned from heaven because his heart was filled with pride and self-exaltation, and he is still at work today. Can you think of ways that pride might show itself in the hearts of people, for example, pride tells us that we have a right to have our own way, even if that way is wrong. Read Proverbs 13:10; Proverbs 16:18; Proverbs 26:12; Daniel 5:20; Psalm 10:4; and Jeremiah 49:16.

   What are some of the consequences that follow when we allow pride to rule in our hearts and minds?

3. Satan, the devil is evil and is still out to destroy God's relationship with man. To understand some of the ways he operates, read the following scriptures:

   Genesis 3:1, 2; Job 1:6-19; Job 2:1-7; Matthew 4:3-11; Mark 4:15; Luke 8:29; John 8:44; John 13:2, 27; 2 Corinthians 11:3,

14; Ephesians 2:2; 2 Thessalonians 2:3-4; 1 Timothy 3:6; James 4:7; and Revelation 12:9.

What methods did he use to deceive the woman?

4. When God confronted Adam and Eve over their disobedience, they did not take responsibility for their sins—Adam blamed Eve, and Eve blamed the serpent. Blaming others and not taking responsibility for our own sins and actions is a prideful tactic the devil uses to keep us from confessing our sins to Jesus. He knows if we confess our sins to Jesus, He will forgive us. Read 1 John 1:8-10.

   As Christians, we are also to confess our sins to one another: Read James 5:16.

5. In Genesis 3:15, God prophesied to the serpent about the coming of Jesus to earth. Why did Jesus come? Read John 6:38-40; Luke 19:10; Daniel 9:24; Hebrews 2:14, 15; and 1 John 3:8.

   Can you think of reasons why God allowed the devil to go on destroying people's lives for thousands of years instead of destroying him at that time?

6. God had told Adam and Eve if they ate of the fruit of the *"tree of the knowledge of good and evil,"* they would die. They were still alive, but death was coming. Besides physical death to Adam and Eve, in what other ways had death come to them?

   In what ways had death come to man, animals, the earth and everything on it?

7. God created mankind to live with Him forever, but now He did not want Adam and Eve to live forever in their sinful state. Read Genesis 3:22-24. What did God do to Adam and Eve?

   Why do you think God placed the *"tree of life"* in the garden and what do you think was its purpose? Read 1 John 5:20. Can you see a correlation between the *"tree of life"* and Jesus?

What do you think would have happened to Adam and Eve and all of creation had Adam and Eve been allowed to eat of the *"tree of life"* and live in the garden forever in their sinful state?

8. What do you think the *"tree of the knowledge of good and evil"* was, and why do you think God put it there?

9. The devil likes to keep sins hidden so that we cannot come to repentance and be saved. He promotes pride, and pride exalts itself against the knowledge of God. Without repentance, there is no salvation. Refusing to acknowledge our sin is pride exalting itself against the knowledge and wisdom of God. Jesus tells us to confess our sins to God and obey God's commands.

Read Matthew 3:1-6; Mark 1:15; Luke 13:3; and 1 John 1:9.

CHAPTER 3

LIFE IN THE FALLEN WORLD

Man's Separation From God

Things for Adam and Eve had certainly changed. They had suddenly been thrust out of the paradise they had known with God into an unknown world they knew nothing about. They would now have to deal with fear and worry and other negative emotions while they learned to survive in a hostile environment. God had cursed the land, so now weeds and stickers would grow, and it would be hard to till the soil to grow grain and vegetables. Adam would have to kill the animals he had named in order to eat and make clothing. It is possible that at that time, the animals had already become hungry and vicious and that some creatures and plants had probably become poisonous. Each day Adam would have to find ways to protect them from the environment, seeking shelter in order to be safe and warm.

It wasn't easy for Eve either. She probably had to learn domestic skills— cooking and making clothes out of animal skins. Adam would now rule over her, and she would have to experience pain in childbirth. It is possible that Adam and Eve may have felt rage towards God over their circumstances, if they had not yet accepted responsibility for their actions. Nothing would give them peace and satisfaction the way God had given it to them. This was not how it was intended to be! Things were out of control, and Satan, pleased about what he had done, but burning with more anger toward God, was determined to defeat God by trying to destroy all of His creation! He would do everything he could to destroy God's creation before God's prophecy about Jesus came true.

Even though God, their Father, would stand back and watch Adam and Eve strive and toil, He would always love them and keep His hand upon them. God is just, and He loved them too much to ignore what they had done. He needed to send them away to suffer hard times so they would be able to recognize their sin and return to love and obey their Father once again. He knew them, and He knew that someday, they would return to Him with repentant hearts. The Bible says *"...God is love"* (1 John 4:8). It must have hurt Him deeply to see His children suffer, just as it hurts earthly parents when their children make bad choices that cause them pain and suffering. He would wait for their return to Him. Ephesians 1:4 says (God) *"...hath chosen us in him* (in Christ) *before the foundation of the world...."* He would pursue an eternal relationship with us with a passion, and He would do it through the children (seed) of Adam and Eve and their descendants.

The Offspring of Adam and Eve

God had given Adam and Eve a desire for sexual intimacy in order to reproduce. When speaking about man and woman, Malachi, the prophet said, *"Has not the one God made you? You belong to him in body and spirit. And what does the one God seek? Godly offspring..."* (Malachi 2:15, NIV®). Now this intimacy would also lead to great suffering and pain in childbirth for Eve, and their hearts would suffer over their children.

In Genesis 4 we find that Eve gave birth to two sons, Cain first, and then Abel. By the time Cain was born, Eve had placed her faith in God again because verse one says she gave credit to God for helping her give birth to Cain.

> *"And in process of time it came to pass, that Cain brought of the fruit of the ground an offering unto the LORD. And Abel, he also brought of the firstlings of his flock and of the fat thereof. And the LORD had respect unto Abel and to his offering: But*

unto Cain and to his offering he had not respect. And Cain was very wroth (became angry), *and his countenance fell"* (Genesis 4:3-5).

Why was God upset with Cain's offering? He had brought the Lord an offering of fruit from his garden. Let's see what the Bible says about it:

"And the LORD said unto Cain, Why art thou wroth? and why is thy countenance fallen (facial expression changed)? *If thou doest well, shalt thou not be accepted? and if thou doest not well, sin lieth at the door. And unto thee shall be his desire, and thou shalt rule over him"* (Genesis 4:6-7).

For some reason, Cain's heart was not right with God, and God knew it. It was Abel's faith that gave him approval with God--his heart was right with God.

"By faith Abel brought a better offering than Cain did. By faith he was commended as righteous, when God spoke well of his offering. And by faith Abel still speaks even though he is dead" (Hebrews 11:4, NIV®).

Whatever feeling had been in Cain's heart (probably jealousy), had turned to sin, which drove him to murder his brother, Abel. 1 John 3:12 tells us why Cain killed Abel: *"And wherefore slew he him? Because his own works were evil, and his brother's righteous."* Cain had inherited his parents' sin nature.

Then the LORD said to Cain, 'Where is your brother Abel?' 'I don't know,' he replied. 'Am I my brother's keeper?' The LORD said, 'What have you done? Listen! Your brother's blood cries out to me from the ground. Now you are under a curse and driven from the ground, which opened its mouth to receive your brother's blood from your hand. When you work the ground, it will no longer yield its crops for you. You will be a restless wanderer on the earth'" (Genesis 4:8-10, NIV®).

The Bible says that God put a mark on Cain so that in his wanderings, no one would take his life. He ended up living in the land of Nod, which was on the eastern side of Eden. Cain's punishment for his sin was similar to that of his parents, Adam and Eve. He lost his home, his family, he would endure a lifetime of hard labor, and he was spiritually separated from God. As we read on in Genesis, we find that Cain had a wife, and she bore sons to him. The Bible doesn't say where Cain's wife came from, or even how she came into existence—that is one of God's mysteries He has chosen to keep to Himself. Later, Cain built the city of Enoch, which he named after one of his sons. Lamech, one of Cain's grandsons, also committed murder, just as Cain had done. Sin has never stopped, and everyone from Adam and Even until now has been born into sin—one generation after another.

> *"As it is written, There is none righteous, no, not one: there is none that understandeth, there is none that seeketh after God"* (Romans 3:10-11).

God sent Cain away with his sinful heart, and when Adam was 130 years old, God gave Eve another son named Seth to take the place of Abel. Later, Seth had a son named E´-nos,*"…then began men to call upon the name of the LORD"* (Genesis 4:26). God continued to bless Adam and Eve with more children, who lived to be over 900 years old. The following list in Genesis 5 establishes their family line from father to son, even though they had daughters, as well: Enos, Cainan, Mahalaleel, Jared, and Enoch, who never died:

> *"…Enoch… became the father of Methuselah. And after he became the father of Methuselah, Enoch walked faithfully with God 300 years and had other sons and daughters. Altogether, Enoch lived a total of 365 years. Enoch walked faithfully*

with God; then he was no more, because God took him away"
(Genesis 5:21-24 NIV®).

*"By faith Enoch was taken from this life, so that he did not
experience death: He could not be found, because God had taken
him away. For before he was taken, he was commended as one
who pleased God"* (Hebrews 11:5, NIV®).

Genesis 5:25-29, NIV®, says, *"Methuselah... became the
father of Lamech...Altogether, Methuselah lived a total of 969
years, and then he died...When Lamech had lived 182 years, he
had a son. He named him Noah and said, 'He will comfort us
in the labor and painful toil of our hands caused by the ground
the LORD has cursed.'"*

Then Lamech continued the family line with Methuselah and
Noah. At the age of 500, Noah became the father of Shem, Ham, and
Japheth.

God Destroys His Creation With a Flood

*"And it came to pass, when men began to multiply on the face of
the earth, and daughters were born unto them, That the <u>sons of
God</u> saw the daughters of men that they were fair; and they took
them wives of all which they chose"* (Genesis 6:1-2).

"The sons of God (ĕlōhîm)...are either angelic beings, or rulers, i.e.
kings (cf. Ps 82:6), or more likely the godly line of Seth. Sons of God...
generally signifies heavenly creatures."[1]

*"There were giants in the earth in those days; and also after that,
when the sons of God came in unto the daughters of men, and they
bare children to them, the same became mighty men which were of
old, men of renown"* (Genesis 6:4).

The Lord became angry because men were taking unto themselves ungodly women, and He limited their years on earth to 125. He began to grieve over mankind because they had become so wicked and violent, and He made the decision to destroy all of His living creation. However, God saw one righteous man who had tremendous faith and who walked with Him, and his name was Noah.

> *"God looked upon the earth, and, behold, it was corrupt; for all flesh had corrupted his way upon the earth. And God said unto Noah, The end of all flesh is come before me; for the earth is filled with violence through them; and, behold, I will destroy them with the earth. Make thee an ark of go'-pher wood* (possibly cypress)[2]*..."* (Genesis 6:11-14).

God selected Noah to establish His covenant with, and He would also spare Noah's family and some of the animals and creatures He had made. How would God destroy *"all flesh?"* He told Noah,

> *"And, behold, I, even I, do bring a flood of waters upon the earth, to destroy all flesh, wherein is the breath of life, from under heaven; and every thing that is in the earth shall die. But with thee will I establish my covenant; and thou shalt come into the ark, thou, and thy sons, and thy wife, and thy sons' wives with thee. And of every living thing of all flesh, two of every sort shalt thou bring into the ark, to keep them alive with thee; they shall be male and female. Of fowls after their kind, and of cattle after their kind, of every creeping thing of the earth after his kind, two of every sort shall come unto thee, to keep them alive. And take thou unto thee of all food that is eaten, and thou shalt gather it to thee; and it shall be for food for thee, and for them"* (Genesis 6:17-22).

> *"Of every clean beast thou shalt take to thee by sevens, the male and his female: and of beasts that are not clean by two, the male and his female. Of fowls also of the air by sevens, the male and the female..."* (Genesis 6:2-3).

"And The LORD then said unto Noah, Come thou and all thy house into the ark; for thee have I seen righteous before me in this generation. Of every clean beast thou shalt take to thee by sevens, the male and his female: and of beasts that are not clean by two, the male and his female. Of fowls also of the air by sevens, the male and the female; to keep seed alive upon the face of all the earth. For yet seven days, and I will cause it to rain upon the earth forty days and forty nights; and every living substance that I have made will I destroy from off the face of the earth" (Genesis 7:1-4).

At 600 years old, Noah obeyed the Lord, and filled the ark with the animals, his sons and their wives, and he and his wife, and <u>God shut the door</u> (Genesis 7:16) on the ark after they were all safe inside. He sent the rain for forty days and forty nights, and the floods stayed on the earth for 150 days.

"By faith Noah, being warned of God of things not seen as yet, moved with fear, prepared an ark to the saving of his house; by the which he condemned the world, and became heir of the righteousness which is by faith" (Hebrews 11:7).

"And all flesh died that moved upon the earth, both of fowl, and of cattle, and of beast, and of every creeping thing that creepeth upon the earth, and every man: All in whose nostrils was the breath of life, of all that was in the dry land, died" (Genesis 7:21-22).

After 150 days, the ark rested on the mountains of Ararat. It took almost three months for the water to decrease enough to be able to see the tops of the mountains. After forty days, Noah sent out a raven and a dove. The raven did not return, but the dove came back to him because it had no place to set her foot. Noah sent her out again after seven days, and she came back with a plucked olive leaf. After seven more days, he sent the dove out again, and she did not return to him. God told Noah:

"Go forth of the ark, thou, and thy wife, and thy sons, and thy sons' wives with thee. Bring forth with thee every living thing that

> *is with thee, of all flesh, both of fowl, and of cattle, and of every*
> *creeping that that creepeth upon the earth; that they may breed*
> *abundantly in the earth, and be fruitful, and multiply upon the*
> *earth"* (Genesis 8:16-17).

When Noah got off the ark, he built an altar and offered burnt offerings of clean beasts and fowls unto the Lord. (These were those that God had told Noah to bring in sevens.)

> *"And the LORD smelled a sweet savor; and the LORD said in*
> *his heart, I will not again curse the ground any more for man's sake;*
> *for the imagination of man's heart is evil from his youth; neither will*
> *I again smite any more every living thing, as I have done. While the*
> *earth remaineth, seedtime and harvest, and cold and heat, and summer*
> *and winter, and day and night shall not cease"* (Genesis 8:21-22).

> *"And God blessed Noah and his sons, and said unto them, Be*
> *fruitful, and multiply, and replenish the earth"* (Genesis 9:1).

God also gave mankind authority over the creatures of the land, sea, and air. He gave Noah permission to kill animals for food, but not to eat or drink their blood.

> *"But flesh with the life thereof, which is the blood thereof, shall ye*
> *not eat* (drain the blood). *And surely your blood of your lives*
> *will I require; at the hand of every beast will I require it, and at the*
> *hand of man; at the hand of every man's brother will I require the*
> *life of man. Whoso sheddeth man's blood, by man shall his blood*
> *be shed: for in the image of God made he man"* (Genesis 9:4-6).

God's Covenant With His Creation

God made a covenant with Noah, his descendants, and with all of His creation to never destroy flesh or the earth again with water.

> *"And God said, This is the token of the <u>covenant</u> which I make between me and you and every living creature that is with you, for perpetual generations: I do set my bow in the cloud, and it shall be for a token* (sign) *of a covenant between me and the earth. And it shall come to pass, when I bring a cloud over the earth, that the bow shall be seen in the cloud: And I will remember my covenant, which is between me and you and every living creature of all flesh; and the waters shall no more become a flood to destroy all flesh. And the bow shall be in the cloud: and I will look upon it, that I may remember the everlasting covenant between God and every living creature of all flesh that is upon the earth. And God said unto Noah, This is the token of the covenant, which I have established between me and all flesh that is upon the earth"* (Genesis 9:12-17).

The Hebrew word translated *covenant* is "bᵉrîyth." The meaning of the word is "...compact.....confederacy...league."[3]

A covenant is a formal agreement between God and His people. It is a promise entirely instituted by God, and when God makes a promise, He keeps it. God made His first covenant with Noah and the earth, but it was not to be His last. The final covenant He would make with mankind would be the new covenant of blood through the blood of Jesus Christ.

Renewal of the Earth

In a way, the flood was God's way of cleansing the earth and bringing a new beginning for the earth and its inhabitants. One of Noah's ancestors, Lamech, had prophesied of this event in Genesis 5:29:

> *"And he called his name Noah, saying, This same shall comfort us concerning our work and toil of our hands, because of the ground which the LORD hath cursed."*

1 Peter 3:18-22, NIV® compares the flood with the baptism of believers in Christ:

> *"...In it* (the ark) *only a few people, eight in all, were saved through water, and this water symbolizes baptism that now saves you also—not the removal of dirt from the body but the pledge of a good conscience toward God. It saves you by the resurrection of Jesus Christ, who has gone into heaven and is at God's right hand—with angels, authorities and powers in submission to Him."*

We find in the scripture above that the water of the flood was symbolic of baptism. Our water baptism "signifies that the Old Adam in us should, by daily contrition and repentance, be drowned and die with all sins and evil lusts and, again, a new man daily come forth and arise, who shall live before God in righteousness and purity forever."[4]

Even though God had cleansed the earth from all evil men and their pollution upon the earth, the sin nature would continue to rule in the hearts of men, and many would still refuse to obey God. It didn't take very long for the full effects of the sin nature to manifest itself again, and Satan would continue to use it to pursue the destruction of God's creation and the souls of men.

Noah planted a vineyard. One day, he drank too much wine and became drunk. When he was laying naked in his tent, his son, Ham, who was the father of Canaan, saw him and called to his brothers, who were outside, to come and see their naked father. They brought a cover and walked over to him backwards so they would not see his naked body and covered him up. After Noah woke up and heard what Ham had done to him, he prophesied a curse on Canaan, the son of Ham:

> *"Cursed be Canaan! The lowest of slaves will he be to his brothers.' He also said, 'Praise be to the LORD, the God of Shem! May Canaan be the slave of Shem. May God extend Japheth's territory; may Japheth live in the tents of Shem, and may Canaan be the slave of Japheth'"* (Genesis 9:25-27, NIV ®).

The Clans of Noah's Sons

Genesis 10 tells us how the new civilizations began after the flood. Japheth's sons were *"...Go´-mer, and Ma´-gog, and Ma´-dai, and Ja´-van, and Tu´-bal, and Me´-shech and Ti´-ras,"* who were known as the Japhethites (Genesis 10:2). *"By these were the isles of the Gentiles divided in their lands; every one after his tongue, after their families, in their nations"* (Genesis 10:5).

Ham's sons were *"...Cush, and Miz´-ra-im* (Egypt), *and Phut and Canaan,"* and were called the Hamites. His son, Cush, established the kingdoms of *"...Babylon, Uruk, Akkad and Kalneh, in Shinar. From that land he went to Assyria, where he built Nineveh, Rehoboth Ir, Calah and Resen..."* (Genesis 10:10-12, NIV®).

> *"Egypt, was the father of the Ludites, Anamites, Lehabites, Naphtuhites, Pathrusites, Kasluhites (from whom the Philistines came) and Caphtorites"* (Genesis 10:13-14, NIV®).

> *"Canaan, was the father of Sidon his firstborn, and of the Hittites, Jebusites, Amorites, Girgashites, Hivites, Sinites, Arvadites, Zemarites, and Hamathites. Later the Canaanite clans scattered and the borders of Canaan reached from Sidon toward Gerar as far as Gaza, and then toward Sodom, Gomorrah, Admah and Zeboyim, as far as Lasha"* (Genesis 10:15-19, NIV®).

Shem's sons were *"E´-lam, and Assh´-ur, and A-rphax´-ad, Lud, and Ar´-am."* Shem and his ancestors moved to the *"eastern hill country"* (Genesis 10:30, NIV®), and became known as the Semites.

The Tower of Babel

As man moved from the east, they settled on a plain in Shinar, and everyone spoke the same language. God had told Noah's family to *"...Be fruitful, and multiply and replenish the earth."* However, as time progressed, men did not want to be scattered over all the earth, but to be in one place together. In order to accomplish this, they started to build a tower to reach the heavens and exalt them selves. Once again, the Lord changed the plans of men: He changed their language so they could not understand each other and scattered them in different parts of the earth (see Genesis 11).

In Conclusion

Even though Adam and Eve were separated from God because of their sin, God did not abandon them. As time went on, He selected Abel and Seth, their sons, to carry on His godly seed. As sin began to increase in the hearts of men, the spilled blood of men also contaminated the earth. God made a decision to bring a flood to destroy all His creation that had the breath of life, with three exceptions: He would save Noah, who was from the seed of Seth, Noah's family, and the creatures He had created. God used the flood to cleanse the earth of sin and brought a new beginning. The sin nature would still exist, and the devil would still reign upon the earth, so evil would still prevail. However, God placed His rainbow in the sky as a sign of His covenant with Noah and the earth and its inhabitants.

In spite of this curse of sin, we have hope—that's why Jesus came. Jesus, God's Son, died a sacrificial death on the cross, to pay for our sins. When we believe in Him and confess that we are sinners, He forgives us, and we are renewed through the saving power of Jesus Christ.

> "Therefore, if any man be in Christ, he is a new creature: old things are passed away; behold, all things are become new" (2 Corinthians 5:17).

"Man lost the image of God when he fell into sin. In believers, a beginning of its renewal is made. Only in heaven, however, will this image be fully restored."[5]

In the next chapter, we are going to meet Abraham, a man of faith who received promises from God, which would lay the foundation for the Judeo religion and the Christian church. It is the beginning of an amazing story of an imperfect man, who didn't always do things right, but who had an incredible faith and respect in the living God. We will read firsthand the promises given to Abraham about the future of his descendants, the Hebrews, the land they would live on, and even the prophecy of the bondage they would be under for 400 years.

Deeper Insights:

1. Cain and Abel both brought sacrifices to the Lord, but God was not happy with Cain's offering.

    Read Hebrews 11:4. Why did Cain's offering displease the Lord, while Able's offering did please Him?

2. The world became a wicked place. The godly men began marrying ungodly women, and the condition of sin had reached an epidemic state. Read 1 Corinthians 5:7-11 and 2 Corinthians 6:14-18 to see what God says about believers being unequally yoked with unbelievers?

3. God was sorry He had created everything and everyone and was ready to destroy all that had the breath of life in them. Then He saw Noah and spared Noah, his family, and the animals.

    What did God see in Noah that He did not see in the rest of mankind at that time that would cause Him to spare Noah and his family? Read Genesis 6:9.

4. After the flood, God made a covenant with Noah and all His creation—He would never bring a flood to destroy all living things again. What sign did God give mankind to remind Him of this promise? Read Genesis 9:11-17.

    Can you think of any reasons why God may have chosen to use a rainbow as His sign?

5. In a way, God used the flood to wash away the corruption and violence of sinful men and the blood of murder spilled on the ground. He gave creation a new start. The Bible compares the flood with the *washing away* of sin with our water baptism after we repent and receive Christ.

   Is it important for us, as believers in Christ, to be baptized? Read Matthew 3:1-6, 16-17; Acts 2:38-39, 22:16.

6. God confounded the men who were building the Tower of Babel.

   Why did God not want them to build the Tower of Babel? Read Genesis 11:4-6 and Luke 1:51.

CHAPTER 4

THE FAITH OF ABRAHAM, PART 1

Abram's Background

Before God gave Abraham his name, he was called Abram. He is known as father Abraham to the Jewish nation. It was to Abram that God gave the first promises about the future of the Hebrews and the exact land on which the Hebrew people were to live. These promises also contained the gospel of Jesus Christ, which would be fulfilled in God's timing through the descendants of Abram. It was with Abram that God established the Hebrew nation and made a covenant with them to be their God. The Bible records nine separate encounters with God and Abram regarding these promises for the future.

The year was about "2000 BC."[1] Noah's son, Shem, had died and many descendants had come through his family line, including a man by the name of Terah. Terah and his three sons, Abram, Nahor, and Haran lived in Ur. Ur "was located on the Euphrates River in lower Mesopotamia, present-day Iraq."[2] Abram was Noah's great grandson.

Over 2,000 years later, after Christ's death, Stephen would give the following historical account about Abram's family to the Sanhedrin in Acts 7:2-3: *"...The God of glory appeared unto our father Abraham, when he was in Mes-o-po-ta´-mi-a, before he dwelt in Har´-an...And said unto him, Get thee out of thy country, and from thy kindred, and come into the land which I shall show thee."*

Haran "was located in Southern Turkey."[3] Both the city of Ur and the city of Haran worshipped many gods, including the moon-god, "Sin."[4] Later, Joshua would proclaim this to the Israelites after Moses' death.

> *"This is what the LORD, the God of Israel, says: Long ago your ancestors, including Terah the father of Abraham and Nahor, lived beyond the Euphrates River and worshipped other gods'"* (Joshua 24:2, NIV®).

So God selected Abram from a family who worshipped false gods (idolatry). God selected Abram and spoke to him because He knew Abram's heart, and He knew he would respond to Him and obey Him.

In this chapter we will see how the persistence of God and His repetitive promises to Abram would make Abram's faith strong. Abram would have much faith and hope to pass down to his descendants. In his encounter with Abram, God used many different ways to speak to him. He appeared to him, gave him dreams, visions, visitors, and He spoke to him directly with His voice. He had no set pattern or ritual, and God was the initiator, not Abram. His love for mankind was strong and compassionate, and His plan to redeem man was unstoppable, regardless of the circumstances that would arise. He would build a foundation for the forthcoming gospel that would change eternity forever.

Abram's First Encounter With God

> *"NOW the LORD had said unto Abram, Get thee out of thy country, and from thy kindred, and from thy father's house, unto a land that I will show thee: And I will make of thee a* **great nation, and I will bless thee, and make thy name great; and thou shalt be a blessing: And I will bless them that bless thee, and curse him that curseth thee: and in thee shall all families of the earth be blessed"** (Genesis 12:1-3).

These promises contained the gospel of Jesus Christ, the forthcoming Messiah. Before Jesus was even born, the gospel was preached about Him. God, Himself, preached this gospel to Abram.

> *"And the scripture, foreseeing that God would justify the heathen through faith, preached before the gospel unto Abraham, saying, In thee shall all nations be blessed. So then they which be of faith are blessed with faithful Abraham"* (Galatians 3:8-9).

> *"That the blessing of Abraham might come on the Gentiles through Jesus Christ; that we might receive the promise of the Spirit through faith"* (Galatians 3:14).

The Greek word translated *Gentiles* is "ĕthnikōs." The meaning of the word is "...heathen...."[5]

After his father died, Abram obeyed God's command to go to the land that God would show him. He was seventy-five years old when he packed up his tent, his wife, Sarai (who was really his half sister through his father), and everything he owned, to go to a place he knew nothing about. His nephew, Lot, and his tribe of people, went along, as well. Abram trusted God to take care of them and provide for them.

> *"By faith Abraham, when he was called to go out into a place which he should after receive for an inheritance, obeyed; and he went out, not knowing whither he went"* (Hebrews 11:8).

Abram's Second Encounter With God

> *"And Abram passed through the land unto the place of Si´-chem, unto the plain of Mo´-reh. And the Ca´-naanite was then in the land. And the LORD appeared unto Abram, and said, **Unto thy seed will I give this land:** and there builded he an altar unto the LORD, who appeared unto him. And he removed from thence unto a mountain on the east of Beth-el, and pitched his*

tent, having Beth-el on the west, and Ha´-i on the east: and there he builded an altar unto the LORD, and called upon the name of the LORD. And Abram journeyed, going on still toward the south" (Genesis 12:6-9).

"Now to Abraham and his seed were the promises made. He saith not, And to seeds, as of many; but as of one, And to thy seed, which is Christ" (Galatians 3:16).

"From there he went on toward the hills east of Bethel and pitched his tent, with Bethl on the west and Ai on the east. There he built an altar to the LORD and called on the name of the LORD. Then Abram set out and continued toward the Negev" (Genesis 12:8-9, NIV®).

Now Abram was not a perfect man. He struggled with fear, and was capable of deceiving others, as we shall see; but he believed God. In Genesis 12:10-20, we find that there was a famine in the land and Abram went to Egypt to find food and security. Abram was afraid that the Egyptians would kill him when they saw what a beautiful woman his wife, Sarai, was. He told Sarai to lie to them and say that she was his sister. Pharaoh took Sarai into the palace and was very kind to Abram, giving him animals and servants; but the Lord inflicted diseases upon Pharaoh and his household to put a stop to Abram's façade. When Pharaoh realized that Sarai was Abram's wife, he sent them all away, including all the gifts he had given Abram, which made Abram a wealthy man. Eventually Abram made his way back to Bethel where he had previously pitched his tent and built an altar, and he called on the name of the Lord. Abram acknowledged God with every move he made by building altars along the way of his journey, praying and believing.

Lot was still moving around with Abram, and he also had wealth of animals and tents. Their herdsmen began quarreling, so they decided to separate. Abram told Lot to choose which area of land he wanted. Lot chose the plain of Jordan, which was well watered and near Sodom; and Abram lived in Canaan.

Abram's Third Encounter With God

> *"And the LORD said unto Abram, after that Lot was separated from him, Lift up now thine eyes, and look from the place where thou art* **northward, and southward, and eastward, and westward:** *For* **all the land which thou seest, to thee will I give it, and to thy seed for ever.** *And I* **will make thy seed as the dust of the earth:** *so that if a man can number the dust of the earth, then shall thy seed also be numbered. Arise, walk through* **the land** *in the length of it and in the breadth of it; for* **I will give it unto thee.** *Then Abram removed his tent, and came and dwelt in the plain of Mam´-re, which is in He´-bron, and built there an altar unto the LORD"* (Genesis 13:14-18).

Abram's Fourth Encounter With God

Genesis 14 gives the account of five kings who had been subject to king Chedorlaomer, king of Elam, for twelve years. They rebelled against king Chedorlaomer and his allies, who were powerful, and went to battle in the valley of Siddim (Salt Sea).

> *"And the vale of Sid´-dim was full of slimepits; and the kings of Sodom and Go-mor´-rah fled, and fell there; and they that remained fled to the mountain. And they took all the goods of Sodom and Go-mor´-ah, and all their victuals* (food), *and went their way. And they took Lot, Abram's brother's son, who dwelt in Sodom, and his goods, and departed. And there came one that had escaped, and told Abram the Hebrew; for he dwelt in the plain of Mam´-re the Am´-orite, brother of Esh´-col, and brother of Aner: and these were confederate with Abram. And when Abram heard that his brother was taken captive, he armed his trained servants, born in his own house, three hundred and eighteen, and pursued them unto Dan.*

43

"And he divided himself against them, he and his servants, by night, and smote them, and pursued them unto Ho´-bah, which is on the left hand of Damascus. And he brought back all the goods, and also brought again his brother Lot, and his goods, and the women also, and the people" (Genesis 14:10-16).

After Abram returned from defeating Chedorlaomer and the kings allied with him, the king of Sodom came out to meet Abram in the valley of Shaveh. At the same time, Melchizedek, the king of Salem, appeared to Abram, bringing bread and wine, and he blessed Abram.

"Blessed be Abram of the most high God, possessor of heaven and earth: And blessed be the most high God, which hath delivered thine enemies into thy hand. And he (Abram) *gave him tithes of all"* (Genesis 14:19-20).

"This Melchizedek was king of Salem and priest of God Most High. He met Abraham returning from the defeat of the kings and blessed him, and Abraham gave him a tenth of everything. First, his name means 'king of righteousness'; then also, 'king of Salem' means 'king of peace'. Without father or mother, without genealogy, without beginning of days or end of life, resembling the Son of God he remains a priest forever.

"Just think how great he was: Even the patriarch Abraham gave him a tenth of the plunder! Now the law requires the descendants of Levi who become priests to collect a tenth from the people—that is, from their fellow Israelites—even though they are also brothers descended from Abraham. This man, however, did not trace his descent from Levi, yet he collected a tenth from Abraham and blessed him who had the promises. And without doubt the lesser person is blessed by the greater. In the one case, the tenth is collected by people who die; but in the other case, by him who is declared to be living. One might even say that Levi, who collects the tenth, paid the tenth through Abraham, because when Melchizedek met

Abraham, Levi was still in the body of his ancestor" (Hebrews 7:1-10, NIV®).

Just what could this scripture be implying?

In Abram's future, the law and the earthly priesthood would be established through the line of Levi, but Levi had not yet been born. So Abram did not know about the law and earthly priesthood system, yet he gave tithes to him. This encounter was very interesting. God had been appearing and speaking to Abram, but this time He came as a person—as God's High Priest. At that time, there was no priesthood or high priest system known to the Hebrews, as God would establish those over 400 years later. In that future time, Aaron would become the first high priest in the line of Levi. So who was this Melchizedek who came to bless Abram? Who was he that Abram recognized as being a High Priest of God and knew to give a tithe to him?

Melchizedek, priest of God Most High, brought bread and wine. Interestingly, Jesus, Who would become the High Priest after His death and resurrection, also shared bread and wine with His disciples at the Lord's Supper (see Luke 22:19-20). He explained to them that the bread represented His body, and the wine represented His blood. He did this just before He established the new blood covenant by His death on the cross.

Melchizedek had come to Abram right when Abram would need the faith to answer the king of Sodom who was on his way to meet with him. As we shall read, Abram will acknowledge God to the king with a new confidence and stronger faith in the living God, Who had delivered his enemies into his hands. This encounter with the priest of the Most High God, gave Abram boldness. Right after Abram's faith had been strengthened, the king of Sodom came and spoke to him.

> *"And the king of Sodom said unto Abram, Give me the persons, and take the goods to thyself. And Abram said to the king of Sodom, I have lift up mine hand* (solemnly promised) *unto the LORD, the most high God, the possessor of heaven and earth, That I will not take from a thread even to a shoelatchet, and that I will not take any thing that is thine, lest thou shouldest say, I have*

made Abram rich: Save only that which the young men have eaten, and the portion of the men which went with me, Aner, Esh´-col, and Mam´-re; let them take their portion" (Genesis 14:21-24).

Abram's Fifth Encounter With God

"AFTER these things the word of the LORD came unto Abram in a vision, saying, Fear not, Abram: I am thy shield, and thy exceeding great reward. And Abram said, Lord GOD, what wilt thou give me, seeing I go childless, and the steward of my house is this El-i-e´-zer of Damascus? And Abram said, Behold, to me thou hast given no seed: and, lo, one born in my house is mine heir.

"And, behold, the word of the LORD came unto him, saying, this shall not be thine heir; ***but he that shall come forth out of thine own bowels shall be thine heir.*** *And he brought him forth abroad, and said,* ***Look now toward heaven, and tell the stars, if thou be able to number them: and he said unto him, So shall thy seed be.*** *And he believed in the LORD; and he counted it to him for righteousness"* (Genesis 15:1-6).

Although Abram was getting old, God had just told him he was going to father a son from his own seed; and Abram believed him. It was his faith—his believing God—that was *"credited to him for righteousness."* Faith is still the key factor for us today. Since Christ died on the cross to pay for our sins, we receive His righteousness when we put our faith in Him as our Savior.

"Even as Abraham believed God, and it was accounted to him for righteousness. Know ye therefore that they which are of faith, the same are the children of Abraham" (Galatians 3:6-7).

Even though Abram would have numerous offspring from his own body, God was also talking about Abram's numerous offspring who would come to believe in Christ. They would be his offspring of faith. God also gave Abram the following dream about Abram's own death, and the assurance that the land of Canaan would belong to Abram's descendants to live upon. He prophesied about the Hebrews and their future bondage in Egypt for 400 years. Everything God was saying was pre-planned by Him.

> God told Abram, *"...Take me a heifer of three years old, and a she goat of three years old, and a ram of three years old, and a turtledove, and a young pigeon. And he took unto him all these, and divided them in the midst, and laid each piece one against another: but the birds divided he not. And when the fowls came down upon the carcases, Abram drove them away.*
>
> *"And when the sun was going down a deep sleep fell upon Abram; and, lo, a horror of great darkness fell upon him. And he said unto Abram, Know of a surety that **thy seed shall be a stranger in a land that is not theirs,** and **shall serve them;** and **they shall afflict them four hundred years; And also that nation, whom they shall serve, will I judge:** and afterward shall they **come out with great substance. And thou shalt go to thy fathers in peace; thou shalt be buried in a good old age. But in the fourth generation they shall come hither again: for the iniquity of the Am´-orites is not yet"* (Genesis 15:9-16, NIV®).

Abram would inherit the land, but would die and not occupy the land. Knowing that did not alter Abram's faith—he still trusted God. As we shall see later, this prophecy of bondage would be fulfilled in Genesis 47. Next we see the word, *covenant*, again. God made a covenant with Abram, indicating the land He was giving to Abram's offspring. This time the Lord gave Abram the boundaries of the land that He was giving to Abram's descendants, and it did not just include the land of the Canaanites.

> *"And it came to pass, that, when the sun went down, and it was dark, behold a smoking furnace, and a burning lamp that passed between those piece. In the same day the LORD made a covenant with Abram, saying,* **Unto thy seed have I given this land, from the river of Egypt unto the great river, the river Eu-phra´-tes: The Ken´-ites, and the Ken´-izzites, and the Kad´-mo-nites, And the Hit´-tites, and the Per´-rizzites, and the Reph´-a-im, And the Am´-orites, and the Ca´-naan-ites, and the Gir´-ga-shites, and the Jeb´-u-sites"** (Genesis 15:18-21).

The Conception of Ishmael

How much plainer could God make this? He had given Abram solid promises, prophesies, a vision, a dream, and had personally come to him. Abram would never have any reason to doubt God. God, the Creator of the universe, had spoken to him and assured him that He had a plan for Abram and the future of the world that would come through his seed. However, Abram was human, and his wife, Sarai, had a plan of her own to "hurry up" God's promises. Like Eve, Sarai's choice would alter human events for eternity.

> *"Now Sar´-a-i, Abram's wife, bare him no children: and she had a handmaid, an Egyptian, whose name was Ha´-gar. And Sar´-a-i said unto Abram, Behold now, the LORD hath restrained me from bearing: I pray thee, go in unto my maid; it may be that I may obtain children by her. And Abram hearkened to the voice of Sar´-a-i"* (Genesis 16:1-2).

Abram did as his wife suggested and took Hagar as his wife and slept with her. When Hagar found out she was pregnant, she began to despise Sarai. Sarai blamed Abram for Hagar's behavior and began to mistreat her, so Hagar ran away from Sarai. While she was out in the desert, an angel of the Lord came to her and told her to go back to Sarai. The angel gave her a promise:

"...I will multiply thy seed exceedingly, that it shall not be numbered for multitude. And the angel of the LORD said to her: Behold, thou art with child, and shalt bear a son, and shalt call his name Ish'-ma-el; because the LORD hath heard thy affliction. And he will be a wild man; his hand will be against every man, and every man's hand against him; and he shall dwell in the presence of all his brethren. And she called the name of the LORD that spake unto her, Thou God seeth me: for she said, Have I also here looked after him that seeth me?"... And Ha'-gar bore Abram a son: and Abram called his son's name, which Ha'-gar bare, Ish'-ma-el" (Genesis 16:10-15).

In Conclusion

God looks at the hearts of men. He saw the heart of Abram; a young man who had been raised in a city and family of idolatry. He called him out to become the father of the Jewish nation, and ultimately, the foundational leader of faith of the Judeo-Christian religions. Why? It was certainly not Abram's perfection or his own righteousness that God was after. As we have seen, he was capable of lying, being fearful, and not always standing up on his own two feet. BUT, God knew that Abram would believe Him—he would have faith in Him and obey Him. He also knew that Abram would teach his children about the promises that had been given to him.

God gave Abram many promises, including a son from his own body. Even though Abram believed God, he obeyed his wife who became impatient and tried to "fix" the problem of her barren condition, herself. With that decision, Ishmael became Abram's son through Hagar. However, Ishmael was not to be the godly seed that would inherit God's promises to Abram. As we shall see in the next chapter, this one decision will cause a problem that will continue throughout eternity. As we journey on with Abram, we will read about more of God's promises to him, and God's decisive plan in carrying out those promises; and we will see how God will put Abram to the ultimate test of faith.

Deeper Insights:

1. Why do you think Abram would risk everything to follow God without knowing God's plan?

2. When God gave Abram this prophetic promise in Genesis 12:3, *"...in thee shall all people on earth will be blessed,"* He was giving a prophecy of the gospel of Jesus Christ.

   Since Jesus died on the cross to pay for our sins, how have all nations been blessed? Read John 3:16; 10:27-29; 11:25-26; Romans 4:6-8; 5:1-2, 6-11; 8:1, 2, 28-34; 2 Corinthians 5:17-19; and Ephesians 1:3-14.

   Read Galatians 3:6-9-14. Who will be blessed and why?

3. Who was Melchizedek? Read Hebrews 7:1-3 to find similarities between Melchizedek and Jesus.

   Abram gave Melchizedek tithes. The sacrificial system, which included tithing to the Levitical priests, had not yet been established. In fact the tribe of Levi from which the priests would come, would later come from Abram's descendants.

   Why do you suppose Abram would tithe to Melchizdek? Who do you think Melchizedek could have been?

4. During some of these first encounters with Abram, God promised him blessings, land for his descendants, numerous offspring, and even a son from his own seed, even though Abram's wife was barren. Knowing all of this, Abram still ran ahead of God and did not wait for the promised son, and there would be repercussions over that decision.

   Having heard these promises from God, why do you think he did not wait for the fulfillment of these promises, but slept with Hagar, his wife's handmaid, to obtain his first child?

5. When Hagar ran away from Sarai and went out into the desert, an angel of the Lord came to her and told her to go back to Sarai. He also gave her a promise about her son. What was that promise? Read Genesis 16:10-13.

CHAPTER 5

THE FAITH OF ABRAHAM, PART 2

Abram's Sixth Encounter With God

"And when Abram was ninety years old and nine, the LORD appeared to Abram, and said unto him, I am the Almighty God; walk before me and be thou <u>perfect</u>" (Genesis 17:1)

The Hebrew word translated *perfect* is "tâmîym." The meaning of the word is "entire...integrity, truth...sound, without spot, undefiled, upright..., whole...."[1]

*"And **I will make my covenant between me and thee**, and **will multiply thee exceedingly**. And Abram fell on his face: and God talked with him, saying, As for me, behold, my covenant is with thee, and thou shalt be a **father of many nations**. Neither shall thy name any more be called Abram, but **thy name shall be Abraham;** for a **father of many nations** have I made thee. And **I will make thee exceeding fruitful**, and I will make nations of thee, and **kings shall come out of thee**. And **I will establish my covenant between me and thee and thy seed after thee in their generations for an everlasting covenant**, to be a God unto thee, and to thy seed after thee. And **I will give unto thee, and to thy seed after thee, the land wherein thou art***

a stranger, all the land of Canaan, for an everlasting possession; and I will be their God" (Genesis 17:2-8).

God changed Abram's name to Abraham. The Hebrew word translated *Abram* is "'Abrâm." The meaning of the word is "...high father...."[2] The Hebrew word translated *Abraham* is "'Abrâhâm." The meaning of the word is "...father of a multitude...."[3]

In this encounter, God gave Abraham some new promises. Kings would come from Abraham. Later, as we will see, kings will come from Abraham's family line, the tribe of Judah, from which will come King Jesus, Who will come from the lineage of king David. The everlasting covenant with Abraham and his descendants was something new, too, but it would come with conditions. Abraham must walk perfect—in integrity and truth, being obedient to the One Who had called him. This covenant with Abraham was a serious matter, affecting the souls of men forever and would be an everlasting covenant for eternity. To seal this everlasting covenant with God, Abraham would also have to meet God's condition of circumcision as a sign of his part of the covenant with God.

The Rite of Circumcision

*"This is my **covenant**, which ye shall keep, **between me and you and thy seed after thee;** Every man child among you shall be circumcised. And ye shall* **<u>circumcise</u>** *the flesh of your foreskin; and it shall be a* **token** (sign) *of the* **<u>covenant</u> betwixt me and you.** *And he that is eight days old shall be circumcised among you, every man child in your generations, he that is born in the house, or bought with money of any stranger, which is not of thy seed. He that is born in thy house, and he that is bought with thy money, must needs be circumcised: and* **my covenant shall be in your flesh for an everlasting covenant.** *And the uncircumcised man child whose flesh of his foreskin is not circumcised, that soul shall be cut off from his people; he hath broken my covenant"* (Genesis 17:9-14).

The Hebrew word translated *circumcise* is "nâmal." The meaning of the word is "...to become clipped...."[4] In the above passage, we are talking about cutting the foreskin on a male to a shorter length. The Hebrew word translated *covenant* is "bᵉrîyth." The meaning of the word is "...in the sense of cutting...; a compact (because made by passing between pieces of flesh)...."[5]

Why would God give such a command? God was establishing a nation under Abraham. He was setting aside a chosen people with whom He would have an everlasting covenant relationship. Circumcision would now become a permanent rite, an outward sign that the Hebrew people belonged to God as His chosen people. They would now be a people who would be in covenant with Him by the cutting off their own flesh—not to mutilate themselves, but to cut away a part of themselves, to consecrate themselves to God.

As believers in Christ, the circumcision rite in our flesh is no longer required, because it was part of the Old Testament covenant. Now, Christ has circumcised our hearts through His blood that was shed on the cross with the death of His own flesh. In speaking to the Gentile church in Colossae, Paul said,

> *"In him* (in Christ) *you were also circumcised with a circumcision not performed by human hands. Your whole self ruled by the flesh was put off when you were circumcised by Christ, having been buried with him in baptism, in which you were also raised with him through your faith in the working of God, who raised him from the dead"* (Colossians 2:11-12, NIV®).

Since Christ's death, we are in His new everlasting covenant, and it is our hearts that have become circumcised. We, too, are held to a high standard of having a pure heart before God—to walk in integrity and truth. Those who were not circumcised in their flesh were not allowed to enter into the everlasting covenant that God made between Himself and Abraham. It is the same today. Those who do not have the Holy Spirit, the Spirit of Christ, will not be able to enter into the new everlasting covenant that has been made through Christ. The sign of our belonging to Christ is the infilling of the Holy Spirit, which bears fruit in us: *"...love, joy, peace, long-suffering, gentleness, goodness, faith, Meekness, temperance..."* (Galatians 5:22)

God changes Sarai's name:

> *"And God said unto Abraham, As for Sar'-a-i thy wife, thou shalt not call her name <u>Sar'-a-i</u>, but **Sarah shall her name be**. And **I will bless her**, and **give thee a son also of her:** yea, **I will bless her**, and she shall be a **mother of nations; kings of people shall be of her**. Then Abraham fell upon his face, and laughed, and said in his heart, Shall a child be born unto him that is a hundred years old? And shall Sarah, that is ninety years old, bear?* (Genesis 17:15-17)

Now we see that God has changed Sar´-ai's name to Sarah. The Hebrew word translated *Sar'ai* is "Sâray." The meaning of the word is "...the wife of Abraham...."[6] The Hebrew word translated *Sarah* is "Sârâh." The meaning of the word is "...a mistress, i.e. female noble:-lady, princess, queen...Abraham's wife...."[7]

God made it clear that He had selected Abraham and Sarah to be the father and mother of many nations, not Abraham and Hagar. Sarah will bear them a son, and it will be from Sarah's womb that God will raise up kings from her, but how would that happen? Sarah was barren and passed the age of child bearing. The Bible says that Abraham laughed to himself about this because he would be 100 years old when the promised son would be born. Abraham was happy, but he also grieved over Ishmael.

> *"And Abraham said unto God, O that Ish´-ma-el might live before thee!*
>
> *"And God said, **Sarah thy wife shall bear thee a son indeed; and thou shalt call his name Isaac: and I will establish***

> *my covenant with him for an everlasting covenant,*
> *and with his seed after him"* (Genesis 17:18-19).

These promises were very important. God made it very clear that the promised son would be named Isaac. The Hebrew word translated *Isaac* is "Yitschâq." The meaning of the word is "...laughter, i.e. mockery...."[8] God was selecting Isaac, the promised son, and his children, to be the godly seed in an everlasting covenant with Him.

> *"And as for Ish´-ma-el, I have heard thee: Behold, I have blessed him, and will make him fruitful, and will multiply him exceedingly; twelve princes shall he beget, and I will make him a great nation. **But my covenant will I establish with Isaac**, which Sarah shall bear unto thee at this set time in the next year"* (Genesis 17:20-21).

Ishmael would later become the father of some of the Arab nations. The promises given to Abraham would not come through Ishmael's family line, but God would also bless Ishmael. Abraham and Sarah had taken things into their own hands, in an attempt to fulfill God's promise of a son. However, Isaac, who would be born the following year, would be the promised son that God, Himself, would provide. Even though Abraham must have felt disappointed about his son, Ishmael, he still obeyed God. He knew God and believed Him.

> *"And Abraham took Ish´-ma-el his son, and all that were born in his house, and all that were bought with his money, every male among the men of Abraham's house; and circumcised the flesh of their foreskin in the selfsame day, as God had said unto him. And Abraham was ninety years old and nine, when he was circumcised in the flesh of his foreskin. And Ish´-ma-el his son was thirteen years old, when he was circumcised in the flesh of his foreskin"* (Genesis 17:23-25).

> *"...And all the men of his house, born in the house, and bought with money of the stranger, were circumcised with him"* (Genesis 17:27).

Abraham's Seventh Encounter With God

The Lord physically appeared to Abraham. Three men came to visit Abraham at his tent. A little later, in Genesis 19:1, we find that two of the men were angels. Abraham knew the Lord was there because he bowed down and spoke to Him:

> *"My Lord, if now I have found favor in thy sight, pass not away, I pray thee, from thy servant. Let a little water, I pray you, be fetched, and wash your feet and rest yourselves under the tree. And I will fetch a morsel of bread, and comfort ye your hearts; after that ye shall pass on: for therefore are ye come to your servant. And they said, So do, as thou hast said"* (Genesis 18:3-5).

While they were all eating a meal that Abraham and Sarah had quickly prepared, the men asked Abraham where Sarah was, and he told them she was in the tent.

> *"And he* (the LORD) *said,* **I will certainly return unto thee according to the time of life;** *and, lo,* **Sarah thy wife shall have a son.** *And Sarah heard it in the tent door, which was behind him. Now Abraham and Sarah were old and well stricken in age; and it ceased to be with Sarah after the manner of women"* (Genesis 18:10-11).

Ironically, Sarah began to laugh to her self, but not out loud; yet the Lord heard her laugh. Remember, God had already prophesied that her son's name would be Isaac, which means "laughter."

> *"And the LORD said unto Abraham, Wherefore did Sarah laugh, saying, Shall I of a surety bear a child, which am old? Is any thing too hard for the LORD? At the time appointed I will return unto thee, according to the time of life, and Sarah shall have a son"* (Genesis 18:13-14).

Sodom's doom

> *"And the men rose up from thence, and looked toward Sodom: and Abraham went with them to bring them on the way. And the LORD said, Shall I hide from Abraham that thing which I do; Seeing that Abraham shall surely become a great and mighty nation, and all the nations of the earth shall be blessed in him? For I know him, that he will command his children and his household after him, and they shall keep the way of the LORD, to do justice and judgment; that the LORD may bring upon Abraham that which he hath spoken of him"* (Genesis 18:16-19).

> *"And the men turned their faces from thence, and went toward Sodom: but Abraham stood yet before the <u>LORD</u>"* (Genesis 18:22).

Here the Hebrew word translated *LORD* is *"Yehôvâh."* The meaning of the word is "...(the) self-Existent or Eternal...Jewish national name of God...the Lord...."[9]

After Abraham learned of God's plan, he became quite concerned because Lot was living in Sodom with his family. Abraham pleaded with God to spare the city even if there were only ten righteous people in it so that Lot and his family would be saved. His plea to God was instrumental in Lot, his wife and two daughters being sent out of Sodom before the destruction of the cities of Sodom and Gomorrah. However, Lot's wife was lost through her disobedience to God's command because she looked back at the cities and was turned into a pillar of salt (Genesis 19).

> *"And it came to pass, when God destroyed the cities of the plain, that God remembered Abraham, and sent Lot out of the midst of the overthrow, when he overthrew the cities in the which Lot dwelt"* (Genesis 19:29).

Why did God destroy Sodom and Gomorrah? What had they done to deserve such punishment? Regarding Sodom and Gomorrah, Scripture tells us:

They were *"…giving themselves over to fornication, and going after strange flesh, are set forth for an example, suffering the vengeance of eternal fire."* NIV® says it this way: They *"…gave themselves up to sexual immorality and perversion…"* (Jude 7).

To get a more complete picture of the perversion of the cities, we find that when the two angels arrived at Sodom, Lot invited them into his house, and the men of the city desired them sexually. The men who lived in the city asked Lot this question: *"…Where are the men which came in to thee this night? Bring them out unto us, that we may know them"* (Genesis 19:5).

God's Intervention

Abraham and Sarah moved *"…into the region of the Negev…"* (Genesis 20:1, NIV®), and we find that, once again, Abraham and Sarah lied to a king to protect Abraham from being killed. Again, Sarah was taken into the palace of a king. This time, though, God spoke to the king and warned him in a dream:

> *"…God came to king A-bim'-e-lech in a dream by night, and said to him, Behold thou art but a dead man, for the woman which thou hast taken; for she is a man's wife. But A-bim'-e-lech had not come near her: and he said, 'LORD, wilt Thou slay a righteous nation? Said he not unto me, She is my sister? And she, even she herself said, He is my brother: in the integrity of my heart and innocency of my hands have I done this. And God said unto him in a dream, Yea, I know that thou didst this in the integrity of thy heart; for I also withheld thee from sinning against me: therefore suffered I thee not to touch her. Now therefore restore the man his wife; for he is a prophet, and he shall pray for thee, and thou shalt live: and if thou restore her not, know thou that thou shalt surely die, thou, and all that are thine"* (Genesis 20:3-7).

King Abimelech immediately released Sarah back to Abraham and gave him animals, slaves, silver, and a choice of where to live anywhere in his land.

Sarah Gives Birth to Isaac

God had intervened. He had a plan for the future, and He knew that very shortly Sarah would become pregnant with Abraham's son. The next year, at the same time as the Lord had said, Sarah gave birth to the son God had promised, and Abraham named him Isaac. Abraham, who was 100 years old, obeyed the Lord and circumcised Isaac when he was eight days old.

> *"And the child (Isaac) grew, and was weaned: and Abraham made a great feast the same day that Isaac was weaned. And Sarah saw the son of Ha'-gar the Egyptian, which she had born unto Abraham, <u>mocking</u>. Wherefore she said unto Abraham, Cast out this bondwoman and her son: for the son of this bondwoman shall not be heir with my son, even with Isaac. And the thing was very grievous in Abraham's sight because of his son"* (Genesis 21:8-11).

The Hebrew word translated *mocking* is "tsâchaq." The meaning of the word is "...to laugh outright...in merriment or scorn...."[10]

Abraham's Eighth Encounter With God

> *"And God said unto Abraham, Let it not be grievous in thy sight because of the lad, and because of thy bondwoman; in all that Sarah hath said unto thee, hearken unto her voice; for in* **Isaac shall thy seed be called.** *And also of the son of the bondwoman will I make a nation, because he is thy seed"* (Genesis 21:12-13).

(The *seed* God was talking about that would come from Isaac, would become those who would someday put their faith in Christ.)

The next morning, Abraham provided Hagar with food and water and sent Hagar and Ishmael off into the desert. God was watching over Hagar and Ishmael, and He saved them when He heard their voices:

> *"And the water was spent in the bottle, and she cast the child under one of the shrubs. And she went, and sat her down over against him a good way off, as it were a bowshot: for she said, Let me not see the death of the child. And she sat over against him, and lift up her voice, and wept. And God heard the voice of the lad; and the angel of God called to Ha'-gar out of heaven, and said unto her, What aileth thee, Ha'-gar? fear not; for God hath heard the voice of the lad where he is. Arise, lift up the lad, and hold him in thine hand; for I will make him a great nation. And God opened her eyes, and she saw a well of water; and she went, and filled the bottle with water, and gave the lad drink. And God was with the lad; and he grew, and dwelt in the wilderness, and became an archer. And he dwelt in the wilderness of Par'-an: and his mother took him a wife out of the land of Egypt"* (Genesis 21:15-21).

Abraham had to drink the bitter cup with the sweet. Abraham and Sarah had wanted children, and had waited over twenty-five years for God to fulfill His promise of a son to them. In the meantime, with Sarah's influence, they had been impatient and had run ahead of God to try and bring God's promise to pass in her own way. Now Abraham had to suffer grief over that decision and send his son Ishmael and his mother, Hagar, away from their family out into the desert. It must have torn Abraham's heart to see him go, but he had God's assurance that Ishmael would become a great nation. Hagar and Ishmael were cast out alone into the desert with wild animals, poisonous creatures, and the hot desert sun not knowing where to go or what would lie ahead. After Hagar had gone back, she had obeyed her mistress, but hate had risen in her heart for Sarah, making it impossible for the two women to stay together. Earlier, God had spoken to Hagar with a promise and a prophecy about Ishmael, and through her faith, she acknowledged God: She said, *"...Thou <u>God</u> seest me..."* (Genesis 16:13).

Here the Hebrew word translated *God* is *"êl."* The meaning of the word is "mighty; espec. The Almighty is the Hebrew word for "...strength, mightily...the Almighty...."[11]

Abraham's Ninth Encounter With God

God was about to put Abraham through the ultimate test.

> *"And it came to pass after these things, that God did tempt Abraham, and said unto him, Abraham: and he said, Behold, here I am. And he said, Take now thy son, thine only son Isaac, whom thou lovest, and get thee into the land of Mo-ri´-ah; and offer him there for a burnt offering upon one of the mountains which I will tell thee of"* (Genesis 22:1-2).

This was the only son Abraham had left, a son for whom he had waited for over twenty-five years. Why would God ask him to kill him? He had already obeyed God and sent his other son away. As we keep reading, we find that Abraham did obey without an argument. Whatever he was going through emotionally, he chose to rise above his feelings and trust and obey God Who had given His promises to him.

> *"And Abraham rose up early in the morning, and saddled his ass, and took two of his young men with him, and Isaac his son, and clave* (split) *the wood for the burnt offering, and rose up, and went unto the place of which God had told him. Then on the third day Abraham lifted up his eyes, and saw the place afar off. And Abraham said unto his young men, Abide ye here with the ass; and I and the lad will go yonder and worship, and come again to you.*
>
> *"And Abraham took the wood of the burnt offering, and laid it upon Isaac his son; and he took the fire in his hand, and a*

knife; and they went both of them together. And Isaac spake unto Abraham his father, and said, My father: and he said, Here am I, my son. And he said, Behold the fire and the wood: but where is the lamb for a burnt offering? And Abraham said, My son, God will provide himself a lamb for a burnt offering: so they went both of them together.

"And they came to the place which God had told him of; and Abraham built an altar there, and laid the wood in order, and bound Isaac his son, and laid him on the altar upon the wood" (Genesis 22:3-9).

This must have been traumatic for Isaac who trusted and loved his father, but the Bible doesn't give any indication that Isaac fought his father. This incident very possibly parallels the heart and reaction of Jesus as he was being prepared for His own crucifixion. In speaking of Jesus, Isaiah prophesied:

"He was oppressed, and he was afflicted, yet he opened not his mouth: he is brought as a lamb to the slaughter, and as a sheep before her shearers is dumb, so he openeth not His mouth" (Isaiah 53:7).

"And Abraham stretched forth his hand, and took the knife to slay his son. And the angel of the LORD called unto him out of heaven, and said, Abraham, Abraham: and he said, Here am I. And he said, Lay not thine hand upon the lad, neither do thou any thing unto him: for now I know that thou fearest God, seeing thou hast not withheld thy son, thine only son from me" (Genesis 22:10-12).

Abraham was willing to offer his son to God as a sacrifice in obedience to Him. It must have been puzzling because God had given the promises for Abraham's descendants through Isaac's seed, and then God had told him to kill that son; but Abraham's faith was tremendous.

He trusted God so much that even if God required him to kill his own son, he knew that God had a reason. God did not want a child-sacrifice—He was testing Abraham's faith and trust in Him.

Hebrews 11:17-19 says, *"By faith Abraham, when he was tried, offered up Isaac: and he that had received the promises offered up his only begotten son, Of whom it was said, That in Isaac shall thy seed be called: Accounting that God was able to raise him up, even from the dead; from whence also he received him in a figure."*

The Bible does not record that God was showing miracles of raising the dead at that time, yet Abraham believed He could. Even if it wasn't God's plan to raise him from the dead, Abraham believed He knew best.

> *"And Abraham lifted up his eyes and looked, and behold behind him a ram caught in a thicket by his horns: and Abraham went and took the ram, and offered him up for a burnt offering in the stead of his son. And Abraham called the name of that place Je-ho´-vah-ji´-reh as it is said to this day, In the mount of the LORD it shall be seen"* (Genesis 22:13-14).

The Hebrew word translated *"Je-ho´-vah-ji´-reh* is *"Yᵉhôvâh yireh."* The meaning of the word is *"...Jehovah will see (to it)...a symbolical name for Mt. Moriah."* [12] Many Bible scholars believe that Jesus was crucified on this same mountain in the land of Moriah.

God provided a ram to be sacrificed instead of Abraham's son. This was exactly what God did for us, too. Jesus, the Lamb of God, was the ram in the thicket that God provided to become the sacrifice to pay for our sins. Accounts of the crucifixion are found in Matthew 27, Mark 15, Luke 23, and John 19, and will be discussed in-depth in Book 2 of this series.

> *"And the angel of the LORD called unto Abraham out of heaven the second time, And said, By myself have I sworn, saith the LORD, for because thou hast done this thing, and hast not withheld thy son, thine only son: That in blessing **I will bless thee**, and in multiplying **I will multiply thy seed as the stars of the heaven**, and as the sand which is upon the sea shore; and*

> *thy seed shall possess the gate of his enemies; And in thy*
> *seed shall all the nations of the earth be blessed; because*
> *thou hast obeyed my voice"* (Genesis 22:15-18).

God solidified His promises: Isaac would become the next descendant to receive the promises given to Abraham. Why did God solidify His promises to Abraham? He did it because Abraham believed and obeyed His voice.

Galatians 4 gives us an allegory of the two covenants of Sarah and Hagar. God had made it perfectly clear—the descendants through Isaac, Sarah's son, would become *"...the children of promise..., born after the Spirit..."* (Galatians 4:28, 29). Sarah is noted as the *"...freewoman...."* The descendants through Hagar, the *"...bondwoman...,"* and her son, Ishmael, would be known as *"...born after the flesh...."*

> *"But as then he that was born after the flesh persecuted him that*
> *was born after the Spirit, even so it is now"* (Galatians 4:29).

When Christ, the promised One, came, He came through the Hebrew lineage of Isaac. He came to save all of mankind, both the Jews and the Gentiles, who would believe in Him. Abraham and his descendants were the *"...children of promise..."* because they believed in the promise of the coming Christ. Now, all who receive Christ as their Lord and Savior become the *"...children of promise..."* and are filled with the Holy Spirit, through faith in Him.

The Region of Moriah

"Abraham's offering (of Isaac) took place on one of the hills on which Jerusalem now stands ('possibly the Temple hill, itself—see 2 Chronicles 3:1')."[13] This journey, from the land of the Philistines, would be about "80 km, which might well have required three days to traverse, and in Genesis the place in question is not a 'mount Moriah' but one of several mountains in a land of that name, and the hills on which Jerusalem stands are visible at a distance. There is no need to doubt therefore that Abraham's sacrifice took place on the site of later Jerusalem, if not on the Temple Hill."[14]

The Temple Hill was the location where Solomon will later build the permanent Temple in Jerusalem, which will be used by the Israelites for a centralized place of worship.

Sarah's Death

Sarah died at 127 years old. Abraham bought some property from the Hittites for a burial site and buried Sarah in the land of Canaan in the cave of Machpelah near Mamre in the field he purchased from Ephron, the Hittite, for 400 shekels of silver (found in Genesis 23).

In Conclusion

Altogether, the Bible records at least nine encounters between God and Abraham, and God gave Abraham the gospel of Jesus Christ—all nations would be blessed. God was the One Who initiated all of His promises, but God did have conditions for these promises. First, Abraham must walk perfectly; second, he must implement the rite of circumcision, which would become an outward sign that Abraham and his descendants were consecrated to God; third Abraham must pass God's ultimate test—he must be willing to give his son, Isaac, back to God. Abraham had stumbled a few times along the way, but he passed his tests of faith and obedience to the living God. After fulfilling his part of the covenant, God awarded to him and his descendants all the promises He had given him.

The law had not yet been written, so Abraham's sexual act with Hagar, his wife's handmaid, may not have been considered as sin. Even so, there would be repercussions over Abraham's decision to run ahead of God. Isaac's children would become known as the children "...*born of the Spirit....*" Ishmael's children would become known as children "...*born of the flesh....*"

As we journey on, we find that once again, God will select godly seed from Isaac's children, and the promises of the everlasting covenant, which had been given to Abraham, will continue on through Isaac's son, Jacob.

Deeper Insights:

1. God's seventh encounter with Abram is powerful. The Lord told Abram to *"walk before me and be thou perfect"* (Genesis 17:1-2). Abram was a man born with the sin nature, so we know that he could not be perfect in the literal sense. What do you think God meant when He told Abram to be perfect?

    As stated in this chapter, the Hebrew word translated *perfect* is "tâmîym." The meaning of the word is "entire...integrity, truth...sound, without spot, undefiled, upright..., whole...."

    Based on the Hebrew meaning of perfect, how does God tell us we ought to walk?"

    Read 1 John 1:7; 3 John 4; Colossians 1:10-13; 2:6-7; 4:5-6; Galatians 5:16-17; and Ephesians 4:1-3, 5:2.

    We cannot be perfect on our own, but God is the One Who makes us perfect. In summary, the meaning of the Greek words translated *perfect/perfected* in the scriptures below is "... to complete thoroughly, i.e. repair...or adjust...accomplish... finish...fulfill...consecrate...."

    Read the following scriptures about the words *perfect/perfected*: 1Peter 5:10 (katartizō)[15]; Hebrews 2:9-10; 10:14-18; (tĕlĕiŏō)[16] Galatians 3:3-9 (ĕpitĕlĕō)[17]; 2 Timothy 3:16-17 (artiŏs)[18]; and Ephesians 4:10-13 (tĕlĕiŏō)[19]. How does God perfect us?

    As believers in Christ, what is accounted to us for righteousness? Read Romans 4:1-5.

2. The Lord commanded Abram to perform the rite of circumcision to seal his covenant with God. It was to be a sign

of the covenant between God and the Hebrews. Those who were not circumcised in their flesh were not included in the everlasting covenant, and the same is true for us today. The Holy Spirit comes to live in those who put their hope in Christ. He is the sign in us that we belong to Christ. If we are not sealed with the Holy Spirit, we will not be included in the new everlasting covenant through the blood of Christ.

What does it mean to be circumcised "...*by the circumcision of Christ?*" (Colossians 2:11)

Read Romans 3:20-22; Colossians 2:9-15; and Philippians 3:3.

What is the fruit of the Holy Spirit, which is evidenced in the lives of Christians?

Read Galatians 5:22-23.

What are the works of the flesh? Read Galatians 5:16-21; Ephesians 5:3-11; and 1 Thessalonians 4:3-8

3. God did not select Ishmael as His godly seed, yet Abraham circumcised him when he was thirteen years old. Does that mean that Ishmael was included in the everlasting covenant with God? Read Romans 9:1-8.

4. The Lord destroyed the two cities of Sodom and Gomorrah because of unrighteousness.

    What were the sins of Sodom and Gomorrah? We have read that sexual perversion was prevalent in Sodom and Gomorrah, but there were other sins, too. Read Genesis 19:4-5; Ezekiel 16:49-50; and Isaiah 3:8-9.

5. Since God had not yet given the law to man, do you think it was considered sin for Abraham to sleep with his wife's handmaid, by his wife's suggestion? Read Romans 5:13.

    What was wrong with Sarah's suggestion?

    Hagar had obeyed her mistress to conceive a son by Abraham. Do you think it was unfair that

Sarah demanded that Hagar and her son, Ishmael, be sent away from Abraham's family?

Read Genesis 16:4-6 and Genesis 21:8-10.

6. Sarah was in her nineties when she conceived Isaac. How was she able to conceive and bare a son? Read Hebrews 11:11.

7. Two covenants had been established with the births of Isaac and Ishmael.

   Read Galatians 4:22-31. What is the difference between those who are "...*born after the flesh*..." and those who are born "...*by promise...?*"

   Can those "*born after the flesh*" become "*children of promise?*" If so, how can they?

8. Abraham had been perfect before God—he was obedient in instituting the rite of circumcision, and his faith was strong, yet God told Abraham to kill his son.

   Why did God ask Abraham to do such a horrible thing? Read Genesis 22:1, 12.

   What was the result of his obedience? Read Genesis 22:15-18.

   The Old Testament is full of parallelisms that point the way to Christ. Read Genesis 22:1-18 and list the ways that this great sacrifice of Abraham compares to the great salvation story for us through Christ.

CHAPTER 6

THE TWELVE SONS OF ISRAEL

The Search For Isaac's Wife

After Sarah had died, and Abraham was getting quite old, he wanted to find a wife for his son, Isaac. In order for the promises to come to his descendants, Isaac must have children. Isaac's descendants must not come from the pagan Canaanites, and a wife must be selected from his own country and his own relatives. Again, we will see God's hand in this situation as He carries out His plan of selecting people to bare His godly seed.

> "One day Abraham said to the man in charge of his household, who was his oldest servant, 'Swear by the LORD, the God of heaven and earth, that you will not let my son marry one of these local Canaanite women. Go instead to my homeland, to my relatives, and find a wife there for my son Isaac.'

> "The servant asked, 'But suppose I can't find a young woman who will travel so far from home? May I then take Isaac there to live among your relatives?'

> "'No!' Abraham warned. 'Be careful never to take my son there. For the LORD, the God of heaven, who took me from my father's house and my native land, solemnly promised to give this land to my offspring. He will send his angel ahead of you, and he will see

to it that you find a young woman there to be my son's wife. If she is unwilling to come back with you, then you are free from this oath. But under no circumstances are you to take my son there"' (Genesis 24:2-9, NLT).

Abraham's chief servant took camels and goods and traveled to Abraham's brother, who lived in the town of Nahor and brought back a wife for Isaac. Her name was Rebekah.

"And Isaac came from the way of the well La'-hai-roi; for he dwelt in the south country. And Isaac went out to meditate in the field at the eventide: and he lifted up his eyes, and saw, and, behold, the camels were coming. And Rebekah lifted up her eyes, and when she saw Isaac, she lighted off the camel. For she had said unto the servant, What man is this that walketh in the field to meet us? And the servant had said, It is my master: therefore she took a veil, and covered herself. And the servant told Isaac all things that he had done. And Isaac brought her into his mother Sarah's tent, and took Rebekah, and she became his wife; and he loved her: and Isaac was comforted after his mother's death" (Genesis 24:62-67).

Abraham's Second Wife and His Death

In Genesis 25, we find that Abraham married another woman, Keturah, *"And she bare him Zimran, and Jok´-shan, and Me´-dan, and Mid´-i-a-n, and Ish´-bak and Shu´-ah"* (Genesis 25:2).

"Keturah's sons are the ancestors of a number of north Arabian peoples. When Abraham died at age 175, Isaac and Ishmael came together and buried him with Sarah in the field he had purchased from the Hittites. All of Keturah's sons had been provided for by Abraham, but Isaac remained his father's sole heir, and on Abraham's death both possessions and promises become his: God 'blessed' Isaac."[1] Even though God had told Abraham he would die and not live to see the

promises fulfilled, Abraham kept his faith and trusted God that what
He had promised for His descendants would come to pass.

Ishmael, the son born to Abraham by Hagar, lived to be 137 years
old, leaving behind his twelve sons. His people lived *"...from Hav´-I-lah
unto Shur, that is before Egypt, as thou goest toward Assyria: and he died in the
presence of all his brethren"* (Genesis 25:18).

Esau and Jacob

Isaac, Abraham's son, was forty years old when he married Rebekah.
She was barren, just as his mother, Sarah, had been. He prayed for her,
and after twenty years, the Lord answered his prayer. During Rebekah's
pregnancy, *"...the children struggled together within her; and she said, If it be
so, why am I thus? And she went to enquire of the LORD"* (Genesis 25:22).
The Lord gave Rebekah a prophecy of His plan for the two twin sons
in her womb:

> *"...Two nations are in thy womb, and two manner of people shall
> be separated from thy bowels; and the one people shall be stronger
> than the other people; and the elder shall serve the younger.*

> *"And when her days to be delivered were fulfilled, behold, there
> were twins in her womb. And the first came out red, all over like
> an hairy garment; and they called his name Esau. And after that
> came his brother out, and his hand took hold on Esau's heel; and
> his name was called Jacob: and Isaac was threescore years old when
> she bare them"* (Genesis 25:23-26).

The Hebrew word translated *Jacob* is "Ya'ăqôb." The meaning of
the word is "...heel-catcher (i.e. supplanter)...."[2]. Esau, the oldest son,
would serve Jacob, the youngest son.

> *"And the boys grew: and Esau was a cunning hunter, a man of
> the field; and Jacob was a plain man, dwelling in tents. And Isaac*

loved Esau, because he did eat of his venison: but Rebekah loved Jacob" (Genesis 25:27-28).

Esau, did not value his birthright and one day when he was hungry, he sold it to his brother, Jacob, for some stew. "As firstborn son, Esau will succeed Isaac as head of the family and inherit a double share of the estate. When he sells his birthright he forfeits all title to the inheritance and to the blessing that goes with it."[3] So, rightfully, Esau's birthright and blessing will go to Jacob, even though Jacob was the youngest son, just as the Lord had prophesied to Rebekah.

Isaac Inherits God's Promises

"And there was a famine in the land, beside the first famine that was in the days of Abraham. And Isaac went unto A-bim´-e-lech king of the Philis´-tines unto Ge´-rar" (Genesis 26:1).

The Lord appeared to Isaac and spoke promises to him, as He had done so many times with his father, Abraham:

*"...Go not down into Egypt; dwell in the land which I shall tell thee of: Sojourn in this land, and I will be with thee, and will bless thee; for **unto thee, and unto thy seed, I will give all these countries**, and I **will perform the oath which I sware unto Abraham thy father;** And I **will make thy seed to multiply as the stars of heaven, and will give unto thy seed all these countries; and in thy seed shall all the nations of the earth be blessed;** Because that Abraham obeyed my voice, and kept my charge, my commandments, my statutes, and my laws"* (Genesis 26:2-5).

Isaac, like his father, Abraham, believed the Lord and obeyed Him. God was now passing down to Isaac the promises He had given to Abraham. While in Beersheba, Isaac had another encounter with the Lord:

> *"...I am the God of Abraham your father; fear not, for I am with thee; and **I will bless thee, and will multiply thy seed for my servant Abraham's sake**"* (Genesis 26:24).

In the meantime, Esau took two Hittite wives, who were descendants of Noah's grandson Canaan, whom Noah had cursed. This was a worry to Isaac and Rebekah, because the Hittite wives did not have faith in the living God, but worshiped idols.

Isaac Blesses His Sons

When Isaac became old and blind, and it was almost time for him to die, he told his eldest son, Esau, to go kill some wild game and cook up a meal for him so he could bless him before he died. Rebekah heard this conversation and wanted Jacob to have the blessing instead of Esau (which was really God's plan all along), so she sent Jacob out to get some game for her to cook. The two of them devised a deceitful plan to cover Jacob with goatskins so he would be hairy like his brother and dressed him in Esau's clothes. This deceit would prove to be a sad story at a high cost. Rebekah and Jacob would deceive Isaac, breaking Isaac's heart, and Rebekah would never see Jacob again. It is evident that God did not choose Jacob because he was perfect. Just like his grandfather Abraham, he was capable of deceit.

Rebekah dressed Jacob in Esau's clothing so that he would smell like his brother, and took goat skins and covered his hands and the back of his neck, so that he would feel hairy like Esau. When she had dressed him, she sent Jacob into Isaac, along with a meal made of goat meat, which she had cooked up to taste like venison. When Isaac asked Jacob who he was, Jacob lied to him:

> *"...I am Esau thy first-born; I have done according as thou badest me: arise, I pray thee, sit and eat of my venison, that thy soul may bless me. And Isaac said unto his son, How is it that thou hast found it so quickly, my son? And he said, Because the*

LORD thy God brought it to me. And Isaac said unto Jacob, Come near, I pray thee, that I may feel thee, my son, whether thou be my very son Esau or not. And Jacob went near unto Isaac his father; and he felt him, and said, The voice is Jacob's voice, but the hands are the hands of Esau. And he discerned him not, because his hands were hairy, as his brother Esau's hands: so he blessed him. And he said, Art thou my very son Esau? And he said, I am" (Genesis 27:19-24).

Isaac believed Jacob, even though he thought he was feeling Esau's hairy hands. He ate what he thought was his cooked meal of venison and drank the wine he had brought him. Then Isaac asked Jacob to come to him and kiss him, and after he smelled his clothes, he blessed him:

"Therefore God give thee of the dew of heaven, and the fatness of the earth, and plenty of corn and wine: let people serve thee, and nations bow down to thee: be lord over thy brethren, and let thy mother's sons bow down to thee: cursed be every one that curseth thee, and blessed be he that blesseth thee" (Genesis 27:27-29).

Later Esau came back with his prepared meal for his father, only to find that his brother had taken his blessing, which he had actually given him earlier when he had sold his birthright. Esau begged his father for a blessing, as well, and Isaac gave him the following blessing:

"...Behold thy dwelling shall be the fatness of the earth and of the dew of heaven from above; and by thy sword shalt thou live, and shalt serve thy brother: and it shall come to pass when thou shalt have the dominion, that thou shalt break his yoke from off thy neck" (Genesis 27:39-40).

Again, we can see that the prophecy God had given to Rebekah had come true.

Esau was hurt and angry and made the decision to kill Jacob after the death of his father, Isaac. When Rebekah realized this, she sent Jacob away, giving her husband, Isaac, the excuse that she didn't want Jacob to stay because he might stay and marry a Hittite woman. When Isaac heard that, he commanded Jacob to never marry a Canaanite woman, but to go to his grandfather's house in Paddan Aram and take a wife from among his uncle Laban's daughters. Then he blessed him with a prayer to receive the promises that God had been given to Abraham. When Esau realized how much his parents were against the Canaanite women, and that Jacob had obeyed his parents, he rebelled and went and married a daughter of Ishmael (Hagar's son). God had selected Jacob as His godly seed because his heart was right, and Esau had a heart of rebellion.

Jacob Inherits God's Promises

Jacob left for Paddan Aram, and when he laid his head down on his pillow of stone, he had a dream in which God came to him and passed down His promises to him:

> *"And he dreamed, and behold a ladder set up on the earth, and the top of it reached to heaven: and behold the angels of God ascending and descending on it. And behold, the LORD stood above it, and said, I am the LORD God of Abraham thy father, and the God of Isaac:* **the land whereon thou liest, to thee will I give it, and to thy seed; And thy seed shall be as the dust of the earth, and thou shalt spread abroad to the west, and to the east, and to the north, and to the south: and in thee and in thy seed shall all the families of the earth be blessed.** *And, behold,* **I am with thee, and will keep thee in all places whither thou goest, and will bring thee again into this land;** *for I will not leave thee, until I have done that which I have spoken to thee of"* (Genesis 28:12-15).

Those promises were a turning point for Jacob. He knew that the Lord had been there, and he made a decision:

> *"And Jacob vowed a vow, saying, If God will be with me, and will keep me in this way that I go, and will give me bread to eat, and raiment to put on, So that I come again to my father's house in peace; then shall the LORD be my God: And this stone, which I have set for a pillar, shall be God's house: and of all that thou shalt give me I will surely give the tenth unto thee"* (Genesis 28:20-22).

Just as Abraham had given Melchizadek a tenth of the plunder, Jacob would also give a tenth to the Lord. The law had still not come into effect or the priesthood, which required tithing.

Jacob Finds a Wife

Jacob didn't know it, but God was about to teach him a lesson on deception. When Jacob arrived in Paddan Aram, he fell in love with Rachel, who was actually his cousin. Jacob stayed and worked a month for her father, Laban. Jacob agreed to work for seven years for the wages of Laban's youngest daughter, Rachel. When the seven years were ended, Laban held a party, and after dark, brought his oldest daughter, Leah, to Jacob; and he unknowingly slept with her. After confronting Laban, who had deceived him, Laban told him that in their country they must not give the youngest daughter before the oldest daughter in marriage. So an agreement was made that Rachel be given to him at that time, but that he would be required to work another seven years to pay for her. Laban had deceived Jacob, as Jacob had deceived his own father.

God could see that Jacob loved Rachel more than Leah, so He opened Leah's womb, and closed Rachel's womb so she could not have children. Back in the days of the Old Testament, it was a disgrace for women to not bare children, because large families were considered to be a blessing from God. God makes it clear in Genesis 29 and 30 that He is the One Who opens and closes the wombs of women. The next part of this true story almost sounds comical as Jacob becomes involved in bed hopping from one competitive wife to the other and from one maidservant to another.

In Genesis 29:32-35, we see that Leah gave birth to four sons, and she gave them these names:

Reuben: *"...for...Surely the LORD hath looked upon my affliction; now therefore my husband will love me."*

Simeon: *"Because the LORD hath heard that I was hated, he hath therefore given me this son also...."*

Levi: *"...Now this time will my husband be joined unto me, because I have born him three sons...."*

Judah: *"Now will I praise the LORD...."*

The line of Levi would eventually become the Levitical priesthood, and the line from Judah would eventually become the royal line of kings that would usher in king David and then King Jesus.

Rachel became jealous of Leah and scolded Jacob for not giving her children and gave him her maidservant, Bilhah, to bear children for her. In Genesis 30:3-8, we see Bilhah gave birth to the following sons:

Dan: *"...God hath judged me, and hath also heard my voice...."*

Naphtali: *"With great wrestlings have I wrestled with my sister, and I have prevailed...."*

Leah had stopped bearing children and gave her servant Zilpah to Jacob to bear children for her. In Genesis 30:9-13, we see that Zilpah gave birth to these two sons:

Gad: *"A troop cometh...."*

Asher: *"Happy am I, for the daughters will call me blessed...."*

Leah's son, Reuben, went out into the fields and brought her some mandrake plants to help make his mother fertile, a belief that was held at that time. When Rachel heard that Leah had the mandrakes, she asked Leah for them with the promise that she could sleep with Jacob that night. Leah then gave birth to another son—**Issachar**: *"...God hath given me my hire, because I have given my maiden to my husband...."* Leah conceived another time, and bore another son—**Zebulun**. *"...God hath endued me with a good dowry; now will my husband dwell with me, because I have born him six sons...."* Then she also bore a daughter and named her Dinah (see Genesis 30:14-21).

> *"...God remembered Rachel, and God hearkened to her, and opened her womb. And she conceived, and bare a son; and said, God hath taken away my reproach: And she called his name* **Joseph** *"* (Genesis 30:22-24).

Jacob now had eleven sons and one daughter.

When it was time for Jacob to take his wives and children and return to his homeland, Laban didn't want him to go because his own wealth had increased by Jacob being there. Jacob struck up a deal with Laban. He would work for him if he could have all of Laban's spotted and speckled cattle and goats and his brown sheep. However, Jacob had a deceptive plan in mind, and Laban, just as Jacob had, would feel the sting of his own deception.

> *"And Jacob took him rods of green poplar, and of the hazel and chestnut tree; and pilled white strakes in them, and made the white appear which was in the rods. And he set the rods which he had pilled before the flocks in the gutters in the watering troughs when the flocks came to drink, that they should conceive when they came to drink. And the flocks conceived before the rods, and brought forth cattle ring-streaked, speckled, and spotted.*
>
> *"And Jacob did separate the lambs, and set the faces of the flocks toward the ring-streaked, and all the brown in the flock of Laban;*

and he put his own flocks by themselves, and put them not unto
Laban's cattle. And it came to pass, whensoever the stronger cattle
did conceive, that Jacob laid the rods before the eyes of the cattle in
the gutters, that they might conceive among the rods. But when the
cattle were feeble, he put them not in: so the feebler were Laban's,
and the stronger Jacob's" (Genesis 30:37-39).

Laban's sons were not happy with Jacob, and they talked among themselves, accusing him of taking their father's possessions. Jacob could also see that Laban wasn't happy either.

"And the LORD said unto Jacob, Return unto the land of thy
fathers, and to thy kindred; and I will be with thee" (Genesis 31:3).

Jacob told his wives about how Laban had deceived him and about what had happened with the cattle, sheep, and goats. He also told them what the Lord had told him to do. Jacob continued, *"And the angel of God spake unto me in a dream, saying, Jacob: And I said, Here am I. And he said, Lift up now thine eyes, and see, all the rams which leap upon the cattle are ring-streaked, speckled, and grizzled: for I have seen all that Laban doeth unto thee. I am the God of Beth-el, where thou appointedst the pillar, and where thou vowedst a vow unto me: now arise, get thee out from this land, and return unto the land of thy kindred"* (Genesis 31:6-13).

Jacob had thought he had caused the changing of the cattle, but the Lord let him know He had made the changes in his favor.

When Jacob was preparing to take his family and his wealth back to the land of Canaan, he didn't tell Laban he was leaving; and to top it off, Rachel stole her father's household gods for an inheritance. When Laban realized that Jacob had left, and his gods were missing, he was mad. He and his relatives spent seven days pursuing Jacob and his family. On the way, God came to Laban in a dream and told him not to say anything, good or bad, to Jacob. When Laban caught up with Jacob, he asked him why he had ran away and stolen his gods. Jacob told Laban he had been afraid that he would take his daughters away from him, but he didn't know anything about the gods. He did not know that Rachel had hidden them under her camel's saddle. Laban searched the camp, but did not find the gods, and Jacob got his chance to remind Laban of all the things he had done to him during those twenty years of service. Jacob and Laban made a covenant agreement together pronouncing God's blessings on each other. They promised to never bring harm to each other again, and then Laban went back home and Jacob continued on his journey.

As Jacob continued on his way to Canaan, *"...the angels of God met him. When Jacob saw them, he said, 'This is the camp of God!' So he named that place Mahanaim"* (Genesis 32:1-2, NIV®). In Hebrew *Mahanaim* means "...double camp...."[4]

God Changes Jacob's Name

As Jacob and his group came nearer to Esau, he sent some messengers ahead to let Esau know he was coming back, and he was asking for his grace. The messengers came back and told Jacob that Esau was coming to meet him with 400 men, which terrified Jacob. He split his camp up into two camps, so that at least one group could try and escape should the other group be attacked. Then Jacob went to God and prayed.

> *"...O God of my father Abraham, and God of my father Isaac, the LORD which saidst unto me, Return unto thy country, and to thy kindred, and I will deal well with thee: I am not worthy of the least of all the mercies, and of all the truth, which thou hast showed unto thy servant; for with my staff I passed over this Jordan; and now I am become two bands. Deliver me, I pray thee, from the hand of my brother, from the hand of Esau: for I fear him, lest he will come and smite me, and the mother with the children. And thou saidst, I will surely do thee good, and make thy seed as the sand of the sea, which cannot be numbered for multitude"* (Genesis 32:9-12).

The next day Jacob, hoping to pacify Esau, selected gifts for Esau from his herds and told the servants to begin to walk in the direction of Esau in three successive groups. Each group was to convey to Esau that the gifts were from Jacob, and that Jacob was on his way. Jacob stayed back and helped his family take all his possessions and ford the stream. Then Jacob stayed the night alone in the camp.

> *"And Jacob was left alone; and there wrestled a man with him until the breaking of the day. And when he saw that he prevailed not against him, he touched the hollow of his thigh; and the hollow of Jacob's thigh was out of joint, as he wrestled with him. And he said, Let me go, for the day breaketh. And he said, I will not let thee go, except thou bless me. And he said unto him, What is thy name? And he said, Jacob. And he said, **Thy name shall be called no more Jacob, but Israel:** for as a prince hast thou power with God and with men, and hast prevailed"* (Genesis 32:24-28).

God changed Jacob's name to Israel. The Hebrew word translated *Israel* is "Yisrâ'êl." The meaning of the word is "...he will rule as God...."[5]

"...*Jacob called that place Peni´-el: for I have seen God face to face, and my life is preserved*" (Genesis 32:30).

Jacob was now crippled because of his encounter with God, but his heart was not crippled—it was now pure before God. What a personal God!

Jacob and Esau Are Reconciled

When Esau arrived at Jacob's camp, he ran to meet Jacob. They held each other, kissed each other, and they both wept. Esau tried to give back the gifts Jacob had given him, but Jacob insisted he keep them. When Esau offered to accompany Jacob and his group, Jacob offered excuses so that they would not leave together. Esau went back to Seir, and Jacob went to Succoth and then on to Shechem in Canaan, where he bought some land to pitch his tent.

While on the way to Bethel, Jacob had an encounter with God, who told him,

> "...*Thy name is Jacob: thy name shall not be called any more Jacob, but **Israel shall be thy name** and he called his name Israel. And God said unto him, **I am God Almighty**: be fruitful and multiply; a nation and a company of nations shall be of thee, and kings shall come out of thy loins; And the land which I gave Abraham and Isaac, to thee I will give it, and to thy seed after thee will I give the land*" (Genesis 35:10-12).

Jacob had just inherited the promises that had been given to Abraham and Isaac, and he obeyed the Lord. As they were moving from Bethel, Rachel died in childbirth with her last son, **Benjamin**. Israel (Jacob) now had twelve sons, which would become known as the *"twelve tribes of Israel."* Israel's father, Isaac, died at the age of 180 years old, and Esau and Jacob both buried their father. Genesis 36 gives the account of Esau's ancestry with his wives from the land of Canaan. Esau would become the father of the Edomites.

In Conclusion

Abraham knew that in order for Isaac's seed to inherit the promises God had given him, Isaac would need a wife, and it had to be a wife from a Hebrew family, not from any other nation. God had prophesied about the twin boys in Rebekah's womb--the older brother, Esau, would serve the younger brother, Jacob. When Esau uncaringly sold his birthright to Jacob for some stew, he forfeited all his rights as the eldest son, giving those rights to Jacob, which was the fulfillment of God's prophecy. Apparently, only Esau and Jacob knew of the forfeiture of his birthright because Isaac was still preparing to give Esau his rightful blessings before he died. Rebekah and Jacob's deceptive plan to give Jacob Esau's blessing came with a dear price—Rebekah would never see her son, Jacob, again. Jacob would have to go through twenty years of labor under a deceptive uncle in order to marry the wife he loved. However, Jacob's marriages with the two sisters, Leah and Rachel bore him twelve sons and one daughter. Jacob's encounter with God's angel changed his heart, which prepared him to faithfully serve the living God and to be a humble servant, which would play a part in the reconciliation between he and his brother, Esau. After that, God also changed Jacob's name to Israel, "...*for as a prince hast thou power with God and with men, and hast prevailed*" (Genesis 32:24-28).

As we move on, we will read an amazing story about love and forgiveness, and we will see a major prophecy fulfilled that God had given Abraham—a prophecy that will change the world forever.

Deeper Insights:

1. God gave Rebekah a prophecy about the twin sons in her womb—the older son would serve the younger. Isaac also confirmed God's prophecy when he unknowingly blessed Jacob, the younger son, with the prophecy that his mother's sons would bow down to him.

   Read Romans 9:4-18 and Hebrews 12:12-17. Why did God select Jacob instead of Esau for his godly seed?

2. God selected godly seed from each generation so that there would be a people, a nation, who would remain faithful to Him. We find that God chose these men to be His godly seed: Seth and Abel from Adam and Eve; Shem from Noah; Isaac from Abraham; and now Jacob from Isaac. God passed down the promises of Abraham to each of these men and to his godly seed, Isaac. What were those promises? Read Genesis 26:2-5 and Genesis 26:24

3. After Sarah died, Abraham married again to Keturah, and she bore him six children. After Abraham died, who inherited his estate? Read Genesis 25:5-6.

Why was Ishmael left out of Abraham's inheritance? Read Galatians 4:22-30.

Who were Ishmael's descendants and what happened to Ishmael? Read Genesis 25:12-18.

4. After learning of Esau's desire to kill Jacob for tricking him, Rebekah sent Jacob to Paddan Aram to find a wife. On that journey, God spoke to Jacob in a dream and passed the promises down to Jacob that He had given to Abraham and Isaac. What were those promises? Read Genesis 28:12-15.

5. After God gave Jacob His promises, Jacob vowed a vow to God. Read Genesis 28:20-22.

   What was Jacob's vow to God?

6. Jacob had deceived his father to obtain his blessing, and Laban deceived Jacob by giving him Leah instead of Rachel, the wife he had been promised. Jacob had to stay and work seven more years to pay for Rachel. God was using this time to bring about His dynamic plan for the future and to teach Jacob a valuable lesson.

   During this period of time, God opened the wombs of four women to give Jacob twelve sons and a daughter. Read Ruth 4:11. What important role did Rachel and Leah play in God's dynamic plan?

7. Jacob devised a plan in order to trick Laban and increase his own flocks. Read Genesis 31:10-13. What did the angel of the Lord confirm to Jacob?

8. Before Rachel left with Jacob, she stole her father's household gods and hid them under her saddle. Laban, upon realizing his gods were gone, and that Jacob had left with his cattle and goods without telling him, left to overtake Jacob. Read Genesis 31:24. How did God intervene on Jacob's behalf?

   Read Genesis 31:38-42. How did Jacob defend himself to Laban, and at the same time, show Laban the error of his ways?

9. On Jacob's journey home from Laban's, he had a wrestling encounter with an angel of God, and God changed Jacob's name to Israel. The angel physically overcame Jacob by dislocating his thigh, but the Bible says that Jacob prevailed. What happened to cause Jacob to change and prevail? Read Hosea 12:2-4 and Genesis 32:24-32, 48:15-16.

10. After Jacob's encounters with God, he was a changed man, who had learned to be humble. Out of fear of Esau, he humbled himself as Esau's servant. What else did Jacob do that may have changed Esau's heart toward him to love and forgive him? Read Genesis 32:9-19.

CHAPTER 7

THE HEBREWS GO TO EGYPT

Joseph Is Sold Into Slavery.

Earlier, God had given Abraham a prophecy that his descendants would live in Egypt and become enslaved for 400 years. The time had come for that prophecy to begin to unfold.

Joseph was one of the twelve sons of Israel (Jacob). He, like his father, believed in and listened to God's Spirit, and *"...Israel loved Joseph more than all his children, because he was the son of his old age: and he made him a coat of many colors* (pieces)" (Genesis 37:3). Joseph's brothers knew that he was their father's favorite son, and they were jealous of him. When their father made a special robe for him, all of his brothers began to hate Joseph. To make matters worse, when Joseph was about seventeen years old, God gave him a prophetic dream, and he shared it with his brothers:

> *"For, behold, we were binding sheaves in the field, and, lo, my sheaf arose, and also stood upright; and, behold, your sheaves stood round about, and made obeisance to my sheaf"* (Genesis 37:7).

The thought of Joseph becoming a ruler over them made them hate him more. When God gave Joseph this second prophetic dream, He shared it with his brothers, as well:

> *"...Behold, I have dreamed a dream more; and, behold, the sun and the moon and the eleven stars made obeisance to me"* (Genesis 37:9).

This time, his father even scolded him for insinuating that their family would bow down to him. However, these prophecies were from God, and they were very close to being fulfilled.

The brothers' hatred grew for Joseph. One day Israel sent Joseph out into the fields to find his brothers who had been tending his flocks. When the brothers saw him coming, they planned how they would kill him, but Reuben (the oldest) talked them out of murdering their brother. When Joseph caught up with his brothers, they took his robe that his father had given him and threw him into a dry cistern. Some Ishmaelite merchants (descendants from Ishmael) from Gilead came by and the brothers sold Joseph to them for about eight ounces of silver, and the merchants took him to Egypt. Reuben was not there when they sold Joseph, because the Bible says he returned to the cistern and found him missing. The brothers had killed a goat and put the goat's blood on Joseph's robe and showed it to their father, Israel, to convince him that an animal had killed Joseph. They did not want their father to know the terrible thing they had done. Brokenhearted, Israel determined that he would never stop grieving over Joseph.

God Selects Another Godly Seed

Meanwhile, Judah left his brothers and married Shuah, the daughter of a Canaanite. They had three sons—Er, Onan, and Shelah.

After Judah found a wife for Er, God killed Er because he was wicked. So Judah sent his other son, Onan, to marry her and bare children for his brother, but he spilled his seed on the ground, and God killed him, as well.

Judah brought Tamar to live in his house with the promise she would marry Shelah when he was grown. Later, Judah's daughter died. After he finished mourning, he decided to go to Timnah to be with his sheepshearers, but he did not give Tamar to Shelah, who was grown.

When Tamar heard Judah was leaving, she devised a plan. She put on the clothes of a harlot and waited for Judah along the way. When he saw her, he did not recognize her—he thought she was a harlot. When Judah asked to have sex with her, she asked what he would give her, and they agreed that he would send her a kid goat. However, Tamar required he leave his signet, his bracelets, and his staff with her until he sent the kid.

Tamar conceived a set of twins from Judah, and after he left, she dressed herself in her widow clothes. Three months later, the news came to Judah that Tamar was pregnant by whoredom, and he wanted to burn her. Tamar brought out the things Judah had left with her as a promise, and said, "...By the man, whose these are, am I with child... (Genesis 38:25).

> *"And it came to pass in the time of her travail, that, behold, twins were in her womb. And it came to pass, when she travailed, that the one put out his hand: and the midwife took and bound upon his hand a scarlet thread, saying, This came out first. And it came to pass, as he drew back his hand,that, behold, his brother came out: and she said, How hast thou broken forth? This breach be upon thee: therefore his name was called Phar'-ez* (Perez). *And afterward came out his brother that had the scarlet thread upon his hand and his name was called Zar'-ah"* (Genesis 38:27-30).

The following scriptures include Perez in the lineage of David, which leads to Christ: Ruth 4:18-22, Matthew 1:3-6, and Luke 3:31-33—Perez, Hezron, Ram, Amminadab, Nahshon, Salmon, Boaz, Obed, Jesse, and David. In this lineage Jesse will become the father of king David: *"A shoot will come up from the stump of Jesse; from his roots a Branch will bear fruit"* (Isaiah 11:1, NIV®). The Branch is in reference to the Messiah, Jesus. Acts 13:23 says,*"Of this man's* (Jesse's) *seed hath God according to his promise raised into Israel a Savior, Jesus."*

Joseph Goes to Egypt

Potiphar, one of Pharaoh's officials, bought Joseph from the Ishmaelites. The Lord was with Joseph, and Potiphar favored him, putting him in charge of his entire household. After a time, Potiphar's wife began to lust over Joseph, who was a handsome man, and began to try and persuade Joseph to sleep with her. Joseph, because of his loyalty to Potiphar and to God, refused her each time. One day, she grabbed him by his cloak, and when he refused her and turned to leave, his cloak stayed behind in her hand. When Potiphar came home, his wife made up a lie that Joseph had been making passes at her, and when she had screamed, he ran leaving his cloak behind. Potiphar believed his wife's story and threw Joseph into prison.

The Lord was with Joseph in prison and granted him favor with the prison warden, who put him in charge of the other prisoners. While he was there two other prisoners came into his charge—Pharaoh's *"chief cupbearer"* and *"chief baker."* After a time, Joseph noticed they were sad and asked them why. They had each had a dream, and there was no one to give them the interpretation. Joseph interpreted both their dreams—the chief cupbearer would be restored to his position with Pharaoh in three days, and the chief baker would be hung in three days. The interpretations came true just as Joseph had said. The chief cupbearer was released to go back to his position with Pharaoh. Joseph asked him to remember him when he went to Pharaoh in hopes he, too, would someday be set free.

Two years later Pharaoh had two dreams, and there was no one in Egypt who could interpret them for him. The chief cupbearer remembered the Hebrew in prison and told him how Joseph could interpret dreams. Pharaoh sent for Joseph, but Joseph knew his gift of interpretation came from God. He gave God glory and said to Pharaoh, *"...It is not in me: God shall give Pharaoh an answer of peace"* (Genesis 41:16).

The Pharaoh's Dreams

> *"...In my dream, behold, I stood upon the bank of the river: And behold, there came up out of the river seven kine (cow), fat-fleshed and well-favored; and they fed in a meadow: And, behold, seven other kine came up after them, poor and very ill-favored and lean-fleshed, such as I never saw in all the land of Egypt for badness:*

And the lean and the ill-favored kine did eat up the first seven fat kine: And when they had eaten them up, it could not be known that they had eaten them; but they were still ill-favored, as at the beginning. So I awoke.

"And I saw in my dream, and, behold, seven ears came up in one stalk, full and good: And, behold, seven ears, withered, thin, and blasted with the east wind, sprung up after them: And the thin ears devoured the seven good ears: and I told this unto the magicians; but there was none that could declare it to me.

"And Joseph said unto Pharaoh, The dream of Pharaoh is one: God hath showed Pharaoh what he is about to do. The seven good kine are seven years; and the seven good ears are seven years: the dream is one. And the seven thin and ill-favored kine that came up after them are seven years; and the seven empty ears blasted with the east wind shall be seven years of famine. This is the thing which I have spoken unto Pharaoh: What God is about to do he showeth unto Pharaoh. Behold, there come seven years of great plenty throughout all the land of Egypt: And there shall arise after them seven years of famine; and all the plenty shall be forgotten in the land of Egypt; and the famine shall consume the land; And the plenty shall not be known in the land by reason of that famine following; for it shall be very grievous. And for that the dream was doubled unto Pharaoh twice; it is because the thing is established by God, and God will shortly bring it to pass"(Genesis 41:17-32).

God gave Joseph wisdom and a plan to save Pharaoh's kingdom:

"Now therefore let Pharaoh look out a man discreet and wise, and set him over the land of Egypt. Let Pharaoh do this, and let him appoint officers over the land, and take up the fifth part of the land of Egypt in the seven plenteous years. And let them gather all the food of those good years that come, and lay up corn under

the hand of Pharaoh, and let them keep food in the cities. And that food shall be for store to the land against the seven years of famine, which shall be in the land of Egypt: that the land perish not through the famine" (Genesis 41:33-36).

When Pharaoh realized the wisdom Joseph had, he put him in charge of everything except those things concerning the throne. Joseph had been hated by his brothers, sold into slavery, and now God had set him up as Pharaoh's right hand man—a man filled with God's wisdom and favor! Pharaoh gave Joseph the ring off his hand, linen clothes, and a gold chain to wear around his neck.

"And in the seven plenteous years the earth brought forth by handfuls. And he (Joseph) *gathered up all the food of the seven years, which were in the land of Egypt, and laid up the food in the cities: the food of the field, which was round about every city, laid he up in the same. And Joseph gathered corn as the sand of the sea, very much, until he left numbering; for it was without number"* (Genesis 41:47-49).

Asenath, who was the daughter of the priest of On, bore Joseph two sons. He gave his firstborn son the name of Manasseh, *"...For God, said he, hath made me forget all my toil, and all my father's house"* (Genesis 41:51). He called his second son Ephraim, *"...For God hath caused me to be fruitful in the land of my affliction"* (Genesis 41:52).

The Time of Famine

God had given Joseph the interpretation of Pharaoh's dreams, which included seven years of plenty and seven years of severe famine.

"And the famine was over all the face of the earth: and Joseph opened all the storehouses, and sold unto the Egyptians; and the famine waxed sore in the land of Egypt. And all countries came

into Egypt to Joseph for to buy corn; because that the famine was
so sore in all lands" (Genesis 41:56-57).

Israel (Jacob) heard about the corn in Egypt and sent ten of his sons to go and buy some corn to bring home; but he kept his youngest son, Benjamin, at home with him. When the sons arrived in Egypt, they were sent to Joseph to buy their corn, but they did not recognize him. As they bowed down to him, Joseph did recognize them and remembered the dreams he had dreamed so long ago. Joseph loved his family, especially his younger brother, Benjamin, because he and Benjamin had the same mother, Rachel. Joseph decided to play this out to bring his father and Benjamin to Egypt, and he wanted to show his brothers he had forgiven them. God was working something out according to His plan. Joseph accused his brothers of being spies, and they told him, *"...Thy servants are twelve brethren, the sons of one man in the land of Canaan; and, behold, the youngest is this day with our father, and one is not"* (Genesis 42:13).

The *"one is not"* they were talking about was Joseph, but they had no idea they were talking to him. After three days, Joseph told them to leave one brother in the prison and go and bring back their youngest brother. The brothers discussed among themselves the plight that had befallen them. Their consciences were bothering them, and they believed that it was punishment because of what they had done to Joseph, even though they did not recognize him now. Reuben reminded the brothers that he had told them not to sin against Joseph. While they were talking amongst themselves, they didn't realize that Joseph could understand what they were saying, because he had been speaking to them through an interpreter. The Bible says Joseph turned away from them and wept after hearing what they were saying, and while they were watching, he bound their brother, Simeon.

Joseph ordered that each of their sacks be filled with corn and their money put back in their sacks, and he sent them on their way. When they stopped for the night, one of the brothers opened his sack and found his silver had been put back in it. When he told his brothers, they were all afraid, wondering what God had done to them. When they arrived home, they told their father, Israel, about everything that happened to them and that they needed to take Benjamin back to Egypt with them. When they emptied their sacks, each one found their own bag of silver. Israel was upset because he had lost Joseph and now Simeon. To top it off, the brothers wanted to take Benjamin back to Egypt with them, as Joseph had commanded. Reuben pleaded with his father, but Israel refused to let Benjamin go. Reuben said, "...*Slay my two sons, if I bring him not to thee: deliver him into my hand, and I will bring him to thee again. And he said, My son shall not go down with you: for his brother is dead, and he is left alone: if mischief befall him by the way in the which ye go, then shall ye bring down my gray hairs with sorrow to the grave*" (Genesis 42:37-38).

As time went on, the famine did not get any better, and Israel and his family were running out of food. He told his sons to go back to Egypt to get more corn. Judah reminded his father that if he did not take Benjamin back with him, they would not be able to get corn. Judah assured his father that he personally would guarantee Benjamin's safety. Israel reluctantly agreed and told the sons to take some extra food products from their own land and to take double their silver because they still had the original silver that had been returned to them.

When they arrived in Egypt with Benjamin, Joseph arranged with his stewards to prepare a meal for them; but the brothers did not know of his plan. They worried that Joseph thought they had not paid for the corn the last time they were there, and they were being taken to Joseph's house to become his slaves. When they arrived at the entrance, they explained to Joseph's steward what happened with the silver. The steward said, "...*Peace be to you, fear not: your God, and the God of your father, hath given you treasure in your sacks: I had your money. And he brought Simeon out unto them*" (Genesis 43:23).

Joseph made sure they were well cared for. He provided water to wash their feet, food for their donkeys, and he made arrangements for them to dine with him. The brothers offered their gifts to Joseph and bowed down to him. After asking about their father, he was deeply moved at the sight of his own mother's son, Benjamin, and left the room to cry. After he gained control of his feelings, he gave the command to serve the food, and Benjamin's plate contained five times more food than anyone else's plate.

Joseph was not done yet. When it was time for his brothers to go home, he gave orders for their sacks to be filled with food, all their silver put in the mouths of their sacks, and Joseph's own silver cup was to be put in Benjamin's sack. After the brothers had left Egypt, Joseph ordered his steward to catch up with them and bring accusation against them for stealing his silver cup.

When the steward caught up with them and accused them, the brothers were in shock, for they knew they had not taken the silver cup. The steward told them if he found the cup in one of their sacks, that brother would become his slave. Of course, the steward found the silver cup in Benjamin's sack. All the brothers went back to Joseph and bowed before him, as Joseph demanded an explanation for their thievery. Joseph told them whoever was found with the cup, would remain as his servant. Judah spoke up to plead with Joseph about not keeping Benjamin as his slave:

> "...We have a father, an old man, and a child of his old age, a little one; and his brother is dead, and he alone is left of his mother, and his father loveth him..." (Genesis 44:20).

> "Now therefore when I come to thy servant my father, and the lad be not with us; seeing that his life is bound up in the lad's life; It shall come to pass, when he seeth that the lad is not with us, that he will die: and thy servants shall bring down the gray hairs of thy servant our father with sorrow to the grave... I pray thee, let thy servant abide instead of the lad a bondman to my lord; and let the lad go up with his brethren. For how shall I go up to my father, and the lad be not with me? lest peradventure I see the evil that shall come on my father" (Genesis 44:30-34).

Joseph Reveals Himself to His Brothers

Joseph commanded everyone to leave his presence, except for his brothers. Joseph cried so loudly that even the Egyptians outside the room heard him. Joseph made himself known to his brothers.

> *"And Joseph said unto his brethren, I am Joseph; doth my father yet live? And his brethren could not answer him; for they were troubled at his presence. And Joseph said unto his brethren, Come near to me, I pray you. And they came near. And he said, I am Joseph your brother, whom ye sold into Egypt. Now therefore be not grieved, nor angry with yourselves, that ye sold me hither: for God did send me before you to preserve life. For these two years hath the famine been in the land: and yet there are five years, in the which there shall neither be earing nor harvest. And God sent me before you to preserve you a posterity in the earth, and to save your lives by a great deliverance. So now it was not you that sent me hither, but God: and he hath made me a father to Pharaoh, and lord of all his house, and a ruler throughout all the land of Egypt"* (Genesis 45:3-8).

The Hebrew word translated *posterity* is "sh°êrîyth." The meaning of the word is "...a remainder or residual (surviving, final) portion... remnant...."[1]

Joseph's Family Arrive in Egypt

God was preserving a remnant of godly seed. Joseph knew that God's hand was upon him for a reason, and did not blame his brothers for selling him into slavery. God knew that a famine was coming. He had arranged for Joseph to go to Egypt to become Pharaoh's right hand man so that Joseph could set up a food system to help the people receive food and not starve during the famine. Israel was a godly man, and his family, would now be brought to Egypt to fulfill God's purposes to preserve posterity in the earth and to save their lives. Joseph told his brothers to quickly go and give this message to their father:

> *"...God hath made me lord of all Egypt: come down unto me, tarry not: And thou shalt dwell in the land of Go´-shen, and thou shalt be near unto me, thou, and thy children, and thy children's children, and thy flocks, and thy herds, and all that thou hast: And there will I nourish thee; for yet there are five years of famine; lest thou, and thy household, and all that thou hast, come to poverty"* (Genesis 45:9-11).

Pharaoh told Joseph to tell his brothers to go and bring their father and their families to Egypt, and he would make sure they had plenty of food and land. He even offered them the wagons in Egypt to bring their family there.

When the brothers went home and told their father what Pharaoh had said, God gave their father, Israel, a vision. God told him, *"....I am God, the God of thy father: fear not to go down into Egypt; for I will there make of thee a **great nation: I will go down with thee into Egypt; and I will also surely bring thee up again:** and Joseph shall put his hand upon thine eyes"* (Genesis 46:3-4).

Israel (Jacob) was 130 years old when he and his offspring, seventy in all, went to Egypt to join Joseph. Everything was just as God had planned, according to His time clock; And Israel would, at last, be with his long-lost son, Joseph, again. So the eleven sons were brought up out of Canaan and taken into Egypt, where they joined Joseph. Jacob's sons would become *"...the twelve tribes of Israel..."* (Genesis 49:28).

> *"And Joseph made ready his chariot, and went up to meet Israel his father, to Go´-shen, and presented himself unto him; and he fell on his neck, and wept on his neck a good while. And Israel said unto Joseph, Now let me die, since I have seen thy face, because thou art yet alive"* (Genesis 46:28-30).

Egyptians did not care much for shepherds, so Joseph told his family to tell Pharaoh that they were all shepherds, so they could all settle together in Goshen. After meeting some of Joseph's brothers, Pharaoh spoke to Joseph:

> *"The land of Egypt is before thee; in the best of the land make thy father and brethren to dwell; in the land of Go´-shen let them dwell: and if thou knowest any men of activity among them, then make them rulers over my cattle. And Joseph brought in Jacob his father, and set him before Pharaoh: and Jacob blessed Pharaoh..."* (Genesis 47:6-7).

Joseph settled his whole family in Goshen, which was the district of Rameses—the best part of the land. Joseph made sure that his family was well nourished. The famine lasted five more years, and Joseph continued to take care of the people in the land. When their money was gone, Joseph possessed their livestock in exchange for food; when their livestock was gone, Joseph bought all their land, and the people served Pharaoh.

God Selects Ephraim Over Manasseh

Before he died, Israel reckoned Joseph's sons, Ephraim and Manasseh as his because of what God had said to him, *"...Behold, I will make thee fruitful, and multiply thee, and I will make of thee a multitude of people; and will give this land to thy seed after thee for an everlasting possession"* (Genesis 48:4).

> *"Now the eyes of Israel were dim for age, so that he could not see. And he brought them near unto him; and he kissed them, and embraced them. And Israel said unto Joseph, I had not thought to see thy face: and, lo, God hath showed me also thy seed. And Joseph brought them out from between his knees, and he bowed himself with his face to the earth.*

"And Joseph took them both, E´-phra-im in his right hand toward Israel's left hand, and Ma-nas´-seh in his left hand toward Israel's right hand, and brought them near unto him. And Israel stretched out his right hand, and laid it upon E´-phra-im's head, who was the younger, and his left hand upon Ma-nas´-seh's head, guiding his hands wittingly; for Ma-nas´-seh was the firstborn. And he blessed Joseph, and said, God, before whom my fathers Abraham and Isaac did walk, the God who fed me all my life long unto this day, the angel which redeemed me from all evil, bless the lads; and let my name be named on them and the name of my fathers Abraham and Isaac; and let them grow into a multitude in the midst of the earth" (Genesis 48:10-16).

Joseph thought his father had made a mistake.

"And when Joseph saw that his father laid his right hand upon the head of E´-phra-im, it displeased him: and he held up his father's hand, to remove it from E´-phra-im's head unto Ma-nas´-seh's head. And Joseph said unto his father, Not so, my father: for this is the firstborn; put thy right hand upon his head. And his father refused, and said, I know it, my son, I know it: he also shall become a people, and he also shall be great: but truly his younger brother shall be greater than he, and his seed shall become a multitude of nations. And he blessed them that day, saying, In thee shall Israel bless, saying, God make thee as E´-phra-im and as Ma-nas´-seh: and he set E´-phra-im before Ma-nas´-seh" (Genesis 48:17-20).

"By faith Jacob, when he was a dying, blessed both the sons of Joseph; and worshiped, leaning upon the top of his staff" (Hebrews 11:21).

Here again we see God making His own selection of godly seed through Israel, their grandfather.

"And Israel said unto Joseph, Behold, I die: but God shall be with you, and bring you again unto the land of your fathers. Moreover I have given to thee one portion above thy brethren, which I took out of the hand of the Amorite with my sword and with my bow" (Genesis 48:21-22).

Then Israel blessed each one of his twelve sons and prophesied over each of them about the future. These blessings are found in Genesis 49. Israel's blessing over Judah included a prophecy of the coming King Jesus, Who would come from the line of Judah:

"Judah is a lion's whelp: from the prey, my son, thou art gone up: he stooped down, he couched as a lion, and as an old lion; who shall rouse him up? The scepter shall not depart from Judah, nor a lawgiver from between his feet, until Shi´-loh come: and unto him shall the gathering of the people be. Binding his foal unto the vine, and his ass's colt unto the choice vine; he washed his garments in wine, and his clothes in the blood of grapes: his eyes shall be red with wine, and his teeth white with milk" (Genesis 49:9-12).

The meaning of the Hebrew word, *Shi´-loh* is "...an epithet of the Messiah...."[2] The word epithet is "a characterizing word or phrase accompanying or occurring in place of the name of a person or thing."[3] "By permission. From Merriam-Webster's Collegiate®Dictionary, 11th Edition ©2012 by Merriam-Webster, Incorporated (www.Merriam-Webster.com).

The Death of Israel

When it was time for Israel to die, he asked Joseph to carry him out of Egypt and back to the land of Canaan where his fathers were buried, because Canaan was the land that God had promised Abraham and his descendants. So at age 147, Israel died, and Joseph ordered the physicians to embalm his body. His body was carried by Joseph and his brothers, assisted by Pharaoh's dignitaries, back to Canaan and buried with the bodies of Abraham and Sarah, Isaac and Rebekah, and Leah "*...in the cave of the field of Mach-pe´-lah, which Abraham bought with the field for a possession of a burying place of E´-phron the Hit´-tite, before Mam´-re*" (Genesis 50:13). Genesis 35:19 states that Jacob's other wife, Rachel, had been buried in Bethlehem after dying in labor giving birth to Benjamin.

After their father died, Joseph's brothers became afraid that Joseph might bring harm to them.

> "*...And they sent a messenger unto Joseph, saying, Thy father did command before he died, saying, So shall ye say unto Joseph, Forgive, I pray thee now, the trespass of thy brethren, and their sin; for they did unto thee evil: and now, we pray thee, forgive the trespass of the servants of the God of thy father. And Joseph wept when they spake unto him. And his brethren also went and fell down before his face; and they said, Behold, we be thy servants*" (Genesis 50:16-18).

> Joseph told them, "*...Fear not; for am I in the place of God? But as for you, ye thought evil against me; but God meant it unto good, to bring to pass, as it is this day, to save much people alive. Now therefore fear ye not: I will nourish you, and your little ones. And he comforted them, and spake kindly unto them*" (Genesis 50:19-21)

The Death of Joseph

When Joseph was 110 years old, he gave this prophecy to his brothers:

> "*...I die: and God will surely visit you and bring you out of this land unto the land which he sware to Abraham, to Isaac, and to Jacob. And Joseph took an oath of the children of Israel, saying, God will surely visit you, and ye shall carry up my bones from hence*" (Genesis 50:24-25).

"By faith Joseph, when he died, made mention of the departing of the children of Israel; and gave commandment concerning his bones" (Hebrews 11:22).

"So Joseph died, being a hundred and ten years old: and they embalmed him, and he was put in a coffin in Egypt" (Genesis 50:26).

In Conclusion

Talk about someone with a hard luck story, Joseph would be the one. At seventeen years old, his brothers hated him and sold him into slavery, and from there he ended up in Egypt. He was falsely accused of lustful acts, and thrown into prison, yet he was innocent and a man of loyalty and integrity. God knew Joseph, and He had a very important plan for his life. He gave Joseph the gifts of wisdom and of dream interpretation. These gifts enabled him to interpret the Pharaoh's dreams and to devise a food plan to be used during the seven-year famine, which had been prophesied in Pharaoh's dreams. When Pharaoh saw Joseph's wisdom, he set him up as the ruler of all the land of Egypt under Pharaoh, which was right where God intended for him to be. Through the circumstances of the famine, Joseph was reconciled to his brothers who had meant to bring him harm. Through the forgiveness in Joseph's heart for his brothers, they were brought to repentance, and God saved Israel's family as *"a posterity in the earth"* (Genesis 45:7)—a remnant of godly seed, and brought them to Egypt. What a beautiful story of the power of love and forgiveness! Upon his death, Israel was buried in the promised land of Canaan with his ancestors.

Abraham, Isaac, and Jacob (Israel) and his twelve Hebrew sons would now be known as the twelve tribes of Israel. God had established a nation of people from the loins of Abraham, and Abraham's faith had continued to be passed down to this remnant of people.

Part of the prophecy God had given to Abraham about his family living in Egypt had been fulfilled, but there was more to that prophecy.

They were going to be enslaved for 400 years. What could possibly happen to change their lives and bring them into bondage?

Deeper Insights:

1. Israel loved Joseph more than his other brothers because he was born to him in his old age.

   What sin(s) do you think was brewing in the brothers' hearts to bring about a hate strong enough to want to kill their brother? Read Proverbs 6:34; 27:4; Song of Solomon 8:6; James 3:14-16; and 1 John 2:9-11.

2. Potiphar's wife was filled with lust for Joseph, and she tried to encourage him to have sex with her. Joseph loved God and had loyalty and integrity in his heart. Keeping God's righteousness in his focus, he chose to flee from Potiphar's wife, instead of choosing fleeting moments of sinful pleasure. Read 2 Timothy 2:22; and 1 Corinthians 6:9-10.

   Read Romans 8:28. Joseph loved God and chose to obey. How did God work things out for his good in this situation?

   What are some things that might have happened if Joseph had not honored God by giving in to Potiphar's wife? For more insight, read Proverbs 6:23-26 and 7:4-27.

3. What moves the heart of God to help us in times of trouble? Read Psalm 91:14-16.

   God gave Joseph wisdom and the gift of dream interpretation for Pharaoh, which helped him win favor with Pharaoh. Joseph knew he had no wisdom of his own and told Pharaoh, *"It is not in me: God shall give Pharaoh an answer of peace"* (Genesis 41:16).

   Why was it important for Joseph to give God the credit for his gifts? Read Genesis 40:8; 2 Corinthians 3:5; Proverbs 3:5-6; 15:33; and 16:18-19.

4. Joseph gathered all the food in the seven years of plenty, and stored it in the storehouses in Egypt, and then came the seven years of famine. When Joseph's brothers came from Canaan to buy corn from Joseph, the governor, they bowed down to him as humble servants, not knowing who he was. Joseph had every reason to want vengeance, but he had forgiven them, and he loved them.

Read the following scriptures to see the tenderness in Joseph's heart for his family. What did Joseph do in each of these cases? Read Genesis 43:26-30; 45:1-8; 45:14-15; 46:29; and 50:17-21.

Read the following scriptures about love: Proverbs 10:12; Matthew 5:44-45; and 1 John 4:7

Read the following scriptures about forgiveness: Ephesians 4:32; Luke 6:37; and Matthew 6:14-15.

5. 5. Read Genesis 37:7, 9. How did Joseph's prophetic dreams that he had at the age of seventeen in Canaan come true in Egypt?

6. When Israel (Jacob) prophesied over all of his sons before he died, he gave a special blessing over Joseph. Read Genesis 49:22-26.

7. Before Israel died, he told Joseph not to bury him in Egypt. Read Genesis 47:30; and 49:29-32. Where did Israel want to be buried?

Joseph, too, wanted to go to the land of Canaan after his death and asked that his bones be carried there when the Israelites return to that land. Read Genesis 50:24-26.

Why was it important to the Patriarchs to be buried in Canaan? Read Genesis 17:8.

CHAPTER 8

GOD DELIVERS HIS PEOPLE

Slavery in Egypt

In the *Late Bronze Age*, somewhere between "1550-1200 BC,"[1] a lot had changed since Joseph brought his father and brothers to Egypt. Joseph and all of his brothers had died, and the twelve (sons), now tribes, of Israel had been in Egypt for some "370 years."[2] They were a large nation under a new Pharaoh. *Who* Joseph was, and *what* he had done to help Egypt and the surrounding areas during the years of famine, were not remembered by this new Pharaoh. As God had prophesied to Abraham, his descendants were under bondage. They had become quite numerous and Pharaoh was using them as slaves to build his store-cities. He had become fearful of them because of their size, and he was afraid they would side with his enemies if war should break out with other nations.

In order to try and decrease their population, Pharaoh began to oppress the Hebrews with forced labor, but their population only grew larger. Finally he ordered the Hebrew midwives to kill all Hebrew baby boys as they were being delivered, but being fearful of God, they refused to obey. They lied to the Pharaoh and told him that the Hebrew women were giving birth before they arrived to assist them. God blessed the Hebrews with even larger numbers, and He also blessed the midwives with families of their own because they feared Him. Frustrated that he could not decrease the Hebrew population, Pharaoh gave the order that every newborn Hebrew boy was to be thrown into the Nile River, and all the newborn Hebrew girls were to be kept alive. The Hebrews were suffering with great oppression and bondage.

Moses

It was during this period of time that the wife of a Hebrew couple gave birth to a son and hid him until he was three months old. Then he, too, was placed in the Nile River, but not by Pharaoh's men. His mother laid him in a tar and pitched basket, which she placed in the reeds along the banks of the river. The baby's sister watched the basket to see where it would go. When Pharaoh's daughter saw the basket in the water, she told her slave girl to bring it to her. When she looked in the basket and saw the baby boy, she felt compassion for the Hebrew child. The baby's sister came and asked Pharaoh's daughter if she would like her to go and bring one of the Hebrew women to nurse the baby, and Pharaoh's daughter sent her out to bring one to her. Of course, the woman who came to nurse the baby boy was his own mother, and Pharaoh's daughter paid her to take the baby and nurse him. As he grew, his mother returned him to Pharaoh's daughter, who took him as her son. She named him Moses because she said, "...*I drew him out of the water*" (Exodus 2:10). What she did not know was that God had selected Moses, before he was born, to lead the Israelites out of bondage and into their promised land of Canaan.

> *"By faith Moses, when he was born, was hid three months of his parents, because they saw he was a proper child; and they were not afraid of the king's commandment"* (Hebrews 11:23).

While living in Pharaoh's house, Moses was educated in all the Egyptian ways and taught to worship the Egyptian gods; but God had different plans for him. When Moses was about forty years old, he went out to watch his own people, the Hebrews, who were being forced to do hard labor. He saw an Egyptian beating a Hebrew, and he killed the Egyptian to protect the Hebrew. The next day he went back and found two Hebrews fighting with each other. In his attempt to be a mediator between the two, one of them said, *"...Who made thee a prince and a judge over us? Intendest thou to kill me, as thou killedst the Egyptian?..."* (Exodus 2:14)

Moses knew then that his murderous act had been found out. News traveled fast, and when Pharaoh found out that Moses had killed an Egyptian, he tried to have Moses killed. Moses fled for his life and went out into the desert.

> *"By faith, Moses, when he was come to years, refused to be called the son of Pharaoh's daughter; Choosing rather to suffer affliction with the people of God, than to enjoy the pleasures of sin for a season: Esteeming the reproach* (dishonor) *of Christ greater riches than the treasures in Egypt; for he had respect unto the recompense of the reward. By faith he forsook Egypt, not fearing the wrath of the king: for he endured, as seeing him who is invisible"* (Hebrews 11:24-27).

Eventually, Moses came to a shepherd's camp in Midian, near Mount Hebron in the Arabian Desert. Midian was located east of the Red Sea and its inhabitants were descendants of Abraham through his wife, Keturah. Jethro (Reuel) was the priest of Midian, and he had flocks and seven daughters. Moses lived there and married Zipporah, one of Jethro's daughters. She gave birth to a son, and they named him Gershom.

God Commissions Moses

The Hebrew people had been crying out to God because of their tremendous suffering under bondage, and *"...God remembered his covenant with Abraham, with Isaac, and with Jacob. And God looked upon the children of Israel and God had <u>respect</u> unto them"* (Exodus 2:25).

The Hebrew word translated *respect* is "yâda'." The meaning of the word is "...to know...."[3] God remembered His covenant with Abraham, Isaac, and Jacob, and He knew their descendants.

One day when Moses was out tending Jethro's flocks on Mount Horeb (Sinaitic mountains),[4] *"...the angel of the LORD appeared unto him in flames of fire out of the midst of a bush: and he looked, and, behold, the bush burned with fire, and the bush was not consumed"* (Exodus 3:2). When Moses went over to see why the bush did not burn up, *"...God called unto him out of the midst of the bush, and said, Moses! Moses. And he said, Here am I"* (Exodus 3:4).

God told Moses, *"... put off thy shoes from off thy feet, for the place whereon thou standest is holy ground. Moreover he said, I am the God of thy father, the God of Abraham, the God of Isaac, and the God of Jacob. And Moses hid his face; for he was afraid to look upon God"* (Exodus 3:5-6).

> The Hebrew word translated *afraid,* is "yârê." The meaning of the word is "to revere...."[5]

> *"And the LORD said, I have surely seen the affliction of my people which are in Egypt, and have heard their cry by reason of their taskmasters; for I know their sorrows; And I am come down to deliver them out of the hand of the Egyptians, and to bring them up out of that land unto a good land and a large, unto a land flowing with milk and honey; unto the place of the Ca´-naanites, and the Hit´-tites, and the Am´-orites, and the Per´-iz-zites, and the Hi´-vites, and the Jeb´-u-sites.*

> *"Now therefore, behold, the cry of the children of Israel is come unto me: and I have also seen the oppression wherewith the Egyptians oppress them. Come now therefore, and I will send thee unto Pharaoh, that thou mayest bring forth my people the children of Israel out of Egypt"* (Exodus 3:7-10).

The Lord called the Israelites *"my people."* He had chosen them. His plan to give them land and to *"bless all nations"* through them would come to pass, and it would begin with Moses. God had commissioned Moses, but he didn't want the job, and he didn't feel qualified. He would make several excuses as to why he wasn't the one who should go before he would finally surrender to God's will. God gave Moses assurance:

"...Certainly I will be with thee; and this shall be a <u>token</u> unto thee, that I have sent thee: When thou hast brought forth the people out of Egypt, <u>ye shall serve God upon this mountain</u>" (Exodus 3:12)

Moses asked God, *"...when I come unto the children of Israel and shall say unto them, The God of your fathers hath sent me unto you; and they shall say to me, What is His name? what shall I say unto them?"* (Exodus 3:13)

"And God said unto Moses, <u>I AM THAT I AM</u>: and he said, Thus shalt thou say unto the children of Israel, <u>I AM</u> hath sent me unto you...thou say unto the children of Israel, The LORD God of your fathers, the God of Abraham, the God of Isaac, and the God of Jacob, hath sent me unto you: this is my Name for ever, and this is my <u>memorial</u> unto all generations" (Exodus 3:14-15).

The Hebrew words translated *I AM* is "hâyâh." The meaning of the words is "...to exist, i.e. be or become, come to pass...."[6]

God told Moses to go to Egypt and tell the Israelite leaders that God has seen what has been happening to them and that He is getting ready to deliver them and take them to the land He had promised to them. He told Moses to tell the elders to go to Pharaoh and ask that he allow them to take the Israelites on a three-day journey out into the desert to make sacrifices to God. He also told him that Pharaoh would refuse to release them, but God would force Pharaoh's hand.

"I will stretch out my hand, and smite Egypt with all my wonders which I will do in the midst thereof: and after that he will let you go. And I will give this people favor in the sight of the Egyptians: and it shall come to pass, that, when ye go, ye shall not go empty: But every woman shall borrow of her neighbor, and of her that sojourneth in her house, jewels of silver, and jewels of gold, and raiment: and ye shall put them upon your sons, and upon your daughters; and ye shall spoil the Egyptians" (Exodus 3:20-22).

The Lord showed Moses the signs that would be used to convince the Israelites that the God of their fathers had, indeed, appeared to him. He told Moses to throw his rod on the ground, and the rod turned into a snake. He told him to take it by its tail, and then it turned back into a rod; He made Moses' hand become leprous and then whole again; and He told Moses that he would take water from the Nile River, which would turn to blood when he poured it on the ground. Even with these signs, Moses was still not willing to go and continued to make more excuses. *"...I am slow of speech and of tongue"* (Exodus 4:10, NIV®), and, *"...please send someone else"* (Exodus 4:13, NIV®).

The Lord became angry with Moses and told him that his brother, Aaron, was already on his way to go with him to speak for him and that the men in Egypt who had wanted to kill him were now dead. Finally, Moses took his wife, sons, and his donkey to carry them on, and went to meet Aaron at the Mount of God, and from there, they began the long journey across the desert. They would go back to Egypt to perform all the miracles that the Lord would command them to perform. God, Himself, would harden Pharaoh's heart so that he would not release the Hebrews.

God gave Moses this warning for Pharaoh: *"... Israel is my son, even my first-born: And I say unto thee, Let my son go, that he may serve me: and if thou refuse to let him go, behold, I will slay thy son, even thy first-born"* (Exodus 4:22-23).

God Promises to Set the Israelites Free

When they arrived in Egypt, Moses and Aaron went to the elders of the Israelites and performed the signs that God had given them and delivered to them the message from God, and the elders believed them. Moses and Aaron requested permission to take the Israelites on a three-day journey to offer sacrifices to their Lord so that the Lord would not strike the Israelites with plagues. Instead of releasing them, however, Pharaoh gave orders for the Israelites to make bricks with no straw. Of course, they weren't able to make as many bricks without straw, and the Hebrew foremen received beatings by the slave drivers. After the beatings, the foremen complained to Pharaoh and discovered that he required the same daily quota be met without the straw. The Israelites blamed Moses and Aaron for their trouble because now things were even harder for them than before. Moses appealed to God, questioning Him as to why He wasn't rescuing the Israelites, but only making it harder on them. The Lord told Moses,

> "...Now thou shalt see what I will do to Pharaoh: for with a strong hand shall he let them go, and with a strong hand shall he drive them out of his land... I am the LORD: And I appeared unto Abraham, unto Isaac, and unto Jacob, by the name of God Almighty, but by my Name JE-HO´-VAH was I not known to them. And I have also established my covenant with them, to give them the land of Canaan, the land of their pilgrimage, wherein they were strangers. And I have also heard the groaning of the children of Israel, whom the Egyptians keep in bondage; and I have remembered my covenant" (Exodus 6:1-5).

The Hebrew word translated JE-HO´-VAH is "Yᵉhôvâh." The meaning of the word is "...(the) self-existent, eternal, Jewish national name of God, the Lord."[7]

> God gave Moses a promise for the Israelites: "...I am the LORD, and I will bring you out from under the burdens of the Egyptians, and I will rid you out of their bondage, and I will redeem you with a stretched out arm, and with great judgments: And I will take you to me for a people, and I will be to you a God: and ye shall know that I am the LORD your God, which bringeth you out from under the burdens of the Egyptians. And I will bring you in unto the land, concerning the which I did swear to give it to Abraham, to Isaac, and to Jacob: and I will give it you for an heritage: I am the LORD" (Exodus 6:6-8).

The Hebrew word translated redeem is "gâ´al." The meaning of the word is "...to redeem (according to the Oriental law of kinship), i.e. to be the next of kin (and as such to buy back a relative's property, marry his widow etc.)...purchase, ransom."[8] God was going to purchase His people from the Egyptians with His judgments.

The Israelites did not listen, because they were tired and discouraged from having been under Pharaoh's cruel conditions. They began blaming Moses and Aaron for their trouble and would not hear the words of God. Then God told Moses to tell Pharaoh again to let the Israelites go. Moses was fearful and made another excuse, *"...Behold, the children of Israel have not hearkened unto me; how then shall Pharaoh hear me, who am of uncircumcised lips?"* (Exodus 6:12) The Lord reassured Moses:

> *"...See, I have made thee a god to Pharaoh: and Aaron thy brother shall be thy prophet. Thou shalt speak all that I command thee: and Aaron thy brother shall speak unto Pharaoh, that he send the children of Israel out of his land. And I will harden Pharaoh's heart, and multiply my signs and my wonders in the land of Egypt. But Pharaoh shall not hearken unto you, that I may lay my hand upon Egypt, and bring forth mine armies, and my people the children of Israel, out of the land of Egypt by great judgments. And the Egyptians shall know that I am the LORD, when I stretch forth mine hand upon Egypt, and bring out the children of Israel from among them"* (Exodus 7:1-5).

Moses was eighty and Aaron was eighty-three when they put aside their fear and obeyed the Lord. When they went to see Pharaoh, Aaron threw his rod on the ground, and it became a snake. When Pharaoh's wise men and magicians threw their rods on the ground, their rods also became snakes, but Aaron's rod ate their rods. God *"...hardened Pharaoh's heart, that he hearkened not unto them; as the LORD had said"* (Exodus 7:13).

God Sends Ten Plagues (Exodus 7)

God was getting ready to redeem the Israelites with His judgments, and it was time for these judgments to begin. The Lord started to bring plagues on Egypt in the form of natural disasters to confound Pharaoh and belittle the Egyptian gods, which were based on nature. God was going to demonstrate His power so that the Egyptians would know He was the Lord. In Exodus 7-10, the Bible records that God brought nine serious plagues upon Pharaoh and Egypt. Before each plague, Pharaoh was warned that the plague was coming, but God hardened Pharaoh's heart so that he would not release the people. Moses and Aaron delivered the messages from God to Pharaoh, and with their rods outstretched in their hands, God performed these mighty miracles before Pharaoh and his men:

Plague of Blood: Every drop of water in Egypt turned into blood—rivers, ponds, pools, and all vessels of wood and stone. God "caused the Nile-god to bring ruin, not prosperity."[9]

Plague of Frogs: Every house, bed, person, oven, and kneading trough were infested with frogs. "The frogs were associated with Egypt's gods of fertility. God caused them to bring disease instead of fruitfulness."[10]

Plague of Gnats or Lice: God infested Egypt with lice made from the dust of the land.

The Plague of Flies: Swarms of flies went throughout all Egypt that corrupting the land.

The Plague on Livestock: God killed all the Egyptian cattle, horses, Asses, camels, oxen, and sheep.

The Plague of Boils: Blisters upon the Egyptians and their animals.

The Plague of Hail: The worst storm Egypt had ever seen, mingled with hail and fire, destroyed the herbs and trees.

The Plague of Locusts: Swarms of locusts were so thick that the people could not see the earth, and they ate everything in the field that the hail had not killed.

The Plague of Darkness: The plague of darkness was so black that the people could not see each other for three days. It was because of God's power that "…The power of Re, the sun-god, was blotted out."[11]

God wasted Egypt, and yet, not one plague came to Goshen where the Israelites lived. God did this to show Pharaoh he was dividing the Israelites from the Egyptians.

God Warns Pharaoh About the Last Plague

Just as God had told Moses to tell Pharaoh in the beginning, He was getting ready to bring the last plague on Egypt—the plague of death of the first-born. Then the Lord told Moses to warn Pharaoh that all first-born, man and beast, would die, even the Pharaoh's first-born son, but the Israelites would be safe. The Lord would make a distinction between Egypt and Israel, once and for all, and Pharaoh would know it.

> *"And Moses said, Thus saith the LORD, About midnight will I go out into the midst of Egypt: And all the first-born in the land of Egypt shall die, from the first-born of Pharaoh that sitteth upon his throne, even unto the first-born of the maidservant that is behind the mill; and all the first-born of beasts. And there shall be a great cry throughout all the land of Egypt, such as there was none like it, nor shall be like it any more. But against any of the children of Israel shall not a dog move his tongue, against man or beast: that ye may know how the LORD doth put a difference between the Egyptians and Israel. And all these thy servants shall come down unto me, and bow down themselves unto me, saying, Get thee out, and all the people that follow thee: and after that I will go out. And he went out from Pharaoh in a great anger. And the LORD said unto Moses, Pharaoh shall not hearken unto you; that my wonders may be multiplied in the land of Egypt. And Moses and Aaron did all these wonders before Pharaoh: and the LORD hardened Pharaoh's heart, so*

that he would not let the children of Israel go out of his land" (Exodus 11:4-10).

Instructions for the Passover

God was going to send the plague of death upon all Egypt's first-born, but He would spare the Israelites, if they would obey His instructions. He told Moses and Aaron,

> *"...This month shall be unto you the beginning of months: it shall be the first month of the year to you. Speak ye unto all the congregation of Israel, saying, In the tenth day of this month, they shall take to them every man a lamb, according to the house of their fathers, a lamb for a house: And if the household be too little for the lamb, let him and his neighbor next unto his house take it according to the number of the souls; every man according to his eating shall make your count for the lamb. Your lamb shall be <u>without blemish</u>, a <u>male of the first year</u>: ye shall take it out from the <u>sheep, or from the goats</u>: And ye shall keep it up until the fourteenth day of the same month: and the whole assembly of the congregation of Israel shall kill it in the evening.*

> *"And they shall take of the <u>blood</u>, and strike it on the <u>two side posts and on the upper doorpost of the houses</u>, wherein they shall eat it. And they shall eat the flesh in that night, roast with fire, and <u>unleavened bread</u>; and with <u>bitter herbs</u> they shall eat it. Eat not of it raw, nor sodden* (to boil up) *at all with water, but roast with fire; his head with his legs, and with the purtenance* (entrails) *thereof. And ye shall let nothing of it remain until the morning; and that which remaineth of it until the morning ye shall burn with fire. And thus shall ye eat it; with your loins girded* (with your cloak tucked into your belt, NIV®), *your shoes on your feet, and your staff in your hand; and ye shall eat it in haste: it is the Lord's Passover"* (Exodus 12:1-11).

"The Passover lamb… speaks of God's protection and provision for His people—Israel is God's first-born. The bitter herbs remind them of their suffering in Egypt."[12] Bitter herbs consist of the following: 'lettuce, chicory, eryngo, horseradish and sow-thistle, although, all these may not have been available in Biblical times.'[13]. "The flat, unleavened bread recalls the haste of their departure. There was no time to use yeast and wait for the bread to rise."[14]

God told them, *"For I will pass through the land of Egypt this night, and will smite all the first-born in the land of Egypt, both man and beast; and against all the gods of Egypt I will execute judgment: I am the LORD. And the blood shall be to you for a* token *upon the houses where ye are: and when I see the blood, I will pass over you, and the plague shall not be upon you to destroy you, when I smite the land of Egypt. And this day shall be unto you for a memorial; and ye shall keep it a feast to the LORD throughout your generations; ye shall keep it a feast by an ordinance forever"* (Exodus 12:12-14).

The Hebrew word translated *token* is "'ôwth." The meaning of the word is "…in the sense of appearing; a signal…as a flag, beacon, monument, omen, prodigy, evidence…sign…."[15]

> *"And it shall come to pass, when ye be come to the land which the LORD will give you, according as he hath promised, that ye shall keep this service. And it shall come to pass, when your children shall say unto you, What mean ye by this service? That ye shall say, It is the sacrifice of the LORD'S passover, who passed over the houses of the children of Israel in Egypt, when he smote the Egyptians, and delivered our houses. And the people bowed the head and worshiped"* (Exodus 12:25-27).

> *"Through faith he (Moses) kept the Passover, and the sprinkling of blood, lest He (God) that destroyed the first-born should touch them"* (Hebrews 11:28).

There can be no doubt of the symbolic significance of the Passover lamb and the blood on the Hebrew doorposts. Jesus is referred to as the

Lamb in many places throughout the New Testament. When He died on the cross as a sacrifice to pay for our sins, Jesus became our Passover Lamb so that we would not die spiritually. 1 Corinthians 5:7 says, *"...For even Christ our Passover is sacrificed for us...."* He was a Lamb without defect.

> 1 Peter 1:18, 19 says, *"Forasmuch as ye know that ye were not redeemed with corruptible things, as silver and gold, from your vain conversation received by tradition from your fathers; but with the precious blood of Christ, as a lamb without blemish and without spot: who verily was foreordained before the foundation of the world, but was manifest in these last times for you...."*

When Jesus came as our Passover Lamb, He did not do it to copy the Jewish traditions of the Passover that were set up in the Old Testament—just the opposite. Those traditions were set in place as symbols to point the way to the real Passover Lamb, Jesus, the Christ, Who has already come to pay for our sins and to purchase us for Himself.

Just as the blood of the Passover lamb was applied to the doorposts to save the Israelites from the angel of death in Egypt, the blood of Jesus, the Passover Lamb, was applied to us at the cross to save us from God's future judgment of our sin. When we accept Jesus as our Lord and Savior, our sins are covered with His blood that He shed when He was tortured and died on the cross for our sins, and God's judgment will pass over us.

The Plague On the Firstborn

> *"And it came to pass, that at midnight the LORD smote all the first-born in the land of Egypt, from the first-born of Pharaoh that sat on his throne unto the first-born of the captive that was in the dungeon; and all the first-born of cattle. And Pharaoh rose up in the night, he and all his servants, and all the Egyptians; and there was a great cry in Egypt; for there was not a house where there was not one dead"* (Exodus 12:29-30).

Pharaoh had killed Israel's firstborn baby sons, and now God had killed Egypt's firstborn sons, including the son of Pharaoh, as well. Not one Israelite family died on whose doorposts was found the blood of the lamb or goat. That night Pharaoh summoned Moses and Aaron and commanded them to take all their people and animals and leave to worship their Lord. Finally, finding himself in ruination and devastation, Pharaoh let the Israelites go. Even the Egyptians urged them to go for fear of dying, themselves.

Just as God had told them to do, the Israelites asked the Egyptians for articles of silver, gold, and clothing, as the Lord had told them to do, and the Egyptians gave to them what they asked for. Then the Israelites left!

In Conclusion

Pharaoh, out of fear of the large Hebrew nation, killed the Israelite baby boys by ordering their drowning in the Nile River in an attempt to decrease the Hebrew population. Little did he know, God was protecting and reserving one special little baby boy who would grow up to deliver the Israelites from Pharaoh's kingdom. When Moses was eighty years old, he had an encounter with the angel of God in the burning bush, where God gave him his marching orders to bring the Israelites out of Egypt. Although Moses did not voluntarily obey, but made excuses why he was not up for the job, God gave Aaron to him as his prophet and sent him on his way in the power and strength of the Lord.

God could have given the Hebrews a speedy exodus, but He wanted to leave signs and wonders that Moses and his descendants would never forget. He wanted them to remember the price that was paid for them and that He was their God. God raised Pharaoh up and hardened his heart to show all the earth His power and His Name.

> *"For the scripture saith unto Pharaoh, Even for this same purpose have I raised thee up, that I might show my power in thee, and that my name might be declared throughout the earth"* (Romans 9:17).

With the plagues, He displayed His wondrous power to Pharaoh and all Egypt, and, at the same time His arm of protection kept the Hebrews, who lived in Goshen, out of harm's way. The gods of nature in Egypt had been humiliated and debased in that process, as well.

When God brought forth the final plague of death, He provided His covering for them by giving them instructions to apply the blood of their unblemished sheep and goats to the top and side posts of their house doors. When God saw the blood, He passed over them. God would be known as their Redeemer and Deliverer. He redeemed them for Himself.

Jesus Christ is our Passover Lamb, our Redeemer. He ransomed us with His own blood. The Greek word *ransom* is translated "antilutrŏn." The meaning of the word is "…redemption-price…atonement…."[16] He did this to set us free from our bondage to sin and to save us from God's judgment and eternal spiritual death.

"For God so loved the world, that he gave his only begotten Son, that whosoever believeth in him should not perish, but have everlasting life" (John 3:16).

After delivering the plague of death, the last of ten plagues, which claimed Pharaoh's own first-born son and the first-born of all of Egypt's families, Pharaoh finally conceded to let the Israelites go. However, as we shall see, it was not to be the last time they would be harassed by Pharaoh. God would still have to deliver His final blow to Pharaoh and His men before the Israelites would be able to start their journey to the land of Canaan.

Deeper Insights:

1. What gave Moses' mother the courage to hide her baby boy, going against the commands of the Pharaoh, and to place her baby son in possible harm's way on the Nile River? Read Hebrews 11:23.

2. Read Acts 7:23-24. What moved Moses' heart to kill the Egyptian?

   Read Hebrews 11:24-27. What did Moses believe that caused him to choose between a life of wealth and power and a life of suffering as a Hebrew?

   Read Hebrews 13:12-13. How did Moses step "outside" to bare the reproach of Christ by choosing the living God over a life of prosperity?

   Can you recall a time when God brought you to a place of decision where your choice meant that you stepped "outside" to bare Christ's reproach?

3. Read Exodus 3:6. What reaction did Moses have when God identified Himself to him from the burning bush?

   Read the following scriptures to see how these forefathers responded to God:

   Noah: Genesis 6:22/Hebrews 11:7

   Abraham: Genesis 22:1-3/Hebrews 11:17-19

   Jacob: Genesis 28:10-22

   Can you recall a time when God personally made Himself known to you? How did you react or respond to God?

4. What are some reasons we should we fear/reverence God? Read Jeremiah 10:7, 10; Psalm 19:9; 130:3-4; Proverbs 1:7; 14:26-27; and Revelations 15:3-4.

5. When God commissioned Moses to bring the Israelites out of bondage in Egypt, he did not want to go, and he made excuses. Can you think of a time when God told you to do something that you did not want to do, something you were not comfortable with?

   Did you make excuses to God to try and get out of it? If so, can you remember what they were?

Did you obey?

When God tells us to do something, He gives us the ability to do it. Read 1 Corinthians 2:1-5; 2 Corinthians 12:9, 10; and Philippians 4:13.

6. Just before the last plague—death of the first-born, of both man and beast, God gave Moses instructions for the Israelites to protect themselves from this plague. The blood on each doorpost would be a sign or evidence to God that those inside were to be spared. God told Moses, *"...and when I see the blood, I will pass over you...."*

Scripture declares Jesus Christ to be the unblemished Lamb of God Who gave up His own lifeblood to pay for our sins and reconcile us to God. Read Isaiah 53:7; 1 Peter 1:18, 19; 1 Corinthians 5:7; John 1:29; and Revelation 5:6, 12; 7:14.

When God sees the blood of the Lamb covering our sins because of our repentance and acceptance of Christ, His judgment for our sins will pass over us. Read 1 John 1:7, 9; and 2:1-2.

7. Why did God harden Pharaoh's heart so that he would not let the people go? Read Exodus 6:6-7; 7:3-5; 10:1-2; and 11:9-10; Romans 9:15-18.

CHAPTER 9

GOD'S COVENANT WITH HIS PEOPLE

The Journey to Mount Sinai

The night of his son's death, Pharaoh ordered the Israelites, who had been in Egypt for 430 years, to take their flocks and herds and leave. When Pharaoh told them to leave, they left in a hurry. The Bible says, *"...the hosts of the LORD went out from the land of Egypt"* (Exodus 12:41). Six hundred thousand men on foot, plus all their women, children, and others who were with them, possibly "2-3 million people,"[1] left in a hurry with all their livestock, flocks, herds, carts, and belongings. They also left with their plunder of silver and gold and other things they had collected from the Egyptians, as God had told them to do. Moses also brought Joseph's remains on the journey with the Israelites to the promised land of Canaan. Joseph had prophesied to his brothers, the children of Israel, when they first came to Egypt: *"...God will surely visit you; and ye shall carry up my bones away hence"* (Genesis 50:25).

Remember What God Has Done

God knew if He led His people to the Red Sea by going through the Philistine country, and they encountered war with the Philistines at that time, they would want to turn around and go back to Egypt. So He led them by way of the desert. When they arrived in Succoth, which was nearly thirty-five miles away from Goshen, God gave Moses instructions about how to observe the Passover. He told them that during the Passover, no bones were to be broken, and no one could eat of the Passover meal unless he was circumcised. He also told him to consecrate their firstborn. "*Sanctify unto me all the first-born, whatsoever openeth the womb among the children of Israel, both of man or beast: it is mine*" (Exodus 13:2).

The Hebrew word translated *sanctify* is "qâdâsh." The meaning of the word is "to be…(make, pronounce or observe as) clean (ceremonially or morally)…consecrate, dedicate…."[2]

Why did He want them to remember?

> "*In days to come, when your son asks you, What does this mean? say to him, With a mighty hand the LORD brought us out of Egypt, out of the land of slavery. When Pharaoh stubbornly refused to let us go, the LORD killed every firstborn in Egypt, both man and animal. This is why I sacrifice to the LORD the first male offspring of every womb and redeem each of my firstborn sons. And it will be like a sign on your hand and a symbol on your forehead that the LORD brought us out of Egypt with His mighty hand*" (Exodus 13:14-16, NIV®).

The Hebrew word translated *redeem*, is "pâdâh." The meaning of the word is "…to sever, i.e. ransom…release, preserve…."[3]

God Parts the Red Sea

When they left Succoth, they camped on the edge of the desert at Etham.

> "*…the LORD went before them by day in a pillar of a cloud, to lead them the way; and by night in a pillar of fire, to give them light; to go by day and night*" (Exodus 13:21).

The Lord knew that Pharaoh would pursue the Israelites, so He misled Pharaoh to assume they were lost and hemmed in between the sea and the desert. God told the Israelites to camp near Pihahiroth, between Migdol and the sea. Then the Lord hardened Pharaoh's heart once again, so he would come after them. When Pharaoh realized he no longer had his slave labor, he pursued the Israelites with his army and over six hundred chariots, and found the Israelites camped near the sea. When the Israelites saw Pharaoh's army, they were afraid and began to blame Moses for their predicament. They wanted to go back to Egypt. Moses told the people, *"...Fear ye not, stand still, and see the salvation of the LORD...The LORD shall fight for you, and ye shall hold your peace"* (Exodus 14:13-14). Then God told Moses what was going to happen:

> *"...speak unto the children of Israel, that they go forward: But lift thou up thy rod, and stretch out thine hand over the sea, and divide it: and the children of Israel shall go on dry ground through the midst of the sea. And I, behold, I will harden the hearts of the Egyptians, and they shall follow them: and I will get me honor upon Pharaoh, and upon all his host, upon his chariots, and upon his horsemen. And the Egyptians shall know that I am the LORD, when I have gotten me honor upon Pharaoh, upon his chariots, and upon his horsemen.*

> *"And the angel of God, which went before the camp of Israel, removed and went behind them; and the pillar of the cloud went from before their face, and stood behind them: And it came between the camp of the Egyptians and the camp of Israel; and it was a cloud and darkness to them, but it gave light by night to these: so that the one came not near the other all the night.*

> *"And Moses stretched out his hand over the sea; and the LORD caused the sea to go back by a strong east wind all that night, and made the sea dry land, and the waters were divided. And the children of Israel went into the midst of the sea upon the dry ground: and the waters were a wall unto them on their right hand, and on their left"* (Exodus 14:15-22).

The Egyptians followed the Israelites into the sea, and the Lord threw the army into confusion, causing their chariot wheels to fall off. The Egyptians realized that the Lord was fighting for the Israelites and tried to turn around.

> *"And the LORD said unto Moses, Stretch out thine hand over the sea, that the waters may come again upon the Egyptians, upon their chariots, and upon their horsemen. And Moses stretched forth his hand over the sea, and the sea returned to his strength when the morning appeared; and the Egyptians fled against it; and the Lord overthrew the Egyptians in the midst of the sea. And the waters returned, and covered the chariots, and the horsemen, and all the host of Pharaoh that came into the sea after them; there remained not so much as one of them. But the children of Israel walked upon dry land in the midst of the sea; and the waters were a wall unto them on their right hand, and on their left. Thus the LORD saved Israel that day out of the hand of the Egyptians; and Israel saw the Egyptians dead upon the seashore"* (Exodus 14:26-30).

> *"By faith they passed through the Red sea as by dry land: which the Egyptians assaying to do were drowned"* (Hebrews 11:29).

God did this to show His power and gain glory for Himself. Psalm 136:13-15 speaks of this incident:

> *"To him which divided the Red Sea into parts: for his mercy endureth for ever: and made Israel to pass through the midst of it: for his mercy endureth for ever: but overthrew Pharaoh and his host in the Red Sea: for his mercy endureth for ever."*

In seeing what God had done for them, the people began to worship the Lord in songs and dancing, using musical instruments. Here are a few excerpts of their song, which is found in Exodus 15:

(Verse 2) *"...The LORD is my strength and song, and he is become my salvation: he is my God, and I will prepare him a habitation; my father's God, and I will exalt him."* (Verse 13) *"Thou in thy mercy hast led forth the people which thou hast redeemed: thou hast guided them in thy strength unto thy holy habitation."* (Verse 21) *""Sing ye to the LORD, for he hath triumphed gloriously: the horse and his rider hath he thrown into the sea."*

God Tests the Israelites

It had been a great time of celebration, and thanking God. They were free from Pharaoh and no longer in bondage as slaves. However, as time passed on, and things got difficult, the Israelites began to forget about God's mighty wonders and deliverance and began to complain about various things. When Moses led the Israelites into the Desert of Shur, they became thirsty after traveling three days. The water they found at Marah was bitter, and the people complained to Moses.

"...and the LORD showed him a tree, which when he had cast into the waters, the waters were made sweet: there he made for them a statute and an ordinance, and there he <u>proved</u> them. And said, If thou wilt diligently hearken to the voice of the LORD thy God, and wilt do that which is right in his sight, and wilt give ear to his commandments, and keep all his statutes, I will put none of these diseases upon thee, which I have brought upon the Egyptians: for I am the LORD that healeth thee" (Exodus 15:25-26).

The Hebrew word translated *prove*, is "nâcâh." The meaning of the word is "...to test...."[4]

While they were in the wilderness of Sin, they again complained to Moses and Aaron when they were hungry and wished God had let them die in Egypt instead of bringing them out in the desert to be killed with hunger.

> *"Then said the LORD unto Moses, Behold, I will rain bread from heaven for you; and the people shall go out and gather a certain rate every day, that I may prove them, whether they will walk in my law, or no"* (Exodus 16:4).

Aaron told the Israelites, *"...your murmurings are not against us, but against the LORD. And Moses spake unto Aaron, Say unto all the congregation of the children of Israel, Come near before the LORD: for he hath heard your murmurings. And it came to pass, as Aaron spake unto the whole congregation of the children of Israel, that they looked toward the wilderness, and, behold, the glory of the LORD appeared in the cloud. And the LORD spake unto Moses, saying,... At even ye shall eat flesh, and in the morning ye shall be filled with bread; and ye shall know that I am the LORD your God"* (Exodus 16:8-12).

God sent quail in the evening and manna—bread, which came after the dew, *"...thin flakes like frost"* (Exodus 16:14, NIV®). The manna was *"...like coriander seed, white; and the taste of it was like wafers made with honey"* (Exodus 16:31). He told Moses that they should gather only as much as they needed and not keep it over until morning. When they disobeyed God and tried to keep it over, it spoiled and filled with maggots. Each day, after they gathered what they needed, the sun would melt away the leftover manna. On the sixth day, they were to gather twice as much and bake and boil it so there would be some left over so they could rest on the *"holy Sabbath to the LORD"* (Exodus 16:23, NIV®), and it would not spoil. This was a day they were now to set aside to God. Moses told them, *"Six days ye shall gather it; but on the seventh day, which is the Sabbath, in it there shall be none"* (Exodus 16:26). Even after what God had said, people still disobeyed and tried to go out and find the manna on the Sabbath, but there was none. God told Moses to set aside some manna so the Israelites would remember what and how the Lord had provided for them:

> *"And Moses said, This is the thing which the LORD commandeth, Fill an omer* (about 2 quarts) *of it to be kept for your generations; that they may see the bread wherewith I have fed you in the wilderness, when I brought you forth from the land of Egypt"* (Exodus 16:32).

God would continue to provide manna for the Israelites to eat for the next forty years *"...until they came unto the borders of the land of Canaan"* (Exodus 16:35).

When the Israelites left the Desert of Sin and camped at Rephidim, they could find no water again. *"...they tempted the LORD, saying, Is the LORD among us, or not?"* (Exodus 17:7) After Moses cried to the Lord, the Lord said, *"...Go on before the people, and take with thee of the elders of Israel; and thy rod, wherewith thou smotest the river, take in thine hand, and go. Behold, I will stand before thee there upon the rock in Hor´-eb; and thou shalt smite* (strike) *the rock, and there shall come water out of it, that the people may drink. And Moses did so in the sight of the elders of Israel"* (Exodus 17:5-6).

The War With the Amalekites

The Egyptians had tried to destroy the Israelites, now the Amalekites, descendants of Esau, were determined to do the same. While they were in Rephidim, the Amalekites attacked them. Joshua led the Israelite men to fight against the Amalekites, and Moses, Aaron and Hur went to the top of a hill where Moses held up his hands with God's rod in his hand. As long as Moses held up his hands, holding the rod, they would begin to win; when his hands came down, the Amalekites began to win. When Moses got tired, Aaron and Hur put a stone under Moses to sit on, and they both held his hands up when he could no longer hold them up by himself. They did this until sunset when Joshua and some men, who were fighting below the hill, won the battle.

> *"And Moses built an altar, and called the name of it Je-ho´-vah-nis'-si: For he said, Because the LORD hath sworn that the LORD will have war with Am´-a-lek from generation to generation"* (Exodus 17:15-16).

The Lord told Moses to write down on a scroll what had happened so that it would be remembered. Moses had become Israel's first judge, and his load was becoming heavy. It was about this time that he assigned good, able men to judge the small matters of the people, while he continued to judge the larger matters.

The Israelites Prepare To Meet the Lord

When the Israelites arrived at the Desert of Sinai in the third month of leaving Egypt and were camped at the foot of Mount Sinai, God gave Moses a conditional promise for them:

> *"Ye have seen what I did unto the Egyptians, and how I bare you on eagles' wings, and brought you unto myself. Now therefore,* ***if ye will obey*** *my voice indeed, and* ***keep my covenant****, then* ***ye shall be a peculiar treasure*** *unto me above all people: for all the earth is mine: And ye shall be unto me a* ***kingdom of priests, and a holy nation...***" (Exodus 19:4-6).

When Moses told the Israelites what God had said, they agreed to do everything the Lord would tell them to do. Then the Lord told Moses of His plan to come down in a dense cloud so that the Israelites would trust Moses when they would hear God speak to him. He told Moses to sanctify the people—they must wash their clothes and abstain from sexual relations in preparation for this event. No one was to go onto the mountain or touch it, unless there was heard a long blast from the ram's horn, or they would be put to death.

> *"And it came to pass on the third day in the morning, that there were thunders and lightnings, and a thick cloud upon the mount, and the voice of the trumpet exceeding loud; so that all the people that was in the camp trembled. And Moses brought forth the people out of the camp to meet with God; and they stood at the* <u>nether</u> *part of the mount. And mount Si´-nai was altogether on a smoke, because the LORD descended upon it in fire: and the smoke thereof ascended as the smoke of a furnace, and the whole mount quaked greatly. And when the voice of the trumpet sounded long,*

and waxed louder and louder, Moses spake, and God answered him by a voice. And the LORD came down upon mount Si'-nai, on the top of the mount: and the LORD called Moses up to the top of the mount; and Moses went up" (Exodus 19:16-20).

The Hebrew the word translated *nether* is "tachtîy." The meaning of the word is "...lower-most part...."[5]

The Lord told Moses to go back down to make sure the people didn't touch the mountain and die, including the <u>priests</u> who were not sanctified. Apparently, in those days there were priests among the people who played the role of a "kôhên...acting priest (although a layman), a chief ruler, prince, principal officer."[6] He also told Moses to bring Aaron and come back up the mountain.

God Gives Moses the Ten Commandments

When Moses and Aaron returned to be with God, He spoke ten commands for the Israelites.

1. *Thou shalt have no other gods before me.*

2. *Thou shalt not make unto thee any graven image, or any likeness of any thing that is in heaven above, or that is in the earth beneath, or that is in the water under the earth: thou shalt not bow down thyself to them, nor serve them: for I the LORD thy God am a jealous God, visiting the iniquity of the fathers upon the children unto the third and fourth generation of them that hate me; and showing mercy unto thousands of them that love me, and keep my commandments.*

3. *Thou shalt not take the name of the LORD thy God in vain: for the LORD will not hold him guiltless that taketh his name in vain.*

4. *Remember the sabbath day to keep it holy. Six days shalt thou labor, and do all thy work: but the seventh day is the sabbath of the LORD thy God: in it thou shalt not do any work, thou, nor thy son, nor thy daughter, thy manservant, nor thy maidservant, nor thy cattle, nor thy stranger that*

is within thy gates: for in six days the LORD made heaven and earth, the sea, and all that in them is, and rested the seventh day: wherefore the LORD blessed the sabbath day, and hallowed it.

5. *Honor thy father and thy mother: that thy days may be long upon the land which the LORD thy God giveth thee.*

6. *Thou shalt not kill.*

7. *Thou shalt not commit adultery.*

8. *Thou shalt not steal.*

9. *Thou shalt not bear false witness against thy neighbor.*

10. *Thou shalt not covet thy neighbor's house, thou shalt not covet thy neighbor's wife, nor his manservant, nor his maidservant, nor his ox, nor his ass, nor any thing that is thy neighbor's."* (Exodus 20:1-17)

While Moses and Aaron had been with the Lord, the Israelites, down below, had been afraid when they saw the thunder, lightning, and smoke. When Moses came down to them, they told him they didn't want God to speak to them, only to Moses. He told them, *"Fear not: for God is come to prove you, and that his fear may be before your faces, that ye sin not. And the people stood afar off, and Moses drew near unto the thick darkness where God was"* (Exodus 20:20-21).

One of the things the Lord was adamant about was idolatry. He was establishing a new way for the Israelites to worship only Him, not idols of false gods like all the other nations did. The Lord told Moses, *"Ye shall not make with me gods of silver, neither shall ye make unto you gods of gold. An altar of earth thou shalt make unto me, and shalt sacrifice thereon thy burnt offerings, and thy peace offerings, thy sheep, and thine oxen: in all places where I record my name I will come unto thee, and I will bless thee. And if thou wilt make me an altar of stone, thou shalt not build it of hewn stone: for if thou lift up thy tool upon it, thou hast polluted it. Neither shalt thou go up by steps unto mine altar, that thy nakedness be not discovered thereon"* (Exodus 20:23-26).

He also gave them laws about how to live together and about servants, criminal situations, restitution, and human relationships.

These laws were harsh and strict, and the disobedience of some of them even meant death. Three feasts were also to be observed: Feast of Unleavened Bread (for when they came out of Egypt), Feast of Harvest (the first fruits of their labors), and the Feast of Ingathering (when they gather their labors out of the field) (see Exodus 23:14-16).

God's angel would lead the Israelites to the land God had prepared for them. If they would obey Him, God would protect them from their enemies, and He would bless them with food, good health, children, and long life. He would also drive their enemies from their land.

> *"I will not drive them out from before thee in one year; lest the land become desolate, and the beast of the field multiply against thee. By little and little I will drive them out from before thee, until thou be increased, and inherit the land"* (Exodus 23:29-30).

The Blood of the Covenant

> *"And Moses wrote all the words of the LORD, and rose up early in the morning, and builded an altar under the hill, and twelve pillars, according to the twelve tribes of Israel. And he sent young men of the children of Israel, which offered burnt offerings, and sacrificed peace offerings of oxen unto the LORD. And Moses took half of the blood, and put it in basins; and half of the blood he sprinkled on the altar. And he took the book of the covenant, and read in the audience of the people: and they said, All that the LORD hath said will we do, and be obedient.*

> *"And Moses took the blood, and sprinkled it on the people, and said, Behold, the blood of the covenant, which the LORD hath made with you concerning all these words. Then went up Moses, and Aaron, Na-dab, and A-bi´-hu, and seventy of the elders of Israel: And they saw the God of Israel: and there was under his feet as it were a paved work of a sapphire stone, and as it were the body of heaven in his clearness. And upon the nobles of the*

children of Israel he laid not his hand: also they saw God, and did eat and drink" (Exodus 24:4-11).

Blueprints and Stone Tablets

"...the LORD said unto Moses, Come up to me into the mount, and be there: and I will give thee tables of stone, and a law, and commandments which I have written; that thou mayest teach them. And Moses rose up, and his minister Joshua: and Moses went up into the mount of God" (Exodus 24:12-13).

He left the elders, Aaron, and Hur in charge of the Israelites at the foot of the mountain.

"And Moses went up into the mount, and a cloud covered the mount. And the glory of the LORD abode upon mount Si'-nai, and the cloud covered it six days: and the seventh day he called unto Moses out of the midst of the cloud. And the sight of the glory of the LORD was like devouring fire on the top of the mount in the eyes of the children of Israel. And Moses went into the midst of the cloud, and gat him up into the mount: and Moses was in the mount forty days and forty nights" (Exodus 24:15-18).

The Hebrew word translated *glory* is "kâbôd." The meaning of the word is "...splendor or copiousness...honour...."[7]

God had a plan, and He told Moses to ask the Israelites to bring the following offerings to him, if they felt to do so in their hearts: *"... gold, and silver, and brass, And blue, and purple, and scarlet, and fine linen, and goats' hair, And rams' skins dyed red, and badgers' skins, and shit'-tim wood, Oil for the light, spices for anointing oil, and for sweet incense. Onyx stones, and stones to be set in the e'-phod, and in the breastplate. And let them make me a sanctuary that I may dwell among them"* (Exodus 25:3-8).

He gave Moses the details of this new Sanctuary, everything in it, and regulations for the consecration of the priests (see Exodus,

Chapters 25-31). God told Moses, *"...there I will meet with thee, and I will commune with thee from above the mercy seat, from between the two cher'-u-bim which are upon the ark of the testimony, of all things which I will give thee in commandment unto the children of Israel"* (Exodus 25:22). God also said that the Sabbath would be a sign between Himself and the Israelites so that they would *"...know that I am the LORD that doth sanctify you"* (Exodus 31:13). When the LORD was through speaking to Moses, He gave him *"...two tables of testimony, tables of stone, written with the finger of God"* (Exodus 31:18).

The Israelites Fall Into Idolatry

While Moses had been gone from the camp for forty days and forty nights, the Israelites down at their camp had become impatient. They grew tired of waiting for Moses, their leader, and decided to ask Aaron to make them gods to lead them.

> *"...Aaron said unto them, Break off the golden earrings, which are in the ears of your wives, of your sons, and of your daughters, and bring them unto me"* (Exodus 32:1-2).

> *"And he received them at their hand, and fashioned it with a graving tool, after he had made it a molten calf: and they said, These be thy gods, O Israel, which brought thee up out of the land of Egypt. And when Aaron saw it, he built an altar before it; and Aaron made proclamation, and said, Tomorrow is a feast to the LORD. And they rose up early on the morrow, and offered burnt offerings, and brought peace offerings; and the people sat down to eat and to drink, and rose up to play"* (Exodus 32:4-6).

The Lord saw the golden calf that Aaron made and told Moses what was going on down at the camp. God wanted to destroy the Israelites and make Moses into a great nation, instead of them, but Moses pleaded with the Lord to spare them and to remember His oath to Abraham, Isaac, and Jacob (Israel). The Lord repented of what He was going to do.

> "And Moses turned, and went down from the mount, and the two tables of the testimony were in his hand: the tables were written on both their sides; on the one side and on the other were they written. And the tables were the work of God, and the writing was the writing of God, graven upon the tables. And when Joshua heard the noise of the people as they shouted, he said unto Moses, There is a noise of war in the camp. And he said, It is not the voice of them that shout for mastery, neither is it the voice of them that cry for being overcome: but the noise of them that sing do I hear" (Exodus 32:15-18).

When they came near the camp, they saw the chaos, revelry, dancing, and the calf. Moses was so angry he threw the stone tablets down and broke them on the foot of the mountain. He burned the calf in the fire, and took the ashes, mixed with water, and forced the Israelites to drink it. When Moses confronted Aaron as to how this idol worship happened, he lied to Moses at first and told him he threw their gold into the fire and the calf came out. Then Aaron told Moses the truth, and Moses took action!

> "And when Moses saw that the people were naked, (for Aaron had made them naked unto their shame among their enemies): Then Moses stood in the gate of the camp, and said, Who is on the LORD'S side? Let him come unto me. And all the Levites from the tribe of Levi rallied to him.
>
> "...Thus saith the LORD God of Israel, Put every man his sword by his side, and go in and out from gate to gate throughout the camp, and slay every man his brother, and every man his companion, and every man his neighbor. And the children of Levi did according to the word of Moses: and there fell of the people that day about three thousand men. For Moses had said, Consecrate

yourselves today to the LORD, even every man upon his son, and upon his brother; that he may bestow upon you a blessing this day" (Exodus 32:25-29).

The next day Moses went to the Lord to try and make atonement for the Israelites. He asked the Lord to forgive the people, or take his own name out of the book that God had written.

"And the LORD said unto Moses, Whosoever hath sinned against me, him will I blot out of my book. Therefore now go, lead the people unto the place of which I have spoken unto thee: behold, mine angel shall go before thee: nevertheless in the day when I visit I will visit their sin upon them. And the LORD plagued the people, because they made the calf, which Aaron made" (Exodus 32:33-35).

The Lord was so angry that He told Moses to go on without Him and take the Israelites to the land He had promised Abraham, Isaac, and Jacob—*"...a land flowing with milk and honey..."* (Exodus 33:3). He would send an angel with them, but He would not go with them because they were a *"...stiff-necked people..."* (Exodus 33:3). He said if He went with them, He might destroy them. When the people heard how God felt, they mourned for what they had done.

Moses' Relationship With God

Moses had a tent (a tabernacle), where he would meet with God. *"...Moses took the tabernacle and pitched it without the camp, afar off from the camp, and called it the tabernacle of the congregation..."* (Exodus 33:7).

This was a place where Moses went to talk with God. When the people needed to find out something from God, they would go to the tent. When it was time for Moses to enter the tent, the people would watch him from their own tents until he went inside. When they would see the Lord's pillar of cloud come down and stay at the entrance of his tent, they would all stand and worship until he was done speaking with the Lord *"...face to face, as a man speaketh unto his friend..."* (Exodus 33:11). Joshua, Moses' aide, stayed in the tent and did not leave when Moses went back to the camp.

Moses was gravely concerned about what God might do with the Israelites, and wanted to know who God would send with him to help him lead them into Canaan.

Moses reminded the Lord that without His presence, they would not be any different than the other people on the earth, and no one would know that they had found grace in His sight. He asked the Lord not to send them if His presence would not be with them. The Lord told Moses, *"...I will do this thing also that thou hast spoken: for thou hast found grace in my sight, and I know thee by name"* (Exodus 33:12).

He said to the Lord, *"...if I have found grace in thy sight, show me now thy way, that I may know thee, that I may find grace in thy sight: and consider that this nation is thy people. And he said, My presence shall go with thee, and I will give thee rest"* (Exodus 33:13-14).

Then Moses said, *"I beseech thee, show me thy glory.*

> *"And he said, I will make all my goodness pass before thee, and I will proclaim the name of the LORD before thee; and will be gracious to whom I will be gracious, and will show mercy on whom I will show mercy. And the LORD said, Thou canst not see my face: for there shall no man see me, and live. And the LORD said, Behold, there is a place by me, and thou shalt stand upon a rock: And it shall come to pass, while my glory passeth by, that I will put thee in a clift of the rock, and will cover thee with my hand while I pass by: And I will take away mine hand, and thou shalt see my back parts: but my face shall not be seen"* (Exodus 33:18-23).

God Renews the Tables of Stone

One day the Lord told Moses to cut two tables out of stone like the ones he had broken and bring them up on Mount Sinai to God. God would rewrite the words He had written on the first stones. When Moses got to the top of the mountain with the tables of stone,"...*the LORD descended in the cloud, and stood with him there, and proclaimed the name of the LORD. And the LORD passed by before him, and proclaimed, The LORD, The LORD God, merciful and gracious, long-suffering, and abundant in goodness and truth, Keeping mercy for thousands, forgiving iniquity and transgression and sin, and that will by no means clear the guilty; visiting the iniquity of the fathers upon the children, and upon the children's children, unto the third and to the fourth generation"* (Exodus 34:5-7).

Moses bowed to the Lord and, once again, stood in the gap for Israel. He said, *"If now I have found grace in Thy sight, O LORD, let my LORD. I pray Thee, go among us; for it is a stiffnecked people; and pardon our iniquity and our sin, and take us for thine inheritance"* (Exodus 34:8-9).

Then the Lord said, *"...I make a covenant: before all thy people I will do marvels, such as have not been done in all the earth, nor in any nation: and all the people among which thou art shall see the work of the LORD: for it is a terrible* (impressive) *thing that I will do with thee"* (Exodus 34:10).

While Moses was up on the mountain receiving the new stone tables, God also gave him other rules for holy living in the new land (see Exodus 34:11-26, NIrV®).

- *"Tear down their altars. Smash their sacred stones. Cut down the poles they use to worship the goddess Asherah.*

- *"Do not worship any other god...my name is Jealous....Do not make statues of gods.*

- *"Be careful not to make a peace treaty with those who live in the land. They commit sin by offering sacrifices to their gods...You will choose some of their daughters as wives for your sons. And those daughters will commit sin by worshiping their gods. Then they will lead your sons to do the same thing.*

- *"Celebrate the Feast of Unleavened Bread. For seven days eat bread that is made without yeast...Do it...in the month of Abib. You came out of Egypt in that month.*

- *"Every male animal that is born first to its mother belongs to me... Sacrifice a lamb to buy back every male donkey that is born first to its mother. But if you do not buy the donkey back, break its neck. Buy back every oldest son. You must not come to worship me with your hands empty.*

- *"Do your work in six days. But you must rest on the seventh day...*

- *"Celebrate the Feast of Weeks. Bring the first share of our wheat crop.*

- *"Celebrate the Feast of Booths. Hold it in the fall.*

- *"Three times a year all of your men must come to worship me...While you are doing that, I will keep others from wanting to take any of your land for themselves. I am the LORD your God.*

- *"Do not include anything that is made with yeast when you offer me the blood of a sacrifice. You must not keep any of the meat from the sacrifice of the Passover Feast until morning.*

- *"Bring the best of the first share of your crops to my house. I am the LORD your God.*

- *"Do not cook a young goat in its mother's milk"* (Canaanite practice of boiling a kid in its mother's milk to increase fertility)[8]

When Moses came down from the mountain, he was glowing with God's glory.

> *"And when Aaron and all the children of Israel saw Moses, behold, the skin of his face shone; and they were afraid to come nigh him. And Moses called unto them; and Aaron and all the rulers of the congregation returned unto him: and Moses talked with them...and he gave them in commandment all that the LORD had spoken with him in mount Si´-nai.*

> *"And till Moses had done speaking with them, he put a veil on his face. But when Moses went in before the LORD to speak with him, he took the veil off, until he came out. And he came out, and spake unto the children of Israel that which he was commanded. And the children of Israel saw the face of Moses, that the skin*

of Moses' face shone: and Moses put the veil upon his face again, until he went in to speak with him" (Exodus 34:30-35).

In Conclusion

After God redeemed His people from bondage in Egypt, He set up Pharaoh to *"show his power and gain glory."* He parted the Red Sea so the Israelites could cross over, and He drowned the Egyptians who were chasing after them. Before the Egyptians died, they knew they had encountered the living God of Israel.

God wanted the people to remember, and to pass down to their children, what He had done for them. He set up instructions for two memorial occasions: the Passover and consecration of their first-born males, both man and beast, which they were to observe after arriving in Canaan.

Even though God had so miraculously rescued the Israelites, they soon forgot how bad Egypt had been and how good God had been to them. Before long, they began complaining and murmuring every time there was a "bump in the road." God was testing them, and providing for them. He was setting them apart from other nations to be a *"kingdom of priests and a holy nation."* In order to do that, He would need to teach them and give them laws to live by so they would honor Him and live safely with each other. God wrote out the Ten Commandments as their basic law and added more specific social laws to go with them. Their relationship with God was bound by a covenant of law—if they would obey His commands, He would bless and protect them.

It was quite apparent the law was needed, because while God was writing out the laws, the Israelites were melting down their gold and worshiping a golden calf. This evil act of idolatry came at a high cost, because Moses ordered the Levites to slay 3,000 people that day. God was ready to give up on the Israelites, but Moses interceded for them. He was concerned that if God's presence did not go with them, there would be nothing to distinguish them from all the other people in the world.

Moses had a beautiful relationship with God, even seeing Him *"face to face,"* and his face would shine with God's glory when he would spend time in His presence. He loved and adored God and was obedient to His every word. Moses found grace in God's sight, and God knew him by name. God's presence would go with Moses, and He would give him peace, but what about the Israelites? God would not forget His promises He made to Abraham, Isaac, and Jacob, and they would still receive the inheritance that He had promised. His Commandments revealed to them His holiness, and He rewrote them on two more tables of stone.

The Lord gave Moses instructions to build a portable sanctuary where He could travel with them in the desert. What would His sanctuary be like? In the next chapter, we will visit the construction site and see what God's portable house will look like.

Deeper Insights:

1. In this chapter we read in several places where the Lord wanted the Israelites and their descendants to remember what He had done for them:

   Remember the Passover. Read Exodus 12:43-49.

   Just as the bones of the sacrificial Passover lamb were not to be broken, the bones of Jesus, our sacrificial lamb, were not broken when He died on the cross. Read John 19:31-33. Why didn't the soldiers break Jesus' legs?

   Consecrate their firstborn—both man and beast.

   God told the Israelites to consecrate (sanctify) all of their first-born males, man and beast, to him. Read Exodus 13:2-3, 8-9, and 12-16. What did God want them to remember?

   As Christians, how are we to be consecrated to Christ? Read Romans 12:1-2. In what ways can we live that out?

Remember the manna. Read Exodus 16:32-34. Why did God want the Israelites and their descendants to put manna in God's Tent of Meeting?

Remember the war with the Amalekites. Read Exodus 17:8-16. Why did God ask Moses to write in a book about the war with the Amalekites?

The Ten Commandments. Why do you think God gave the Israelites the Ten Commandments and the additional laws? Read Galatians 3:24-25.

Why do you think God went to the trouble to write the Ten Commandments a second time?

2. Read Exodus 15:1-18. After reading this song of Moses, why do you think God brought them to the brink of disaster before delivering them?

3. Read Exodus 15:22-25; 16:2-4; and 20:18-20. What does Scripture say is the reason God allowed the Israelites to suffer hardships? Why would He want to prove them?

4. After God had given Moses His words and laws, all the Israelites agreed to obey what God had told them. Then Moses wrote the words down, which was called the book of the covenant (Exodus 24:7). Read Exodus 24:4-8 to see how Moses sealed the covenant between God and the Israelites.

What had to die with the shedding of blood under the old covenant of law?

Read Hebrews 12:18-24. The new covenant in Christ required the shedding of blood, as well.

Who had to die with the shedding of blood under the new covenant?

5. The Israelites brought their jewelry to Aaron, and he made them a golden calf to worship.

141

What does the New Testament have to say about idols? Read 1 Corinthians 5:9-11, 10:19-22; 2 Corinthians 6:16; Galatians 5:19-21; 1 Thessalonians 1:9-10; and 1 John 5:21.

Even though we may not call them idols, there are people, places, and things we devote ourselves to in place of God. Can you name some of them? Why do we do that?

6. When we are not content with what God has allowed us to have in our lives, we can easily fall into anxiety, murmuring, greed, and envy, just as the Israelites did. Read 1 Corinthians 10:1-10; Hebrews 13:5-6; and James 3:13-16.

Moses was so angry about the Israelites that he threw to the ground the stone tablets that God's finger had written on and broke them. God was so angry about what the Israelites had done that He said He would not go with them to the land He had promised to them. Moses interceded for the Israelites and grace was found from God.

As Christians today, we have Christ, Who also makes intercession for us in heaven. We also have the Holy Spirit Who intercedes for us when we don't even know what to say.

Read Hebrews 7:22-25 and Romans 8:26-27, 34.

CHAPTER 10

GOD'S PORTABLE HOUSE

Christ in The Tabernacle

God had given Moses instructions to build a Tabernacle so that He could live in the midst of His people. This new Tabernacle would be located inside the camp, and God's presence would be inside the Most Holy Place within the Tabernacle. The Tabernacle would be *"...a copy and shadow of what is in heaven. This is why Moses was warned when he was about to build the tabernacle: 'See to it that you make everything to the pattern shown you on the mountain'"* (Hebrews 8:5, NIV®).

The Tabernacle would be portable and made in pieces so that it could be packed up, transported and re-assembled as the Israelites traveled through the desert. It would be a visible sign to the Hebrews, and to other nations, that they belonged to God and that He and His power were with them at all times.

Earlier, when Moses had asked the people to bring offerings for the Tabernacle, they had brought even more than was needed. Skilled people were asked to do the construction work and tailor work, including those who were master craftsmen, designers, embroiderers, and weavers. God told Moses, *"...in the hearts of all that are wisehearted I have put wisdom, that they may make all that I have commanded thee"* (Exodus 31:6).

God was very specific about how the Tabernacle and its furnishings were to be built, and it must be built from the inside (from the Ark in the Most Holy Place where God would live) to the outside courtyard. He was also specific about the placement of everything within the

Tabernacle and courtyard, the ornate patterns to be engraved on each object, the colors that were to be used. It was there, in God's house, that He would establish a way for the Hebrew children to make atonement and be reconciled to Him.

As we are now able to look back at the Tabernacle, we can see the Father, Son, and the Holy Spirit throughout its structure. It contained symbolic previews of the plan of redemption through Jesus Christ, which would happen in God's timing. In this chapter, we will be catching a few glimpses of these previews. Even though God's instructions called for building the Tabernacle from the inside out, we are going to walk through it in just the opposite manner, taking the steps in the order in which we come to Christ to receive our salvation. We will begin our Tabernacle tour at the entrance of the Courtyard, which was the entrance to the surrounding area of the Tabernacle. It was in the Courtyard that the Hebrew worshipers took part in the atonement process.

All Illustrations shown in this chapter are by Joe Olivio.

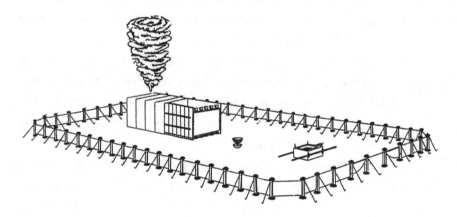

Courtyard

The perimeter of the Courtyard measured 150' long x 75' wide and was made of curtains, which were hung on posts and bases (see Exodus 38:9-29; and Exodus 27:9-19). There was one 30' wide entrance to the

Courtyard (the Gate), and it was located on the eastern side toward the sunrise (see Exodus 28:16). Each person had to enter into the Courtyard through this Gate to receive reconciliation and atonement. There was no other way into the Courtyard.

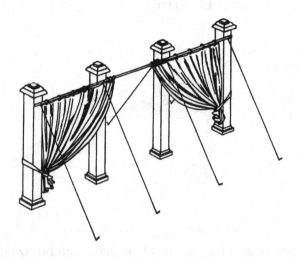

For those who chose to enter in by the Gate to confess their sins and sacrifice their animals as a substitute for themselves, there would be atonement and reconciliation with God. For those who chose not to enter in by the Gate into the Courtyard, there was no atonement and no reconciliation with God. Only those who were obedient to God's commands would be under God's blessings. The Gate was figurative of our coming to Jesus to receive forgiveness for our sins.

> *"Open to me the gates of righteousness: I will go into them, and I will praise the LORD: this gate of the LORD, into which the righteous shall enter. I will praise thee: for thou hast heard me, and art become my salvation. The stone which the builders refused is become the <u>head stone of the corner</u>"* (Psalm 118:19-21).

The Bible says that Jesus is the *"head stone of the corner,"* and He says, *"I am the door: by me if any man enter in, he shall be saved...."* (John 10:9).

When the Israelites walked through the curtain door, they would be standing in front of the Altar of Burnt Offering (the Brazen Altar).

The Altar of Burnt Offering

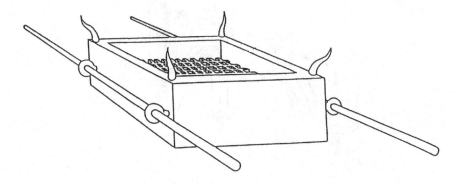

This Altar was made of acacia wood, overlaid with bronze (brass), and measured about 4 ½′ feet high by about 7 ½′ feet long and wide. It was hollow and had a network of bronze grating. There was a horn at each of its corners overlaid with bronze (see Exodus 27). Its bronze utensils consisted of *"...pots to remove the ashes, and its shovels, sprinkling bowls, meat forks and firepans"* (Exodus 27:3, NIV®).

Only priests were allowed to serve at, and be in charge of, the Altar (see Exodus 27:1-8; Numbers 18:3, 7). Unblemished animals were burned on it as sacrificial substitutes for the people to bring atonement for their sins. Just as God had required the lamb's blood to be on the doorposts in Egypt, the blood of the sacrificed animals would once again bring them into God's safety net. Their sins, which separated them from God, would be atoned for by the sacrifice of an animal. It was a substitution system that God, their Father, had divinely set up for them to be reconciled to Him. The Altar of Burnt Offering is symbolic of Christ's death on the cross, where He sacrificed Himself to pay for our sins through the shedding of His own blood. He was a sacrificial Lamb without sin—*"...For even Christ our passover is sacrificed for us..."* (1 Corinthians 5:7).

"...Christ also suffered for us, leaving us an example, that ye should follow his steps: Who did no sin, neither was guile found in his mouth..." (1 Peter 2:21-22).

"Forasmuch as ye know that ye were not redeemed with corruptible things, as silver and gold, from your vain conversation received by tradition from your fathers; But with the precious blood of Christ, as of a lamb without blemish and without spot: Who verily was foreordained before the foundation of the world, but was manifest in these last times for you" (1 Peter 1:18-19).

The Bronze Basin (Laver)

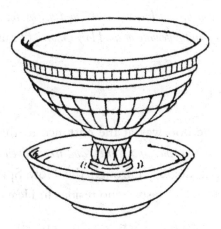

The Basin was used for washing the priests' hands and feet, a place of cleansing. It was to be placed *"...between the tent of meeting and the altar, and put water in it"* (Exodus 30:18, NIV®).

The basin was made *"...from the mirrors of women who served at the entrance to the tent of meeting"* (Exodus 38:8, NIV®).

"Aaron and his sons are to wash their hands and their feet with water from it. Whenever they enter the tent of meeting, they shall wash with water so that they will not die. Also, when they approach the altar to minister by presenting a food offering to the

LORD, they shall wash their hands and feet so that they will not die" (Exodus 30:19-21, NIV®).

The Basin was symbolic of Christ's sanctifying us (purifying and cleansing us) through baptism and the Holy Ghost.

"...Christ also loved the church, and gave himself for it; That he might sanctify and cleanse it with the washing of water by the word, That he might present it to himself a glorious church, not having spot, or wrinkle, or any such thing; that it should be holy and without blemish" (Ephesians 5:25-27).

"But after that the kindness and love of God our Savior toward man appeared. Not by works of righteousness which we have done, but according to his mercy he saved us, by the washing of regeneration, and renewing of the Holy Ghost" (Titus 3:4-5).

The Tabernacle

The Curtain for the doorway at the entrance to the Tabernacle was made of *"...blue, and purple, and scarlet, and fine twined linen, wrought with needlework"* (Exodus 26:36). Through the Holy Spirit (the Spirit of Christ), we have access to Jesus, who resides in Heaven.

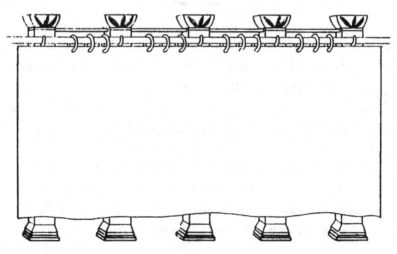

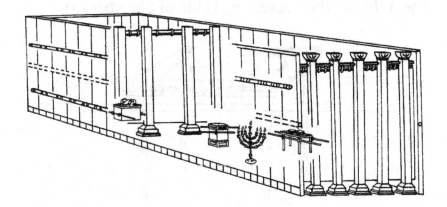

The Tabernacle (also called the Tent of Meeting) housed two rooms—the Holy Place and the Most Holy Place. "In its stricter technical meaning the term 'tabernacle' refers to a set of ten linen curtains, which when draped round a structure of wooden frames formed God's dwelling-place."[1] The frame of the Tabernacle was made of acacia wood covered with "*...rams' skins dyed red, and a covering above of badgers' skins*" (Exodus 26:14). Exodus 26 and 36 give the full description of how this curtain and the curtains around the Tabernacle were to be made. This portable Tabernacle was the focal point of the Israelite's covenant of law and worship, and it went with them wherever they traveled. The instructions God gave Moses about the Tabernacle are found in Exodus 26:1-37.

The Holy Place

The Holy Place (called "*sanctuary*" in Hebrews 9:2) was the first room through the doorway of the Tabernacle. This was the room in which the priests came daily to perform their service to the Lord within the Tabernacle. "*...the priests went always into the first tabernacle, accomplishing the service of God*" (Hebrews 9:6). The following items were in the Holy Place:

The Table of the Presence (Table of Shewbread)

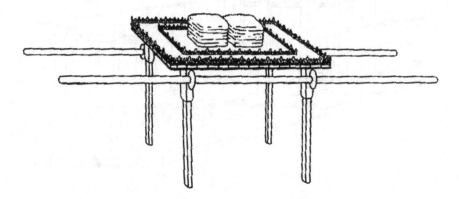

The Table was made of acacia wood, measuring about 3′ long x 1 1/2′ wide x 2 1/4′ high, which was transported by rings and gold-covered poles.

> *"...they overlaid it with pure gold and made a gold molding around it. They also made around it a rim a handbreadth wide and put a gold molding on the rim. They cast four gold rings for the table and fastened them to the four corners, where the four legs were"* (Exodus 37:10-13, NIV®).

The Table was covered over with a blue woven cloth and the Articles (the showbread, gold plates, dishes, bowls, and pitchers) were placed on the cloth (see Numbers 4:7). The Table was placed on the north side of the Holy Place in the Tabernacle opposite of the Lampstand (see Exodus 26:35).

There were twelve loaves of bread that were placed in two rows (six in each row), on the table, representing the twelve tribes of Israel. The ingredients to make the bread were provided by the twelve tribes of the children of Israel for each Sabbath, and the priests would then prepare the bread for the Table. The bread was not to be removed from the Table until the new bread was ready to replace it—it was to be offered continually.

"And thou shalt put pure frankincense upon each row, that it may be on the bread for a memorial, even an offering made by fire unto the LORD. This bread is to be set out before the LORD regularly, Sabbath after Sabbath, on behalf of the Israelites, as a lasting covenant" (Leviticus 24:7-8).

The priests, who were the intercessors for the Israelites, were allowed to eat the Bread: *"And it* (the bread) *shall be Aaron's and his sons; and they shall eat it in the holy place: for it is most holy unto him of the offerings of the LORD made by fire by a perpetual statute"* (Leviticus 24:9).

The Table is figurative of our hearts, as we believe in Christ and become intimate with Him, entering into an everlasting covenant with the living Bread of Life. Christ told His disciples about this Bread during the Lord's Supper, the night before He died: *"Take, eat: this is my body, which is broken for you: this do in remembrance of me"* (1 Corinthians 11:24).

The Lampstand (the Golden Candlestick)

The Lampstand was used *"...for light, with its accessories, lamps and oil for the light"* (Exodus 35:14, NIV®), and was the only light in the Tabernacle (see Exodus 25:31-40). It was ornately designed with *"...cups shaped like almond flowers with buds and blossoms."*

The Hebrew word translated *almond* is "shâqad." The meaning of the word is *"...to be alert...sleepless...to be on the lookout...wake, watch (for)."*[2] The Lampstand included seven lamps and was made of pure gold. It was placed opposite the Table on the south side of the Holy Place in the Tabernacle (see Exodus 37:17-24). The Israelites were to furnish the oil to keep the Lamp burning.

> *"And thou shalt command the children of Israel, that they bring thee pure olive oil beaten for the light, to cause the lamp to burn always without the veil, which is before the testimony...it shall be a statute for ever unto their generations on the behalf of the children of Israel"* (Exodus 27:20-21).

The Lampstand typified Christ, the light of the world: *"In him was life; and the life was the light of men"* (John 1:4). Jesus said, *"...I am the light of the world: he that followeth me shall not walk in darkness, but shall have the light of life"* (John 8:12).

> *"For God, who commanded the light to shine out of darkness, hath shined in our hearts, to give the light of the knowledge of the glory of God in the face of Jesus Christ"* (2 Corinthians 4:6).

As we look at the illustration of the Lampstand, with its shaft and branches, it is easy to understand the following Scripture: *"I am the vine, ye are the branches: He that abideth in me, and I in him, the same bringeth forth much fruit: for without me ye can do nothing"* (John 15:5).

Just as the oil burned in the lamp to give light in the Tabernacle, the Holy Spirit, the Spirit of Christ, shines in us to give us life. Jesus said, *"He that believeth on me, as the scripture hath said, out of his belly shall flow rivers of living water. (But this spake he of the Spirit, which they that believe on him should receive..."* (John 7:38-39).

"...Eye hath not seen, nor ear heard, neither have entered into the heart of man, the things which God hath prepared for them that love him. But God hath revealed them unto us by his Spirit: for the Spirit searcheth all things, yea, the deep things of God" (1 Corinthians 2:9-10).

Sacred Anointing Oil

This was a sacred oil made of specific amounts of the following spices: *"...pure myrrh...sweet cinnamon...sweet calamus...cassia...and of olive oil..."* (Exodus 30:23-24).

It was used *"...to anoint the Tent of Meeting and the ark where the tablets of the covenant are kept. Anoint the table for the holy bread and all of its articles. Anoint the lampstand and the things that are used with it. Anoint the altar for burning incense. Anoint the altar for burnt offerings and all of its tools. And anoint the large bowl together with its stand. You must set them apart so that they will be very holy. Anything that touches them will be holy"* (Exodus 30:26-29, NIrV®).

The priests were also anointed with this oil so they could serve God as His priests, but no one else was to have it poured on them; and the formula was not to be copied for any other purpose. The anointing oil sanctified those people and things that were anointed with it (see Exodus 30:1-33).

When we receive Christ, it is the Holy Spirit Who sanctifies us. He gives us the gift of His Holy Spirit to sanctify us and set us apart. Without the Holy Spirit, we cannot be saved.

"...but ye are washed, but ye are sanctified, but ye are justified in the name of the Lord Jesus, and by the Spirit of our God" (1 Corinthians 6:11).

The Golden Altar of Incense

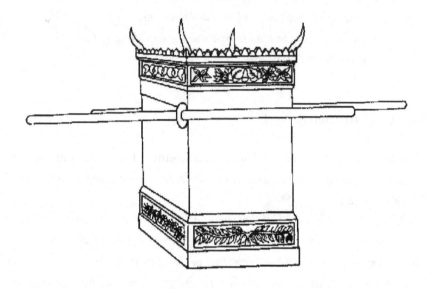

This Altar was made of acacia wood, overlaid with pure gold, with a gold crown around it. It measured about 1 ½′ long and wide and about 3′ feet high, and a horn was made on each corner (see Exodus 30:1-10; and Exodus 37:25-28). It was set in the Holy Place *"...in front of the curtain* (veil) *that housed the Ark and its Atonement Cover and the presence of God"* (Exodus 30:6).

> *"Aaron must burn fragrant incense on the altar every morning when he tends the lamps. He must burn incense again when he lights the lamps at twilight so incense will burn regularly before the LORD for the generations to come. Do not offer on this altar any other incense or any burnt offering or grain offering, and do not pour a drink offering on it. Once a year Aaron shall make atonement on its horns. This annual atonement must be made with the blood of the atoning sin offering for the generations to come. It is most holy to the LORD"* (Exodus 30:7-10, NIV®).

The offering of incense was symbolic of Christ, Who is our High Priest. He intercedes for us in heaven with the Father.

"Wherefore he (Jesus) is able also to save them to the uttermost that come unto God by him, seeing he ever liveth to make intercession for them" (Hebrews 7:25).

"Likewise the Spirit also helpeth our infirmities: for we know not what we should pray for as we ought: but the Spirit itself maketh intercession for us with groanings which cannot be uttered. And he that searcheth the hearts knoweth what is the mind of the Spirit, because he maketh intercession for the saints according to the will of God" (Romans 8:26-27).

Incense

The Incense used in the Tabernacle was made with the following ingredients, and only priests were allowed to offer this incense.

"Then the LORD said to Moses, "Take fragrant spices--gum resin, onycha and galbanum—and pure frankincense, all in equal amounts, and make a fragrant blend of incense, the work of a perfumer. It is to be salted and pure and sacred. Grind some of it to powder and place it in front of the ark of the covenant law in the tent of meeting, where I will meet with you. It shall be most holy to you. Do not make any incense with this formula for yourselves; consider it holy to the LORD. Whoever makes any like it to enjoy its fragrance must be cut off from his people" (Exodus 30:34-38, NIV®).

The Lord wanted incense to be wherever His name was acknowledged: *"My name will be great among the nations, from where the sun rises to where it sets. In every place incense and pure offerings will be brought to my name, because my name will be great among the nations, says the LORD Almighty"* (Malachi 1:11, NIV®).

Among the Israelites, only priests were allowed to offer this incense. Incense was also used as a "symbol of prayer"[3] in the Old Testament: *"Let my prayer be set forth before thee as incense; and the lifting up of my hands as the evening sacrifice"* (Psalms 141:2).

The Curtain—Veil of the Covering (See Exodus 35:12.)

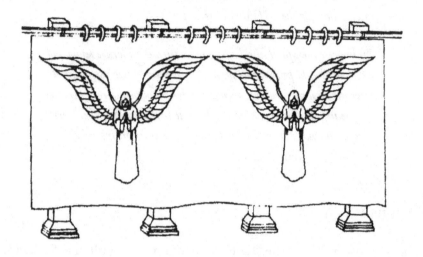

The Curtain hung between the Most Holy Place and the Holy Place, and shielded the Most Holy Place where God dwelt because God is pure and holy and cannot be in the presence of sin or look upon it (see Exodus 26:33). In speaking of God, Habakkuk said, *"Thou art of purer eyes than to behold evil, and canst not look on iniquity..."* (Habakkuk 1:13).

Just as Moses had covered his face with a veil because of the radiance of God's glory, the veil in the Tabernacle shielded the very presence of God and His glory.

The veil was symbolic of Christ, our Mediator, Who now stands between God, the Father, and us. At his death, *"Jesus, when he had cried again with a loud voice, yielded up the ghost. And, behold, the veil of the temple was rent in twain (torn) from the top to the bottom; and the earth did quake, and the rocks rent* (were broken apart)" (Matthew 27:50-51). At that point, Jesus' body became the veil between mankind and God, the Father, giving everyone who believes in Christ access to the Father through His body.

> *"Having therefore, brethren, boldness to enter into the holiest by the blood of Jesus, By a new and living way, which he hath consecrated for us, through the veil, that is to say, his flesh; And having a high priest over the house of God; Let us draw near with a true heart in full*

assurance of faith, having our hearts sprinkled from an evil conscience, and our bodies washed with pure water" (Hebrews 10:19-22).

The Most Holy Place (Holy of Holies)

This was the inner room in the Tabernacle where God lived among His people. This room housed the Ark and its Atonement Cover (the Mercy Seat) and the golden censer (fire pan). On the Day of Atonement, *"...only the high priest entered the inner room, and that only once a year, and never without blood, which he offered for himself and for the sins the people had committed in ignorance. The Holy Spirit was showing by this that the way into the Most Holy Place had not yet been disclosed as long as the first tabernacle was still functioning"* (Hebrews 9:7-8, NIV®).

This Scripture shows that this Tabernacle was only temporary and that there would someday be a way into the Most Holy Place, into the presence of God, the Father. Today, we know that way is Jesus.

Jesus said, *"I am the way, the truth, and the life: no man cometh unto the Father, but by me"* (John 14:6).

The Ark

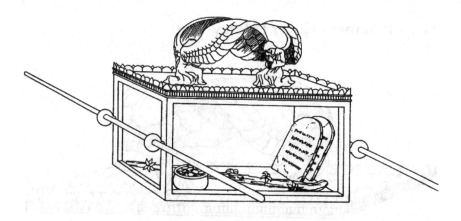

The Ark was a chest made of shit´-tim (acacia from its scourging thorns)[4] wood, overlaid and crowned with pure gold. It measured *"...two cubits*

and a half shall be the length thereof, and a cubit and a half the breadth thereof, and a cubit and a half the height thereof" (Exodus 25:10). It contained the two tablets on which God had written the Ten Commandments (God's law); and the quart of manna, which God had told them to set aside to remember His provision of bread for them. Of this manna, Jesus said,

> *"Our fathers did eat man´-na in the desert; as it is written, he gave them bread from heaven to eat. Then Jesus said unto them, Verily, verily, I say unto you, Moses gave you not that bread from heaven; but my Father giveth you the true bread from heaven. For the bread of God is he* (Jesus) *which cometh down from heaven, and giveth life unto the world. I am the bread of life: he that cometh to me shall never hunger; and he that believeth on me shall never thirst"* (John 6:31-35).

Later on, the Ark would also contain Aaron's rod, a reminder of their rebellion (see Exodus 7:11-12 and Numbers 17:1-10). When the Ark was transported, it was carried by poles, which were inserted into rings on its sides, as was the other furniture (Ark information can be found in Exodus 16:33, 34; Exodus 25:10; Exodus 37:1-5). The "Ark, having been made of wood and gold symbolized Christ's humanity and deity."[5]

The Atonement Cover (Mercy Seat)

This was the lid of the Ark, and it was made of pure gold.

"Then he made two cherubim (cherubs)[6] out of hammered gold at the ends of the cover. He made one cherub on one end and the second cherub on the other; at the two ends he made them of one piece with the cover. The cherubim had their wings spread upward, overshadowing the cover with them. The cherubim faced each other, looking toward the cover" (Exodus 37:6-9, NIV®).

The presence of God is what made the Tabernacle holy. God told Moses, *"There, above the cover between the two cherubim that are over the ark of the covenant law, I will meet with you and give you all my commands for the Israelites"* (Exodus 25:22, NIV®).

On the Day of Atonement (only once a year) the high priest would sprinkle the blood of the sacrificed animals upon and before the Atonement Cover (the Mercy Seat) to make atonement for the Holy Place because of his own sins and the sins of Israel. At that time, God would also appear in a cloud above it.

The Greek word translated *propitiation* is "hilastēriŏn." The meaning of the word is "...an atoning victim or the lid of the Ark (in the Temple), mercy seat...."[7] The Atonement Cover, which was sprinkled with the blood of the sacrificed animal, became the atoning victim, and God would forgive their sins. Christ, Who became the atoning victim for us when He died on the cross, became our Atonement Cover, our Mercy Seat. Paul says in Romans 3:23-25:

> *"For all have sinned, and come short of the glory of God; Being justified freely by his grace through the redemption that is in Christ Jesus: Whom God hath set forth to be a propitiation* (atoning victim that turns away God's anger) *through faith in his blood, to declare his righteousness for the remission of sins that are past, through the forbearance of God."*

When we ask Jesus to forgive us our sins, God sees us as righteous, because we have Christ's righteousness. He no longer sees our sins, but He does see the cleansing blood of Christ, which has washed them away!

Atonement Money

This was money the Lord commanded each Israelite, twenty and older, to bring to Him as a ransom for his life. This money was to be paid each time a census was taken, and it was to be used for the service of the Tabernacle. It was to be a "...*memorial* (reminder) *unto the children of Israel before the LORD to make atonement for your souls*" (Exodus 30:16).

"Theologically the tabernacle as a dwelling-place of God on earth is of immense importance, as being the first in the series: tabernacle, Temple, the incarnation, the body of the individual believer, the church."[8]

Moses Consecrates Aaron and His Sons As Priests

When all the pieces of the Tabernacle and the priestly garments were completed, the Israelites brought them to Moses to inspect, and Moses was pleased that they were as the Lord had commanded. The Lord instructed Moses how to set up the Tabernacle, consecrate it, and anoint it with oil.

> *"Take the anointing oil and anoint the tabernacle and everything in it; consecrate it and all its furnishings, and it will be holy. Then anoint the altar of burnt offering and all its utensils; consecrate the altar, and it will be most holy. Anoint the basin and its stand and consecrate them. Bring Aaron and his sons to the entrance to the tent of meeting and wash them with water. Then dress Aaron in the sacred garments, anoint him and consecrate him so he may serve me as priest. Bring his sons and dress them in tunics. Anoint them just as you anointed their father, so they may serve me as priests. Their anointing will be to a priesthood that will continue for all generations to come"* (Exodus 40:9-15, NIV®).

Here we see the beginning of the *"kingdom of priests,"* as God had prophesied. Hundreds of years later, after Christ died, He became our High Priest:

> *"Having therefore, brethren, boldness to enter into the holiest by the blood of Jesus, By a new and living way, which he hath consecrated for us, through the veil, that is to say, his flesh; And having a high priest over the house of God; Let us draw near with a true heart in full assurance of faith..."* (Hebrews 10:19-23).

1 Peter 2:9 says that believers in Christ are priests, *"...a chosen generation, a royal priesthood, a holy nation, a peculiar people...."*

As God had required, Moses built God's dwelling place from the inside out, beginning with the Ark, setting everything in its place.

"So the tabernacle was set up on the first day of the first month in the second year" (Exodus 40:17, NIV®).

After Moses set up the Tabernacle pieces according to the instructions of the Lord, the Lord inhabited the Tabernacle.

"...a cloud covered the tent of the congregation, and the glory of the LORD filled the tabernacle. And Moses was not able to enter into the tent of the congregation, because the cloud abode thereon, and the glory of the LORD filled the tabernacle. And when the cloud was taken up from over the tabernacle, the children of Israel went onward in all their journeys: But if the cloud were not taken up, then they journeyed not till the day that it was taken up. For the cloud of the LORD was upon the tabernacle by day, and fire was on it by night, in the sight of all the house of Israel, throughout all their journeys" (Exodus 40:34-38).

"...the glory of the Lord appeared in the Cloud" (Exodus 16:10).

The Hebrew word translated *glory* is "kâbôd." The meaning of the word is "splendor or copiousness...honor...."[9]

This has only been a glimpse of God's Tabernacle, the shadow of His redemptive process. We cannot even begin to imagine the eternal aspect of this copy of an eternal pattern. It was a home for God in which He lived in the midst of His people, the Israelites. Not in any way, does this give us a complete understanding and purpose of all the symbols, colors, numbers, and structures God used in its design. Even so, as we have read, it is easy to recognize Christ there. God purposefully set up the Tabernacle with the previews of Jesus to point the way to Him. Since Christ came, we can now look back and see God's plan of redemption within the Tabernacle and Courtyard. The gospel (the good news) of our Salvation was really prophesied about right there.

THE TABERNACLE
GOD'S PLAN OF REDEMTION THROUGH JESUS CHRIST
THE PERFECT TABERNACLE Heb. 9:11

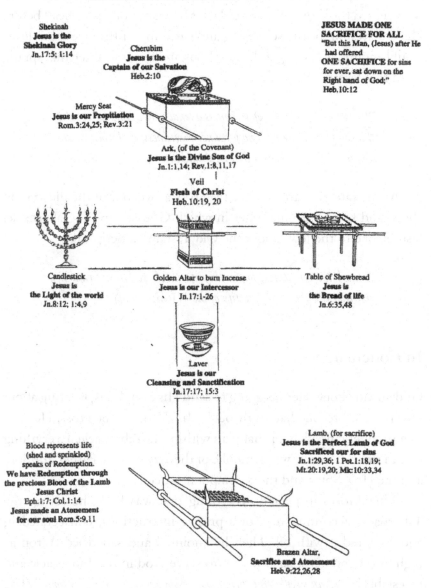

Shekinah
Jesus is the
Shekinah Glory
Jn.17:5; 1:14

Cherubim
Jesus is the
Captain of our Salvation
Heb.2:10

JESUS MADE ONE
SACRIFICE FOR ALL
"But this Man, (Jesus) after He
had offered
ONE SACHIFICE for sins
for ever, sat down on the
Right hand of God;"
Heb.10:12

Mercy Seat
Jesus is our Propitiation
Rom.3:24,25; Rev.3:21

Ark, (of the Covenant)
Jesus is the Divine Son of God
Jn.1:1,14; Rev.1:8,11,17

Veil
Flesh of Christ
Heb.10:19, 20

Candlestick
Jesus is
the Light of the world
Jn.8:12; 1:4,9

Golden Altar to burn Incense
Jesus is our Intercessor
Jn.17:1-26

Table of Shewbread
Jesus is
the Bread of life
Jn.6:35,48

Laver
Jesus is our
Cleansing and Sanctification
Jn.17:17; 15:3

Blood represents life
(shed and sprinkled)
speaks of Redemption.
We have Redemption through
the precious Blood of the Lamb
Jesus Christ
Eph.1:7; Col.1:14
Jesus made an Atonement
for our soul Rom.5:9,11

Lamb, (for sacrifice)
Jesus is the Perfect Lamb of God
Sacrificed our for sins
Jn.1:29,36; 1 Pet.1:18,19;
Mt.20:19,20; Mk:10:33,34

Brazen Altar,
Sacrifice and Atonement
Heb.9:22,26,28

Even the wood used in the Tabernacle was significant: the Tabernacle frames and boards and the Ark, the Altar of Incense, the Table, and the Altar of Burnt Offering were all made of shittim (acacia) wood. There are different speculations as to why the Lord chose acacia wood, but Strong's Concordance gives the Hebrew meaning of Acacia wood as "from its scourging thorns."[10] It could be that the Acacia wood represented the thorns that would later be placed on Jesus' head before His crucifixion, or the scourging and suffering of the cross that Jesus would endure; or the symbolism of Jesus and the acacia tree that sprang up in the desert:

> *"For he shall grow up before him as a tender plant, and as a root out of a dry ground: he hath no form nor comeliness; and when we shall see him, there is no beauty that we should desire him"* (Isaiah 53:2).

At any rate, we can embrace the cross as we look at the illustration above and see the divine order in which God set up the Tabernacle. Jesus spoke to the Jews about the Old Testament Scriptures:

> *"Search the scriptures, for in them ye think ye have eternal life: and they are they which testify of me"* (John 5:39)

In Conclusion

God already knew He was going to send His Son, Jesus, to bring about salvation and reconciliation through His death on the cross. He gave us a prophetic preview of that plan within the Tabernacle. Everything within the Tabernacle was symbolic of the *Trinity*—the Father, the Son, and the Holy Spirit and the redemption process.

After Moses inspected everything that was built, he set up the Tabernacle according to God's precise instructions, consecrated it, and anointed it with oil. Then he anointed and sanctified Aaron as high priest and his sons as priests to serve God in the Tabernacle and to establish *"...an everlasting priesthood throughout their generations."* The beginning of a *"kingdom of priests"* had begun.

Since Christ died for mankind, all who believe in Him as their Lord and Savior become living sanctuaries where God, the Spirit (the

Holy Spirit), comes to live in each believer. The Holy Spirit makes intercession for us to the Father when we don't even know what to pray. He is with us as we go in and out and carry on our daily business, and He helps us along the way. The Bible says He is the Spirit of Christ: *"But ye are not in the flesh, but in the Spirit, if so be that the Spirit of God dwell in you. Now if any man have not the Spirit of Christ, he is none of his"* (Romans 8:9). What kind of an incredible God would want to come and live in people who are still prone to sin through their sin nature? A God Who loves us and wants to give us His mercy. He knows all about us—our sins, failures, weaknesses, and our infirmities—and yet, he still wants to be with us.

In the next chapter, we will find out how the priests perform the rituals God set up for them to use in the Tabernacle to bring about atonement and reconciliation for the Israelites.

Deeper Insights:

1. We can catch many glimpses of God's plan of salvation through Christ in the earthly Tabernacle, but it was not revealed to mankind until Jesus came, in fact, it was hidden. How can we know it now? Read 1 Corinthians 2:7-10.

2. Listed below are the Gate and the items in the Courtyard, which were outside of the Tabernacle in its surrounding area. View the Cross in the Tabernacle illustration on page 163 as you read each Scripture. Try to identify how each step listed here is symbolic of the plan of salvation through Jesus Christ.

   Step #1: They entered through the Gate at the eastern side of the courtyard (We now come to Jesus to be saved).

   What does Jesus call Himself? Read Matthew 7:13-14 and John 10:7, 9.

   What does Jesus mean when He says the Gate is strait and the way is narrow?

Step #2: They brought their sacrificial animal to the priest at the Altar of Burnt Offering. We come to our sacrificial lamb, Jesus, and acknowledge that we are sinners. It was the place where the sinner humbly confessed his sins and offered his animal to be sacrificed as a substitute for himself to pay for his sins. The animal gave its life and blood to pay the death penalty for him, and he received atonement and reconciliation with God.

What did Christ do for us? Read 1 Peter 1:18-20.

What did he save us from? Read Titus 2:11-14; Romans 5:6-11; and Revelation 20:11-14.

Hebrews 12:29 says, *"For our God is a consuming fire."* Just as the fire that burned in the Altar of Burnt Offering consumed the sin sacrifices of the worshiper, the Holy Spirit and the blood of Christ purge (cleanse) us from our sins when we come to our sacrifice, Jesus Christ, and confess our sins. Read Hebrews 1:3; and 1 John 1:7-9.

The animal that was sacrificed as a sin offering and shed its blood on this Altar is figurative of Christ. Read Isaiah 53:10-11.

Step #3: The priests washed in the water in the Basin (Laver) before they could minister at the Altar of Burnt Offering or enter the Tabernacle. After we come to Christ as our Savior, we are to be baptized with water. Even Jesus came to John to be baptized with water. Matthew 3:13-17.

What does Jesus tells us we are to do? Read Acts 2:38.

Exodus 38:8 says that the foot of the basin was made from the brass looking glasses (mirrors) of the women who ministered at the door of the Tabernacle. Can you speculate why God would have wanted the foot of the cleansing basin to be made of the women's mirrors?

3. The priests served in the "Holy Place," also called the "sanctuary." View the Cross illustration. Try to identify how

each step listed here is symbolic of the plan of salvation through Jesus Christ.

Step #4: The Table of Presence, which held the twelve loaves of bread. These are symbolic of our fellowship with Jesus, Who is our Bread of Life. Can you picture Jesus, the Bread of Life, waiting to fill the table of our hungry hearts with Himself—to have intimate fellowship with us.

Jesus proclaims that He is the Living Bread—He is our provider, just like He was for the Israelites in the desert. What does He promise us in John 6:47-51?

Leviticus 24:7 says that <u>frankincense</u> was to be put upon each row of bread for a memorial.

The Hebrew word translated *frankincense* is "lᵉbônâh." The meaning of the word is "...from its whiteness or perhaps that of its smoke...."[11]

Read Matthew 2:11. What gift did the wise men give to baby Jesus after they worshipped Him?

Step #5: The Golden Candlestick, the Lampstand, with its shaft and branches, offered the only light within the Tabernacle to light the room where the priests ministered before God. The shaft of the lampstand is figurative of Christ, and the branches are figurative of the believers in Christ.

Christ gives life to His believers and sustains them with life and light by the Holy Spirit, Who is the Spirit of Christ. Read John 15:5-6.

What does Jesus say about believers in Him? Read Matthew 5:14.

Step #6: Sacred Anointing Oil was made from a formula given by God to be used to anoint the Tabernacle, the things in the Tabernacle, and the priests. This oil was figurative of the Holy Spirit, Who anoints, sanctifies (makes holy), and fills those who believe in Christ.

What does the Bible say about Christians being full or filled with the Holy Spirit? Read Acts 2:4; Ephesians 5:18-21; Galatians 5:16-26; and Romans 8:14.

There will be further discussion in the next chapter about the Altar of Incense and the Most Holy Place as we study about the sacrificial system.

CHAPTER 11

THE SACRIFICIAL SYSTEM

The Need For Sacrificial Offerings

The sin nature, which had started in the garden in Eden through Eve, and then Adam, has been passed down to every person that has ever been born. *"For there is not a just man upon the earth that doeth good, and sinneth not"* (Ecclesiastes 7:20).

Sin is serious business with God because it violates His holiness. *"But your iniquities have separated you from your God; your sins have hidden his face from you, so that he will not hear"* (Isaiah 59:2, NIV®).

The Bible says that God is the *"Shepherd and Bishop"* of our souls (I Peter 2:25). So He provided a temporary way to bring man back into relationship with Himself, and He implemented that way through the Israelites. *"...Without shedding of blood is no remission"* (Hebrews 9:22). The Greek word translated *remission* is "aphĕsis." The meaning of the word is "...freedom, pardon...deliverance, forgiveness, liberty...."[1]

He told the Israelites, *"For the life of the flesh is in the blood: and I have given it to you upon the altar to make atonement for your souls: for it is the blood that maketh an atonement for the soul"* (Leviticus 17:11).

The Hebrew word translated *atonement* is "kâphar." The meaning of the word is "...cleanse, disannul, forgive, be merciful, pacify, pardon... purge...reconcile (-liation)."[2]

God said the blood would make the atonement for the soul, but what is the soul? The Hebrew word translated *soul*, is "nephesh." The meaning of the word is "...a breathing creature...sense (bodily or

169

mental)...heart...mind."[3] God loves us so much that He provided a way for our hearts and minds to be forgiven and cleansed so we could have peace with Him and live with Him forever, even after our physical death here on earth.

Most of the Israelites worked hard at tending their animals, gardening, and using their skills in crafting, and their animals and crops were the most valuable things they had. Since God required blood for atonement, they would need to sacrifice their animals, which were precious and costly to them. They could not give just any animal—God wanted their best animal—one without blemish, perfect. This was to be the animal that would take their place after they placed their hand on its head signifying they were transferring their sins to the animal. The animal's death brought reconciliation between them and God.

God lived among His people; and along with that, the combination of the sacrificial system, the law of holy living, and the rite of circumcision would become the "stamp" on the Israelites that would set them apart from the rest of the world as His chosen people.

God told the Israelites, *"Sanctify yourselves therefore, and be ye holy: for I am the LORD your God. And ye shall keep my statutes, and do them: I am the LORD which sanctify you"* (Leviticus 20:7-8). *"And ye shall be holy unto me: for I the LORD am holy, and have severed you from other people, that ye should be mine"* (Leviticus 20:26).

Understanding even a little about the sacrificial system, with its rituals, can give us a true appreciation of what Christ has done for us. He no longer requires these rituals for our atonement, because Christ became the once-and-for-all sacrifice.

The information below has been provided to shed a little light on the sacrificial system. It is not meant to be complete, because there were many variations of the rituals, depending on the set of circumstances of the offerer. More information can be found in the first seven chapters of Leviticus, where the laws and regulations of the various offerings are recorded in great detail.

The Offerings

The word *sacrifice* is described as: "...(1) an act of offering to a deity something precious: the killing of a victim on an altar; (2) something offered in sacrifice; (3a) destruction or surrender of something for the sake of something else; (3b) something given up or lost; (4) loss..."[4] "By permission. From Merriam-Webster's Collegiate® Dictionary, 11th Edition ©2012 by Merriam-Webster, Incorporated (www.Merriam-Webster.com)."

"...In the Old Testament, fire symbolizes judgment...and fire may symbolize cleansing...It can be applied to any offering which was wholly or partially consumed by fire. Thus it was applied to the burnt offering; the cereal/grain offering; peace offering; the guilt offering; the consecration offering."[5]

Various Offerings Used In the Tabernacle

Burnt Offering (See Leviticus 1 and Leviticus 6:8-13.)

This was "...the only one in which the whole animal was burnt on the Altar of Burnt Offering; a token of dedication."[6] This offering was "...a *"sweet savor unto the LORD"* (Leviticus 1:17).

The Hebrew word translated *savor* is "rêyach." The meaning of the word is "odor...scent, smell."[7] It could be that when God smelled the burnt up offering, which represented the burning up of their sins, the scent became a pleasing aroma to Him because the offerer was being reconciled to Him. He was pleased with the heart of the offerer. Christ's sacrifice was also a fragrant offering to God. *"And walk in love, as Christ also hath loved us, and hath given himself for us an offering and a sacrifice to God for a sweet-smelling savor"* (Ephesians 5:2).

People who have accepted Christ as their Lord and Savior are a pleasing aroma to God, too.

> *"For we are unto God a sweet savor of Christ, in them that are saved, and in them that perish"* (1 Corinthians 2:15).

The offerer had <u>three choices</u> from which to select a Burnt Offering:

- A male animal from the herd (bull) without defect (unblemished)

  The offerer would voluntarily bring his unblemished animal to the Altar of Burnt Offering inside the Gate, where he was responsible for slaughtering it. Before he killed the bull, he would lay his hand on its head, acknowledging to God that he was the sinner, and that he was transferring his sins to the animal that was going to die in his place for his sins. The animal then became the victim that would *"...be accepted for him to make atonement for him"* (Leviticus 1:4).

  After the offerer slaughtered his animal before the Lord, the priests would take the blood of the animal and sprinkle it against the Altar of Burnt Offering on all sides. Then the offerer would skin it and cut it into pieces. After the priests had tended the fire, and arranged the wood on the fire, they would arrange the parts, head, and fat on the wood that was on the fire. The offerer would then wash the inner parts and the legs with water, and the priest would burn all of it on the Altar *"... to be a burnt sacrifice, an offering made by fire, of a sweet savor unto the LORD"* (Leviticus 1:9).

- A male animal from the flock (goat or sheep) unblemished (their best)

  The ritual was similar to the above, except the animal was to be slaughtered before the Lord on the north side of the Altar.

- A dove or a young pigeon (for those who could not afford an animal from the herd or flock). This offering had the same meaning, but in this case, *"...The priest shall bring it to the altar, wring off the head and burn it on the altar; its blood shall be drained out on the side of the altar. He is to remove the crop and the feathers, and throw them down east of the altar where the ashes are. He shall tear it open by the wings, not dividing it completely and then the priest shall burn it on the wood that is on the altar. It is a burnt offering, a food offering, an aroma pleasing to the LORD"* (Leviticus 1:15-17, NIV®).

"...The burnt offering is to remain on the altar hearth throughout the night, till morning, and the fire must be kept burning on the altar. The priest shall then put on his linen clothes, with linen undergarments next to his body, and shall remove the ashes of the burnt offering that the fire has consumed on the altar and place them beside the altar. Then he is to take off these clothes and put on others, and carry the ashes outside the camp to a place that is ceremonially clean. The fire on the altar must be kept burning; it must not go out"' (Leviticus 6:9-12, NIV®).

Grain Offering (Meal or Meat Offering) (See Leviticus 2 and Leviticus 6:14-18.)

Many times this offering was offered at the same time as the Peace Offerings and Burnt Offerings. The priest would take the offering to the Altar and take out a memorial portion and burn it on the Altar *"... to be an offering made by fire, of a sweet savor unto the LORD: And the remnant of the meat offerings shall be Aaron's and his sons': it is a thing most holy of the offerings of the LORD made by fire"* (Leviticus 2:2-3).

All Grain offerings had to be made without yeast or honey, because yeast and honey could not be used in an offering made by fire. These offerings had to be seasoned with salt. "Yeast and honey caused fermentation...Salt, on the other hand, was a preservative and a reminder of the solemn covenant meal."[8] There were different ways to prepare the Grain offerings: fine flour with oil and incense; fine flour cakes without yeast mixed with oil or wafers made without yeast and spread with oil, baked in an oven; fine flour mixed with oil without yeast, crumbled and oil poured on it, prepared on a griddle; fine flour and oil cooked in a pan; grain offering of firstfruits: crushed heads of new grain with oil and incense on it. Meat offerings were firstfruits of *"...green ears of corn dried by the fire, even corn beaten out of full ears"* (Leviticus 2:14-15) with oil and frankincense on it.

Fellowship Offering (Peace Offering) (See Leviticus 3 and Leviticus 7:11-36.)

This thank offering was used for restoring fellowship with God and others. It was very similar to the Burnt Offering, but a fat offering was included for the Lord, which was the choicest part.

Sin Offering (SeeLeviticus 4:1-5:13 and Leviticus 6:24-30.)

This was an offering made *"...when anyone sins unintentionally and does what is forbidden in any of the LORD'S commands"* (Leviticus 4:2, NIV®). Unintentional sins included these situations: if an anointed priest sinned, brought guilt on the people; or Israelite community, leader, or a member of the community sinned unintentionally; or if a person sinned by not speaking up, instead of testifying the truth he knew; or if a person touched human uncleanness; or if a person took an oath to do anything—good or evil. When a person was too poor to bring an animal, doves, or pigeons, he could bring a tenth of an ephah of fine flour with no oil or incense for his Sin Offering. There were various rituals for the Sin Offering, depending upon the circumstances.

Guilt Offering (Tresspass Offering) (See Leviticus 5:14-6:7 and Leviticus 7:1-10.)

This offering pertained more to social offenses and sins against the Lord's holy things:

> *"...When anyone is unfaithful to the LORD by sinning unintentionally in regard to any of the LORD's holy things..."* (Leviticus 5:15, NIV®).

> *"If anyone sins and does what is forbidden in any of the LORD's commands, even though they do not know it, they are guilty and will be held responsible"* (Leviticus 5:17, NIV®).

"...If anyone sins and is unfaithful to the LORD by deceiving his neighbor about something entrusted to him or left in their care or something stolen, or if they cheat their neighbor, or if they find lost property and lie about it, or if they swear falsely, about any such sin that people may commit..." (Leviticus 6:2-3, NIV®).

The rituals were much the same as the Sin Offering. The sinner would bring a ram, without blemish, unto the Lord and confess his sins, but he would also make a payment for restitution and penalties for the harm done. A fifth of that value was to be given to the priest. The priest would make atonement for him and forgive him. In regards to sinning against the commandments, the sinner would bring a ram, without blemish, and a trespass offering to the priest. The priest would then make atonement for him and forgive him.

"Anyone who eats the fat of an animal from which food may be presented to the LORD must be cut off from their people. And wherever you live, you must not eat the blood of any bird or animal. Anyone who eats blood, must be cut off from their people" (Leviticus 7:25-27, NIV®).

The Levitical Priesthood

God had said that Israel was called to be *"...a priestly kingdom and a holy nation..."* (Exodus 19:6), and He had already determined who the first priests would be. God told Moses, *"And take thou unto thee Aaron thy brother, and his sons with him, from among the children of Israel, that he may minister unto me in the priest's office, even Aaron, Nadab and A-bi´-hu, El-e-a´-zar and Ith´-a-mar, Aaron's sons"* (Exodus 28:1). Aaron was a descendant from the tribe of Levi.

In summary, the priests were to be responsible for "...keeping the tabernacle, lighting the lamps, continuing the sacred fire, covering the furniture when it was time for the tabernacle to be moved, burning incense in the Holy Place, offering sacrifices, praying blessings on the people, purifying the unclean, diagnosing leprosy, blowing the trumpets, carrying the Ark when it was time for it to be moved, and teaching the Israelites the Law."[9]

The Sacred Garments

All Illustrations shown in this chapter are by Joe Olivio.

High priest in his garments of glory and beauty. Ex.28:1-43; 29:1-28; 39:1-3
A type of Christ our Great High Priest High and Exalted. Heb.7:24-26; 8:12
Seven articles of clothing, speak of Divine Perfection.

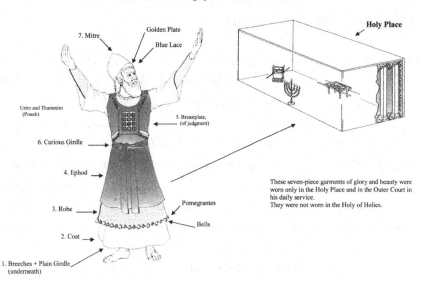

7. Mitre

Golden Plate

Blue Lace

Holy Place

Urim and Thummim
(Pouch)

5. Breastplate,
(of judgment)

6. Curious Girdle

4. Ephod

3. Robe

Pomegrantes

Bells

2. Coat

1. Breeches + Plain Girdle
(underneath)

These seven-piece garments of glory and beauty were worn only in the Holy Place and in the Outer Court in his daily service.
They were not worn in the Holy of Holies.

In Exodus 28:2-4, God had told Moses, *"And thou shalt make holy garments for Aaron thy brother for glory and for beauty, And thou shalt speak unto all that are wisehearted, whom I have filled with the spirit of wisdom, that they may make Aaron's garments to consecrate him, that he may minister unto me in the priest's office. And these are the garments which they shall make...."*

The Headbands and Undergarments (Exodus 39:28): The headbands were made of linen, and the undergarments were made of *"...fine twined linen."* And a girdle of fine twined linen, and blue, and purple, and scarlet, of needlework."

> *"Make linen undergarments as a covering for the body, reaching from the waist to the thigh. Aaron and his sons must wear them whenever they enter the tent of meeting or approach the altar to minister in the Holy Place, so that they will not incur guilt and die..."* (Exodus 28:42-43, NIV®).

The Tunic (Exodus 39:27): It was worn under the robe and was made of fine white linen.

The Robe (Exodus 39:22-26): It was made entirely of blue woven cloth, with pomegranates made of *"...blue, AND purple, and scarlet, and twined linen"* around the hem of the robe. Bells made of pure gold were attached to the hem in between the pomegranates. The robe was worn under the ephod.

> *"Aaron must wear it when he ministers. The sound of the bells will be heard when he enters the Holy Place before the LORD and when he comes out, so that he will not die"* (Exodus 28:35, NIV®).

Ephod (Exodus 39:2-7, NIV®): The Ephod was a garment worn by the high priest, and it was made *"...of gold, and of blue, purple and scarlet yarn, and of finely twisted linen. They hammered out thin sheets of gold and cut strands to be worked into the...yarn and linen, the work of skilled hands. They made shoulder pieces...woven waistband...They mounted the onyx stones in gold filigree settings* *and engraved them like a seal with the names of the sons of Israel. Then they fasten them on the shoulder pieces of the ephod as memorial stones for the sons of Israel, as the LORD commanded Moses."* The ephod was worn by the high priest. *"Aaron is to bear the names on his shoulders as a memorial before the LORD"* (Exodus 28:12, NIV®).

The Sash (Exodus 39:29): This was *"...a girdle of fine twined linen, and blue, and purple, and scarlet, of needlework...."*

Breastplate (KJV), **Breastpiece** (NIV®) **of Judgment** (Exodus 39:8-21): This was a 9" square piece of material made *"...of gold, blue, and purple, and scarlet yarn, and fine twisted linen."* Twelve stones were mounted on it in four rows: (row 1) *"...sardius, topaz, and a carbuncle..."* (row 2) *"...emerald, a sapphire, and a diamond"* (row 3) *"...ligure (jacinth), an agate, and an amethyst"* (row 4) *"...a beryl, an onyx, and a jasper...set in ouches (settings) of gold...."* Each stone was engraved with a name of one of the *"twelve tribes of Israel."* The Breastplate was then attached to the front of the Ephod and the waistband with braided chains made of pure gold.

> *"Whenever Aaron enters the Holy Place, he will bear the names of the sons of Israel over his heart on the breastpiece of decision as a continuing memorial before the LORD. Also put the <u>Urim and the Thummim</u> in the breastpiece, so they may be over Aaron's heart whenever he enters the presence of the LORD. Thus Aaron will always bear the means of making decisions for the Israelites over his heart before the LORD"* (Exodus 28:29-30, NIV®).

"The Urim and Thummim were the official means for casting lots to a 'yes' or 'no' from God...and were carried in the priestly ephod."[10]

In his prophecy of Christ, Isaiah 59:17 says, *"For he* (Jesus) *put on righteousness as a breastplate, and a helmet of salvation upon his head; and he put on the garments of vengeance for clothing, and was clad with zeal as a cloak."*

The Mitre (Turban) (Exodus 39:28): It was worn on the head and made of fine linen.

The Holy Crown (Leviticus 8:9): It was worn around the bottom edge of the mitre (the turban).

The Plate: It was attached to the front of the crown with a blue cord and was made out of pure gold and engraved on it were the words, *"… HOLINESS TO THE LORD…"* (Exodus 39:30).

> *"It will be on Aaron's forehead, and he will bear the guilt involved in the sacred gifts the Israelites consecrate, whatever their gifts may be. It will be on Aaron's forehead continually so that they will be acceptable to the LORD"* (Exodus 28:38, NIV®).

The tunic, mitre, headbands and undergarments, and the sash were to be worn by Aaron's sons, as well as Aaron, *"…to give them dignity and honor"* (Exodus 28:40, NIV®).

We can't help but reminded of Ephesians 6:11-18, which tells believers, who are the priesthood of Christ, to wear spiritual protection:

> *"Put on the whole armor of God, that ye may be able to stand against the wiles of the devil. For we wrestle not against flesh and blood, but against principalities, against powers, against the rulers of the darkness of this world, against spiritual wickedness in high places. Wherefore take unto you the whole armor of God, that ye may be able to withstand in the evil day, and having done all, to stand. Stand therefore, having your loins girt about with truth, and having on the breastplate of righteousness; And your feet shod with the preparation of the gospel of peace; Above all, taking the shield of faith, wherewith ye shall be able to quench all the fiery darts of the wicked. And take the helmet of salvation, and the sword of the Spirit, which is the word of God: Praying always with all prayer and supplication in the Spirit, and watching thereunto with all perseverance and supplication for all saints."*

The Consecration of Aaron and His Sons

When it was time for Aaron and his sons to be ordained by God to serve in the Tabernacle, God commanded Moses to perform ordination rituals, while the entire assembly watched from the entrance of the Tent of Meeting. Remember, God had selected Moses, when he was a baby, from the Levite tribe— the tribe selected to become the priesthood for Israel, and he had already been performing priesthood duties. Moses washed Aaron and his sons with water, and then dressed Aaron in the priestly garments. He anointed and consecrated the Tabernacle and everything in it and then dressed Aaron's sons with tunics, sashes, and headbands. Moses offered three offerings unto the Lord: a Sin-Offering where Aaron and his sons laid their hands on its head to make atonement for themselves; a Burnt Offering for *"...a sweet savor, and an offering made by fire unto the LORD"* (Leviticus 8:21); and an offering for their consecration.

> *"...Aaron and his sons laid their hands upon the head of the ram. And he slew it; and Moses took of the blood of it, and put it upon the tip of Aaron's right ear, and upon the thumb of his right hand, and upon the great toe of his right foot. And he brought Aaron's sons, and Moses put of the blood upon the tip of their right ear, and upon the thumbs of their right hands, and upon the great toes of their right feet: and Moses sprinkled the blood upon the altar round about"* (Leviticus 8:22-24).

After that, Moses took the fat from the tail, organs, and right thigh and added an unleavened cake of bread from the basket that was set before the Lord, and he gave them to Aaron and his sons as a wave offering. He burned them on the Altar of Burnt Offering as *"...consecrations for a sweet savor..."* (Leviticus 8:28). Then for Moses' consecration, he waved the breast before the Lord.

To finish the ceremony, Moses took the anointing oil and blood, which was upon the Altar and applied them to Aaron and his sons' clothing, sanctifying them. Moses gave them this command:

"...Boil the flesh at the door of the tabernacle of the congregation: and there eat it with the bread that is in the basket of consecrations, as I commanded, saying, Aaron and his sons shall eat it. And that which remaineth of the flesh and of the bread shall ye burn with fire. And ye shall not go out of the door of the tabernacle of the congregation in seven days, until the days of your consecration be at an end: for seven days shall he consecrate you. As he hath done this day, so the LORD hath commanded to do, to make an atonement for you...keep the charge of the LORD, that ye die not: for so I am commanded" (Leviticus 8:31-35).

After their consecration, Aaron and his sons presented sacrifices for a Sin Offering, Burnt Offering, and a Peace Offering in the presence of the elders and the children of Israel. God required that the Israelites bring a baby goat for a Sin Offering and one-year old calves and lambs for a Burnt Offering, a bullock and a ram for Peace Offerings, and a meat and oil offering. After the ceremony was complete, Moses and Aaron *"...came out, and blessed the people, and the glory of the LORD appeared unto all the people. And there came out a fire from before the LORD, and consumed upon the altar the burnt offering and the fat: which when all the people saw, they shouted, and fell on their faces"* (Leviticus 9:23-24).

Aaron's sons Nadab and Abihus went against God's command. They *"...took their censers, put fire in them and added incense; and they offered unauthorized fire before the LORD, contrary to his command. So fire came out from the presence of the LORD and consumed them, and they died before the LORD"* (Leviticus 10:1-2, NIV®). Moses commanded Mishael, Elzaphan, and Uzziel to carry their bodies outside of the camp.

The Lord told Moses, *"...Speak unto Aaron thy brother, that he come not at all times into the holy place within the veil before the mercy seat, which is upon the ark* (the Most Holy Place); *that he die not: for I will appear in the cloud upon the mercy seat"* (Leviticus 16:1-2).

The Day of Atonement (Leviticus16:1-34)

"...Atonement is to be made once a year for all the sins of the Israelites" (Leviticus 16:34, NIV®).

Aaron was the first appointed high priest to serve in God's earthly Tabernacle. The Day of Atonement was the only day that the high priest would be allowed to enter the Most Holy Place, where God resided, and he must come dressed only in his white tunic and undergarments. It was a Sabbath day of rest, and all the Israelites would be required to fast and rest on that day—they were not to do any work. It was also the day that a scapegoat would carry the sins of the people outside the camp.

"This is how Aaron is to enter the Most Holy Place: He must first bring a young bull for a sin offering and a ram for a burnt offering. He is to put on the sacred linen tunic, with linen undergarments next to his body; he is to tie the linen sash around him and put on the linen turban. These are sacred garments; so he must bathe himself with water before he puts them on. From the Israelite community he is to take two male goats for a sin offering and ram for a burnt offering. Aaron is to offer the bull for his own sin offering to make atonement for himself and his household. Then he is to take the two goats and present them before the LORD at the entrance to the tent of meeting. He is to cast lots for the two goats—one lot for the LORD and the other for the scapegoat. Aaron shall bring the goat whose lot falls to the LORD and sacrifice it for a sin offering. But the goat chosen by lot as the scapegoat shall be presented alive before the LORD to be used for making atonement by sending it into the desert as a scapegoat.

"Aaron shall bring the bull for his own sin offering to make atonement for himself and his household, and he is to slaughter the bull for his own sin offering. He is to take a censer full of burning coals from the altar before the LORD and two handfuls of finely ground fragrant incense and take them behind the curtain. He is

to put the incense on the fire before the LORD, and the smoke of the incense will conceal the atonement cover above the tablets of the covenant law, so that he will not die. He is to take some of the bull's blood and with his finger sprinkle it on the front of the atonement cover; then he shall sprinkle some of it with his finger seven times before the atonement cover.

"He shall then slaughter the goat for the sin offering for the people and take its blood behind the curtain and do with it as he did with the bull's blood: He shall sprinkle it on the atonement cover and in front of it. In this way he will make atonement for the Most Holy Place because of the uncleanness and rebellion of the Israelites, whatever their sins have been. He is to do the same for the tent of meeting, which is among them in the midst of their uncleanness. No one is to be in the tent of meeting from the time Aaron goes in to make atonement in the Most Holy Place until he comes out, having made atonement for himself, his household and the whole community of Israel. Then he shall come out to the altar that is before the LORD and make atonement for it. He shall take some of the bull's blood and some of the goat's blood and put it on all the horns of the altar. He shall sprinkle some of the blood on it with his finger seven times to cleanse it and to consecrate it from the uncleanness of the Israelites.

"When Aaron has finished making atonement for the Most Holy Place, the tent of meeting and the altar, he shall bring forward *the live goat* (the scapegoat). *He is to lay both hands on the head of the live goat and confess over it all the wickedness and rebellion of the Israelites—all their sins—and put them on the goat's head. He shall send the goat away into the wilderness in the care of someone appointed for the task. The goat will carry on itself all their sins to a remote place; and the man shall release it in the wilderness"* (Leviticus 16:3-22, NIV®).

Then Aaron would take off the clothes he had worn when he had entered into the Most Holy Place and leave them in the Tent of Meeting.

He would then *"...bathe himself with water in a holy place..."* (Leviticus 16:24, NIV®) and put on his regular clothes before performing the atonement ceremony for himself and the Israelites. The priest, who took the scapegoat out, must wash his clothes and bathe before returning to camp.

> *"The bull and the goat that were used for sin offering, whose blood was brought into the Most Holy Place to make atonement, must be taken outside the camp; their hides, flesh and intestines are to be burned up"* (Leviticus 16:27, NIV®).

The priest who burned the bull and goat must bathe and wash his clothes with water before he could return to camp.

Jesus is our Atonement Cover, our Mercy Seat. With His own blood, He bought us and paid for our sins. Our part is to believe that He is the Son of God and that God raised Him from the dead, then come to Him and confess our sins, asking for His forgiveness. There is nothing more that can be done to make atonement for our souls.

The Offering Place In the Courtyard

Ceremonies of all burnt offerings and sacrifices were to be performed at the Altar of the Tabernacle and nowhere else.

> *"...Whatsoever man there be of the house of Israel, or of the strangers which sojourn among you, that offereth a burnt offering or sacrifice, And bringeth it not unto the door of the tabernacle of the congregation, to offer it unto the LORD; even that man shall be cut off from among his people"* (Leviticus 17:8-9).

Try to imagine what it must have been like in the Tabernacle courtyard where all the animals were being slaughtered. There were probably between two and three million Israelites, all required by God to come to this place at different times. The ground would have been dusty from the dirt or sand, with spilled and spattered blood from the slaughtered animals all around within the courtyard near the Altar of Burnt Offering. Most of the people were probably barefoot, or at the least, in sandals, walking in the blood and the feces of all the animals that were waiting their turn to be sacrificed inside and outside the eastern entrance to the Tabernacle. There would have been a lot of noise with the animals crying out, the priests praying, and the people yelling and talking. Mixed smells, of manure, urine, dirty animal hair, sweaty and dirty bodies, blood, and the smoke coming from burning wood and animals filled the air. This was their place of worship, the place to receive atonement. This was the place where their God had chosen to live among them and reconcile His people to Himself.

In Conclusion

God provided a temporary way for the Israelites to receive atonement that pointed to Christ. It was also a way that would show them their need for a Savior because of their inability to obey the law. They believed in and put their faith in the promise given to Abraham that all nations would be blessed, but they didn't know that it would be Christ Who would come through their descendants to bless them. We can see the implementation of God's plan of salvation when we look at the sacrificial system. Their animals died for them on the altar, and the blood of their animals made the atonement, bringing them back into reconciliation with God.

God selected the priests, the clothes they were to wear, and He set up the rituals they were to follow as the Israelites came to them to receive atonement. They were servants of God to serve the Israelites and guide them to live holy lives.

God set the Israelites apart from the rest of the world as a holy nation unto Himself to preserve a remnant of people who would pass down their faith to their children until the time of Christ. Not only would they be redeemed through the blood of Christ to live in heaven with Him forever, but they would also be saved from Gods wrath on "the day of the Lord." The "day of the Lord" is still to come in our future, but it will come, because God says it will. God knew exactly what He was doing. Many years of history and preparation would have to go by before the Savior would come—but as we look back at our own history, we know that He did come in the *"...fullness of time..."* (Galatians 4:4).

> *"When Christ came as high priest of the good things that are already here, he went through the greater and more perfect tabernacle that is not man-made, that is to say, not a part of this creation. He did not enter by means of the blood of goats and calves; but he entered the Most Holy Place once for all by his own blood, having obtained eternal redemption.*

> *"The blood of goats and bulls and the ashes of a heifer sprinkled on those who are ceremonially unclean sanctify them so that they are outwardly clean. How much more, then, will the blood of Christ, who through the eternal Spirit offered himself unblemished to God, cleanse our consciences from acts that lead to death, so that we may serve the living God! For this reason Christ is the mediator of a new covenant, that those who are called may receive the promised eternal inheritance—now that he has died as a ransom to set them free from the sins committed under the first covenant"* (Hebrews 9:11-15).

The Lord had established the Law, the sacrificial system to bring reconciliation, and appointed the priests to serve them and teach them His holy standards. Now He would give them some serious practical rules on how to survive in the pagan land of Canaan He had promised to them.

Deeper Insights:

1. Read Exodus 30:1-10 to understand the purpose of the Altar of Incense. The sweet-smelling smoke from the burning incense would rise to the Lord, Who was present on the other side of the veil (the curtain between the Holy Place and the Most Holy Place). On the Day of Atonement, this step of burning incense was highly significant, in that without it, the high priest would die.

    Why did the high priest need to carry the incense into the Most Holy Place? Read Leviticus 16:13.

    What else did the high priest take into the Most Holy Place and what did he do with it?

    Read Leviticus 16:14-19.

2. God set up the Levitical priesthood, and He had requirements that the priests must follow. Read the following scriptures and identify what some of those requirements were:

    Leviticus 10:8-18; and Leviticus 21:1-24.

3. Prior to entering into the Most Holy Place with the blood of the bull, Aaron had selected two goats and cast lots for them to see which one would be sacrificed to the Lord and which one would be used as a scapegoat. He would sacrifice the selected goat and offer it up for the sins of the people, bringing its blood into the Most Holy Place, sprinkling in front of, and before, the Mercy Seat. The high priest would also make atonement for the whole Tabernacle in the same way.

    What did the high priest do with the other goat? Read Leviticus 16:20-22.

    Read Leviticus 16:23-28. What happened to the bull and goat, whose blood was sprinkled on and before the Atonement Cover of the Ark?

4. God set up this sacrificial system as a temporary way for atonement, yet the Bible says this system was not adequate. After reading Hebrews 9:6-10 and 10:1-4, 11, identify what each of the inadequacies were.

   In Hebrews 9:6-10, what do you think God meant by "...*the time of reformation*..." in the KJV or the "...*time of the new order*..." in the NIV®?

5. When Christ died, the Bible says He became a High Priest. Why was He a better High Priest than those within the Levitical priesthood that was set up so long ago? Read Hebrews 9:9-28 and Hebrews 10:10-14.

CHAPTER 12

SURVIVAL SKILLS FOR CANAAN

Rules For Holy Living in Canaan

God knew about the land He was sending the Israelites into. It was populated with people who worshiped many gods. Some of these gods like "El...Baal, i.e., Hadad the storm-god... Dagon... the goddesses Asherah, Astarte, and Anath—like Baal—had multi-coloured personalities and violent characters...goddesses of sex and war; and Kothar-and-Hasis... artificer-god... and other lesser deities abounded."[1] "In Canaan, prostitution and fertility rites were all mixed up with worship. In Israel, by sharp contrast, anything suggesting the sexual or sensual is strictly banned from the worship of God."[2]

The Canaanites were pagans, steeped in all forms of immorality and idolatry. Living among them would become a snare to the Israelites if they were not totally grounded in their God. So the laws and rules for living were set up as a result of God's mercy, justice, and faithfulness.

Instructions for Healthy Eating (Leviticus 11:1-47)

- *"You can eat any animal that has hoofs that are separated completely in two...it must also chew the cud"* (Leviticus 11:3, NIrV®).

- "Blood is forbidden, so the animal must be slaughtered by cutting the throat and allowing as much blood as possible to drain away"[3]

- *"Whatsoever hath no fins nor scales in the waters, that shall be an abomination unto you"* (Leviticus 11:12).

- You may not eat the following birds: *"...eagles, vultures and black vultures...red kites...black kites...ravens...horned owls, screech owls, gulls...hawks...little owls, cormorants, and great owls, and ospreys...storks, hoopoes, bats and all kinds of herons"* (Leviticus 11:13-19, NIrV®).

- You may not eat *"...every flying insect that walks on all fours,"* except, you can eat *"...locusts, katydids, crickets, and grasshoppers"* (Leviticus 11:20-22, NIrV®).

- Meat and milk were never to be cooked or eaten together. "Neutral foods, such as fish,

- eggs, grain, vegetables and fruit can be eaten with either meat or milk products."[4]

Regulations For Health and Holiness

God set up regulations regarding the following situations: purification after childbirth (Leviticus 12:1-8); infectious Skin Diseases (Leviticus 13:1-46; 14:1-32); mildew (Leviticus 13:47-59; 14:33-57); and discharges causing uncleanness (Leviticus 15:1-33). Discharges had to do with semen, menstrual, and other abnormal discharges. Leviticus, chapters 19-27, record many laws having to do with holy living, communal living, penalties and punishments, feasts, priestly duties, immorality, harvests, tithes and offerings, redeeming servants and the poor, and hygiene.

God said, *"Thou shalt not avenge, nor bear any grudge against the children of thy people, but thou shalt love thy neighbor as thyself: I am the LORD"* (Leviticus 19:18).

Special days were to be celebrated:

- *"The Sabbath of Rest...ye shall do no work therein: it is the Sabbath of the LORD in all your dwellings"* (Leviticus 23:3).

- *"The LORD'S Passover"* (Leviticus 23:5)

- *"The feast of unleavened bread unto the LORD"* (Leviticus 23:6-8)

- *"Firstfruits"* (Leviticus 23:10-23)

- *"Memorial of blowing trumpets"* (Leviticus 23:24-25)

- *"Day of atonement"* (Leviticus 23:27-32)

- *"The feast of tabernacles"* (Leviticus 23:34-36)

- *"Sabbath years: A Sabbath of rest unto the land"* (Leviticus 25:1-7)

- *"The year of Jubilee"* (Leviticus 25:8-34): "The fiftieth year, following the seventh seven, is an extra fallow year for the land, which reverts back to its original owner. It is a time when those who have fallen on bad times have their freedom and property restored...It reminds the people that the land belongs to God: and it prevents the wealthy from amassing land."[5]

Devoted People, Animals, and Things (Leviticus 27:1-33)

Persons, animals, crops, houses, land, and tithes could all be redeemed. All firstborn sons and animals, and the firstfruits of their crops, were automatically devoted to the Lord and could not be redeemed.

> *"...Nothing that a man owns and <u>devotes</u> whether a human being or an animal or family land—may be sold or redeemed; everything so devoted is most holy to the LORD"* (Leviticus 27:28, NIV®).

In this passage the Hebrew word translated *devotes* is "charam." The meaning of the word is "to devote to religious uses...."[6]

> *"No person <u>devoted</u> to destruction may be ransomed; they are to be put to death"* (Leviticus 27:29, NIV®).

In this passage, the Hebrew word translated *devoted* is "kheh´-rem." The meaning of the word is...usually a doomed object...."[7]

Blessings and Curses (Leviticus 26:1-46)

Blessings: They will have rain for crops and fruit trees and plentiful food; they will have victory over their enemies and live in peace and safety; they will have God's favor, become large in numbers; and God will keep His covenant with them. He will be their God, and they will be His people.

Curses: If the Israelites would refuse to obey God's commandments and hate His judgments, breaking covenant with Him, would cause and allow punishments, seven times over, to come upon the Israelites for their continued rebellion: They would experience such things as fear, diseases, afflictions, plagues, and wild animals that would eat their children and cattle, and they would be taken over and ruled by their enemies. If they continued to turn away from Him, He would set His face against them to break their stubborn pride: He would abhor them, and they would eat their own children; and God will turn their cities into ruins and lay waste their sanctuaries; and He would bring His sword against them and scatter them among the nations.

Sins That Would Bring a Death Sentence:

God's standards were high, and He could not allow sin to run rampant—it would destroy everyone. Some sins were an automatic death sentence: blaspheming God (Leviticus 24); false doctrines (Deuteronomy 13); sacrificing children (Leviticus 20); divination, witchcraft (Exodus 22, Leviticus 20); Sabbath-breaking (Numbers 15); apostasy (Deuteronomy 13); idolatry (Deuteronomy 17); kidnapping (Deuteronomy 21); cursing and smiting parents (Deuteronomy 21); juvenile rebellion (Deuteronomy 21); adultery (Leviticus 20, Deuteronomy 22); bringing their sacrifices to someone or someplace other than the priest (Leviticus 17); eating blood (Leviticus 17, 20); unlawful sexual relations (Leviticus 18, 20)—these included nakedness and sex with relatives, homosexuality, sex with animals, sex with women who are on their periods; sex involving the religion of the god, Molech; rape (Deuteronomy 22); and murder (Deuteronomy 19:4-13).

> "...Ye shall be _holy_ for I the LORD your God am holy"
> (Leviticus 19:2).

In this passage, the Hebrew word translated *holy* is "qâdôsh." The meaning of the word is "sacred (ceremonially or morally)."[8]

God set up this covenant of law for a reason: Israel was a to be a holy nation, set apart from all other nations—they were not to mix with other cultures. Not only did the law set them apart, but it taught them fear and respect for the Lord, Who would in return bless them with good health, mentally, physically, and spiritually. The law was given to them as a covering of protection, not something to harm them or rob them. Salvation for mankind would come at a high cost to the Israelites. God loved the Israelites whom He had chosen to usher in the Christ; but if they broke His commandments, His discipline would still come. His mercy would also come when they repented and accepted His discipline.

> *"If they shall confess their iniquity, and the iniquity of their fathers, with their trespass which they trespassed against me, and that also they have walked contrary unto me; And that I also have walked contrary unto them, and have brought them into the land of their enemies; if then their uncircumcised hearts be humbled, and they then accept of the punishment of their iniquity: Then will I remember my covenant with Jacob, and also my covenant with Isaac, and also my covenant with Abraham will I remember; and I will remember the land. The land also shall be left of them, and shall enjoy her sabbaths, while she lieth desolate without them: and they shall accept of the punishment of their iniquity: because, even because they despised my judgments, and because their soul abhorred my statutes. And yet for all that, when they be in the land of their enemies, I will not cast them away, neither will I abhor them, to destroy them utterly, and to break my covenant with them: for I am the LORD their God. But I will for their sakes remember the covenant of their ancestors, whom I brought forth out of the land of Egypt in the sight of the heathen, that I might be their God: I am the LORD"* (Leviticus 26:40-45).

People today are the same as the Israelites were back then—we still sin, and we still need boundaries. In Matthew 22:37-40, we find that Jesus summed the whole law up into two commandments:

> *"'...Thou shalt love the Lord thy God with all thy heart, and with all thy soul, and with all thy mind.* (found in Deuteronomy 6:5). *This is the first and great commandment. And the second is like unto it, Thou shalt love thy neighbor as thyself"* (found in Leviticus 19:18). *On these two commandments hang all the law and the prophets."*

These laws have now been written on the hearts and in the minds of those who love Jesus Christ, God's Son. We should not look to the law as a way to work out our salvation and avoid punishment, but we should look to Jesus Christ, Who paid for our sins and gives us the free gift of eternal life, washing away our sins and clearing our consciences. When we love God, we will want to honor Him with obedience.

The Bible says that Jesus Christ is God, the Son, and He is *"...the same yesterday, and today, and forever"* (Hebrews 13:8). He is still merciful and forgiving, and He is still just, but disobedience will still bring His discipline and consequences to us because of our sins. If we believe in Him, He will discipline us in much the same way that a loving parent disciplines his own children, not to harm us, but to help us learn from our sins. The Good News is written in I John 1:9, *"If we confess our sins, he is faithful and just to forgive us our sins, and to cleanse us from all unrighteousness."*

In Conclusion

God had shown His character to Moses. He was full of mercy and grace, goodness and truth, and a forgiver of sins; and He was also just. He made a covenant to do marvelous works in the midst of the Israelites. He was preparing to send them into a dark, pagan land, and His holy laws and standards would help them remember who they were—a peculiar people, set apart by God. His laws were, in essence, their protection and cover. Not only would God bless them if they obeyed His laws, but they would also avoid pitfalls and God's punishment for their sins. If they obeyed Him, they would see His marvelous works being done on their behalf.

God knew the Israelites would sin, so He gave them His promises of mercy and forgiveness if they would confess their sins to Him and humbly accept His punishment. He would always remember the covenant He had made with their ancestors.

Now that the rules and regulations had been set up for living holy, the Israelites were getting excited about going into the land God had promised them. However, some things would still need to be set in order. There would be enemies in the land that they would have to conquer. An army would need to be selected to fight those battles; their tribes would need to be placed in divisions; and spies would still need to be sent out to spy out the land so they would know what to expect. How will God organize all these people so they are ready to live within their camp divisions and be called together in an organized manner? What will the spies find when they enter the land of Canaan?

Deeper Insights:

1. God knew that He was going to lead the Israelites into a pagan land full of all kinds of sin and idolatry. He set up rules so that the Israelites would not intermingle and intermarry with the people of that land. He did not want them to adopt the cultures and traditions of the pagans. Why do you think that was so important to Him?

2. God gave rules for health and hygiene to the Israelites to protect them from illness and disease. Look back over the lists of these health and hygiene rules and see if you can find practical reasons why God might have given these rules to them.

3. God is holy, and He wanted His people to live holy, too—to be a light to the nations. They must remain faithful to Him so

they would not fall into sin. Obedience to Him would ensure that there would remain a remnant of faithful people who would pass their faith down to their children. He laid down the boundaries, and there was punishment, and sometimes death, for those who disobeyed. However, if they would confess their sins to the Lord, He would remember His covenant with their ancestors. Read Leviticus 26:40-45.

4. Read 2 Corinthians 3:4-11. What are the major differences between the old covenant under Moses and the new covenant under Christ? What does the written law do? What does the Spirit give?

5. The law protected the Israelites and brought God's blessings to them if they obeyed Him, but it also brought consequences to them if they disobeyed Him. Even though we, as believers in Christ, do not live under the old covenant of law, but under grace, God has placed those same Ten Commandments in our hearts and minds. Read Hebrews 10:16-17.

6. As believers in Jesus Christ, we no longer live under the covenant of law, but we live under the covenant of grace through Christ Who reconciled us back to God. When we confess our sins, God remembers His blood covenant through His Son, Jesus, and forgives us. Does that mean that we do not have consequences for our sins? Read 1 Corinthians 6:9-20 and Colossians 3:1-11, 25.

7. God, out of His great love for the Israelites, punished them so they would learn to obey Him. Today God still disciplines those He loves. Read Hebrews 12:5-11.

Can you think of any times when God disciplined you? Did you respond or react to Him?

When the discipline was complete, could you look back and see God's hand of mercy and love for you?

8. What do you think God has given believers as a deterrent from sin? Read Romans 2:14-16. What happens when we choose to disobey God and His laws? Read Galatians 6:7-8.

    God is merciful to us. When He reveals to us, and convicts us of our sin, we have hope. What can we do to realign ourselves with Jesus and clear our consciences? Read 1 John 1:7, 9 and 2:1-2.

9. In looking at our own world today, the world that affects our own personal lives, can you think of traditions, cultures, religions, or common practices that are being practiced that do not line up with the Bible?

10. Jesus tells us to go out into the world and preach the *good news* of Jesus Christ, so we are to mingle with, and love people with, His love. However, loving and sharing Christ with other people does not necessarily mean we do everything unbelievers do. Read 2 Corinthians 6:14-18.

    Has God drawn the line in the sand in any area of your life where He has set you aside to live holy and separate? If so, why do you think He has done that?

CHAPTER 13

UNBELIEF AND REBELLION

Selecting An Army and Tabernacle Servants

It had been two years since the Israelites had left Egypt. In order for the Israelites to reach the Jordan River and cross over to conquer the land of Canaan, they would need an army to drive the enemies from the land. The Lord instructed Moses to take a census to find out how many men would be eligible to serve in this new army. Moses counted all the men, twenty years and older, who were able to serve in the army, which totaled about 603,550 men, not counting the Levites, who God had set apart to minister to Him by serving in the priesthood. The Lord told Moses:

> *"I have taken the Levites from among the people of Israel. I have taken them in place of the oldest son who is born to each woman in Israel. The Levites belong to me. That is because every male that is born first to a mother is mine. In Egypt I struck down all of the males that were born first. I did it when I set apart for myself every male that is born first to a mother in Israel. That is true for men and animals alike. They belong to me. I am the LORD"* (Numbers 3:11-13, NIrV®).

The Levites were commanded to be in charge of *"...the tabernacle of testimony...all the vessels..." "...minister to it* (the Tabernacle)..." and *"...camp round about the Tabernacle"* (Numbers 1:50). They would also be responsible for taking down the Tabernacle and setting it up. The specific tasks of the Levites are recorded in Numbers 4.

Camp Divisions and Regulations

With such large numbers of people in the tribes, it would be absolutely necessary for order to be kept in the camp, and when it came time to travel. During their camping times, the Tabernacle would be located in the center of the Hebrew camp, with the Israelite tents camped around it. Levi had three sons: Gershon, Kohath, and Merari, and their tribes were called the Kohathites, Gershonites, and Merarites. They were instructed to camp directly around the Tabernacle: Gershonites on the west side; Merarites on the north side; and Kohathites on the south side. Moses, Aaron, and his sons, those in charge of the Sanctuary, were instructed to camp on the east side of the Tabernacle. If anyone else approached the Sanctuary, they would be put to death. The rest of the tribes were assigned specific locations within the camp behind the tribes listed above. *"Every man of the children of Israel shall pitch by his own standard, with the ensign* (banner) *of their father's house..."* (Numbers 2:2). However, all people with infectious skin diseases were to be sent outside the camp. When the camp order had been established, Moses pronounced this priestly blessing upon the Israelites:

> *"The LORD bless thee, and keep thee: the LORD make his face shine upon thee, and be gracious unto thee: the LORD lift up his countenance upon thee, and give thee peace. And they shall put my name upon the children of Israel; and I will bless them"* (Numbers 6:24-26).

> *"Whenever Moses went into the Tabernacle to speak with the LORD, he heard the voice speaking to him from between the two cherubim above the Ark's cover—the place of atonement—that rests on the Ark of the Covenant. The LORD spoke to him from there"* (Numbers 7:84-89).

The lampstand, with its lamps, was set up and lit according to the Lord's commands, and a ceremony was performed to set apart the Levites and to make atonement for them. When the Levites began to perform their service in the Tabernacle, the Lord established their years of service:

> "...from twenty and five years old and upward they shall go in to wait upon the service of the tabernacle of the congregation: And from the age of fifty years they shall cease waiting upon the service thereof, and shall serve no more: But shall minister with their brethren in the tabernacle of the congregation, to keep the charge, and shall do no service..." (Numbers 8:22-26).

In the first month of the second year after they had left Egypt, the Israelites celebrated the Passover on the fourteenth day of that month to remember what God had done for them. Purification ceremonies were performed for those who had become unclean by being in the presence of dead bodies so they could become clean and participate.

Leaving Mount Sinai

Every day, from evening till morning the cloud covered the Tabernacle and appeared to look like fire at night.

> "And when the cloud was taken up from the tabernacle, then after that the children of Israel journeyed: and in the place where the cloud abode, there the children of Israel pitched their tents. At the commandment of the LORD the children of Israel journeyed, and at the commandment of the LORD they pitched: as long as the cloud abode upon the tabernacle they rested in their tents" (Numbers 9:17-18).

"…Whether it was by day or by night, when the cloud was taken up, they journeyed" (Numbers 9:21).

It was by the Lord's command that determined how long they camped and when they set out to travel. God set up a way to signal all the people in the camp so they could respond to various commands in an orderly manner, without chaos and confusion. He told Moses to make two silver trumpets, each made from one whole piece, and only Aaron and his sons would be allowed to blow them. They would blow the trumpets to call the people together as an assembly, call the leaders together, and to get ready for travel. During wartime, they would blow them so they would be remembered before the Lord their God and be saved from their enemies. They would also blow the trumpets when they offered burnt and peace offerings to remind them of the Lord. Each occasion would require a different trumpet blast signal.

"And it came to pass on the twentieth day of the second month, in the second year, that the cloud was taken up from off the tabernacle of the testimony" (Numbers 10:11).

So after the Tabernacle had been taken down and made ready for travel, Moses led them on their first journey out of the Sinai wilderness. The divisions of the camp set out in a marching order given by God, according to each tribe.

"And they departed from the mount of the LORD three days' journey: and the ark of the covenant of the LORD went before them in the three days' journey, to search out a resting place for them. And the cloud of the LORD was upon them by day, when they went out of the camp. And it came to pass, when the ark set forward, that Moses said, Rise up, LORD, and let thine enemies be scattered; and let them that hate thee flee before thee. And when it rested, he said, Return, O LORD, unto the many thousands of Israel" (Numbers 10:33-36).

Trouble in the Camp

It seemed that things should have been at an all-time high with the Israelites, but they weren't. The people were still complaining about wanting to go back to Egypt when they were unhappy about something. When they complained or acted out, the Lord would become angry and bring a consequence.

They complained about not being able to hear God when He spoke, and He sent fire and burned the outskirts of their camp. Moses prayed, and the fire died down.

When they complained about not having meat—only manna, Moses became upset, and he complained to God that his burden with the people was too much for him to carry. So the Lord told Moses to bring seventy elders to the Tent of Meeting, and He would put His Spirit on them to help Moses. God was going to give meat to the Israelites, but not in the way they were expecting. Moses gave them this message from the Lord:

> "...Sanctify yourselves against tomorrow, and ye shall eat flesh: for ye have wept in the ears of the LORD, saying, Who shall give us flesh to eat? for it was well with us in Egypt: therefore the LORD will give you flesh, and ye shall eat. Ye shall not eat one day, nor two days, nor five days, neither ten days, nor twenty days; But even a whole month, until it come out at your nostrils, and it be loathsome unto you: because that ye have despised the LORD which is among you, and have wept before him, saying, Why came we forth out of Egypt?" (Numbers 11:18-20)

> "When Moses questioned the Lord as to whether there would be enough meat to feed the people for a month, the Lord said, "...Is the LORD's hand waxed short? thou shalt see now whether my word shall come to pass unto thee or not" (Numbers 11:23).

After Moses gathered the elders, "...the LORD came down in a cloud, and spake unto him, and took of the spirit that was upon him, and gave it unto *the seventy elders: and it came to pass, that when the spirit rested upon them, they prophesied, and did not cease"* (Numbers 11:25).

God sent a wind that drove in so much quail that it was piled about three feet high on the ground for *"...a day's walk in any direction"* (Numbers 11:31, NIV®). The people gathered at least sixty bushels each and shared with each other; but while they were still eating the meat, the Lord sent a plague and killed everyone who had craved and lusted for other food.

At Haeroth, Miriam and Aaron complained against Moses because he had married a Cushite (Ethiopian) woman. The Lord called the three of them to the Tabernacle, and He told them,

> *"...If there be a prophet among you, I the LORD will make myself known unto him in a vision, and will speak unto him in a dream. My servant Moses is not so, who is faithful in all mine house. With him will I speak mouth to mouth, even apparently, and not in dark speeches; and the similitude of the LORD shall he behold: wherefore then were ye not afraid to speak against my servant Moses? And the anger of the LORD was kindled against them; and he departed. And the cloud departed from off the tabernacle; and, behold, Miriam became leprous, white as snow: and Aaron looked upon Miriam, and, behold, she was leprous"* (Numbers 12:6-10).

Moses prayed to the Lord for her healing, and the Lord commanded that she be confined outside the camp for seven days until He healed her, and then she was allowed to come back to the camp.

Spies Are Sent to Check Out Canaan

Before the Israelites would be able to cross over the Jordan into Canaan, the Lord told Moses to send out one man from each ancestral tribe to go explore the land.

*"...Get you up this way southward, and go up into the mountain:
And see the land, what it is; and the people that dwelleth therein,
whether they be strong or weak, few or many; And what the land
is that they dwell in, whether it be good or bad; and what cities
they be that they dwell in, whether in tents, or in strongholds; And
what the land is, whether it be fat or lean, whether there be wood
therein, or not. And be ye of good courage, and bring of the fruit
of the land. Now the time was the time of the first ripe grapes"*
(Numbers 13:17-20).

The twelve men explored the land for forty days and came back
with a cluster of grapes so big they carried it on a pole between them,
and they also brought back pomegranates and figs. They gave Moses a
report of what they found in the land:

*"...the people be strong that dwell in the land, and the cities are
walled, and very great: and moreover we saw the children of Anak
there. The A-mal'-ek-ites dwell in the land of the south: and the
Hit'-tites, and the Jeb'-u-sites, and the Am'-orites, dwell in the
mountains: and the Ca'-naanites dwell by the sea, and by the
coast of Jordan. And Caleb stilled the people before Moses, and
said, Let us go up at once, and possess it; for we are well able to
overcome it"* (Numbers 13:27-30).

However, the other men who had gone with Caleb, painted a
frightening picture. They said,

*"...We be not able to go up against the people; for they are stronger
than we. And they brought up an evil report of the land which
they had searched unto the children of Israel, saying, The land,
through which we have gone to search it, is a land that eateth up the
inhabitants thereof; and all the people that we saw in it are men of a
great stature. And there we saw the giants, the sons of Anak, which
come of the giants: and we were in our own sight as grasshoppers,
and so we were in their sight"* (Numbers 13:31-33).

The Israelites began to yell and cry, grumbling against Moses and Aaron, wishing they had died in Egypt. They questioned why God had brought them into the wilderness to die by their enemies. They even talked of choosing a new leader to take them back to Egypt. Moses, Joshua, and Caleb were grieved at the rebellion they heard. Joshua and Caleb pleaded with the people to not rebel against the Lord and that, with God's help, they could "...*swallow*..." the people of the land. The Lord was ready to strike them all down with a plague, but again Moses interceded for them in prayer, asking Him to pardon the Israelites.

> *"And the Lord said, "I have pardoned according to thy word: But as truly as I live, all the earth shall be filled with the glory of the LORD. Because all those men which have seen my glory, and my miracles, which I did in Egypt and in the wilderness, and have tempted me now these ten times, and have not hearkened to my voice; Surely they shall not see the land which I sware unto their fathers, neither shall any of them that provoked me see it: But my servant Caleb, because he had another spirit with him, and hath followed me fully, him will I bring into the land whereinto he went; and his seed shall possess it"* (Numbers 14:18-24).

This generation would not be going into their promised land! In fact, God would make them wander around in the desert for forty years until they died off. God told Moses to take the Israelites back toward the desert and the Red Sea.

The Lord said, *"Your carcases shall fall in this wilderness; and all that were numbered of you, according to your whole number, from twenty years old and upward, which have murmured against me, Doubtless ye shall not come into the land, concerning which I sware to make you dwell therein, save Caleb the son of Je-phun'-neh, and Joshua the son of Nun. But your little ones which ye said should be a prey, them will I bring in, and they shall know the land which ye have despised. But as for you, your carcases, they shall fall in this wilderness. And your children shall wander in the wilderness forty years, and bear your whoredoms, until your carcases be wasted in the wilderness. After the number of the days in which ye searched the land, even forty days, each day for a year, shall ye bear your iniquities, even forty years, and ye*

shall know my breach of promise. I the LORD have said, I will surely do it unto
all this evil congregation, that are gathered together against me: in this wilderness they
shall be consumed, and there they shall die" (Numbers 14:29-35).

After that, the men who had given the bad report were struck down
with a plague from the Lord. The Israelites mourned and recognized
their sin. Then they made a decision to obey the Lord and enter into
the land the Lord had promised them, but it was too late. The Lord
had already spoken, and Moses warned them not to go because the
Lord would not be with them. Some of them did try to go in without
Moses and the Ark of the Lord's covenant (the Lord's presence), but the
Amalekites and Canaanites attacked them and beat them clear down
to Hormah.

This was a hard time, because God required obedience from
the people He had freed from slavery—the people He had set apart
from all other nations. Obeying God was the only way they would
be able to survive in the hostile land and have God's blessings and
protection, and He wanted them to learn this. The Lord even gave
them more laws to live by, such as ordinances for sacrifices, and the re-
enforcement of death for Sabbath breakers. There would be offerings
for unintentional sins, but those who sinned defiantly—intentionally,
would be cut off from his people, and his guilt would remain on him.
God gave them a new command regarding their clothing to help them
remember His laws:

> *"...make tassels on the corners of your garments, with a blue cord*
> *on each tassel. You will have these tassels to look at so you will*
> *remember all the commands of the LORD, that you may obey*
> *them and not prostitute yourselves by going after the lusts of your*
> *own hearts and eyes"* (Numbers 15:38-39, NIV®).

Even after all that God had done and said, resentment, once again,
rose up in the camp. Korah, Dathan, and Abiram led a group of 250
leaders of the community to oppose Moses and Aaron for raising
themselves up above everyone else to be their leader.

Moses told Korah, *"...Take you censers* (firepans) *...And put fire therein, and put incense in them before the LORD tomorrow: and it shall be that the man whom the LORD doth choose, he shall be holy: ye take too much upon you, ye sons of Levi"* (Numbers 16:6-7).

Moses continued, *"Seemeth it but a small thing unto you, that the God of Israel hath separated you from the congregation of Israel, to bring you near to himself to do the service of the tabernacle of the LORD, and to stand before the congregation to minister unto them? And he hath brought thee near to him, and all thy brethren the sons of Levi with thee: and seek ye the priesthood also? For which cause both thou and all thy company are gathered together against the LORD: and what is Aaron, that ye murmur against him?"* (Numbers 16:9-11).

Moses told Dathan and Abiram to go before the Lord, but they refused, blaming Moses for their not being allowed to go into Canaan. So Moses was angry and asked the Lord not to accept their offering. The next day when they all appeared before the Lord with 250 censers with fire and incense in them, the Lord told Moses and Aaron, *"Separate yourselves from among this congregation, that I may consume them in a moment"* (Numbers 16:21).

Moses and Aaron pleaded with the Lord to not destroy everyone because of one man's sin. As the Lord spoke, Moses told the assembly, *"...Move back from the tents of these wicked men! Do not touch anything belonging to them, or you will be swept away because of all their sins. So they moved away from the tents of Korah, Dathan and Abiram. Dathan and Abiram had come out and were standing with their wives and children and little ones at the entrance to their tents* (Numbers 16:26-27, NIV®).

Moses told them that they would know that these men had treated the Lord with contempt if the Lord opened the earth and swallowed them and everything that belonged to them.

> *"As soon as he finished saying all this, the ground under them split apart and the earth opened its mouth and swallowed them, with their households and all Korah's men and all their possessions. They went down alive into the grave, with everything they owned; the earth closed over them, and they perished and were gone from the community"* (Numbers 16:31-33, NIV®).

After the Lord sent fire out and burned up the 250 men who were offering their incense, He commanded that Aaron's son, Eleazar, take the censers out of the smoldering remains and hammer them into sheets to overlay the Altar, to *"...be a sign to the Israelites"* (Numbers 16:38, NIV®). Eleazar made the plates for the Altar *"To be a memorial unto the children of Israel, that no stranger, which is not of the seed of Aaron, come near to offer incense before the LORD; that he be not as Koŕ-ah, and as his company: as the LORD said to him by the hand of Moses"* (Numbers 16:40).

The very next day the Israelites again began to grumble against Moses and Aaron:

> *"...Ye have killed the people of the LORD. And it came to pass, when the congregation was gathered against Moses and against Aaron, that they looked toward the tabernacle of the congregation: and, behold, the cloud covered it, and the glory of the LORD appeared. And Moses and Aaron came before the tabernacle of the congregation. And the LORD spake unto Moses, saying, Get you up from among this congregation, that I may consume them as in a moment. And they fell upon their faces"* (Numbers 16:41-45).

Moses told Aaron to put incense in his censer and go to the assembly to make atonement for them, but the plague had already started from the Lord. Aaron stood in their midst to make atonement, and the plague stopped; but 14,700 people died that day from the plague that God sent upon them.

Aaron's Rod Buds

The Lord was tired of the Israelites grumbling over who should be in charge of His Tabernacle. He would establish this once and for all. He told Moses to take one staff (rod) from each leader of each Israelite ancestral tribe, a total of twelve staffs. He told him to write each leader's name on his staff and to write Aaron's name on the Levite staff. As the

Lord commanded, the staffs were taken into the Tabernacle and laid before the testimony where the Lord met with Moses.

> *"And it shall come to pass, that the man's rod, whom I shall choose, shall blossom: and I will make to cease from me the murmurings of the children of Israel, whereby they murmur against you"* (Numbers 17:5).

> *"And it came to pass, that on the morrow Moses went into the tabernacle of witness; and, behold, the rod of Aaron for the house of Levi was budded, and brought forth buds, and bloomed blossoms, and yielded almonds"* (Numbers 17:8).

> *"And the LORD said unto Moses, Bring Aaron's rod again before the testimony, to be kept for a token against the rebels; and thou shalt quite take away their murmurings from me, that they die not"* (Numbers 17:10).

So Aaron's rod traveled along with the Israelites in the Ark of the Covenant, along with the stone tablets—the Ten Commandments, and the manna in the jar. The Lord made Aaron and his sons responsible for all problems involving the sanctuary and the priesthood.

The Lord told Aaron, "Therefore thou and thy sons with thee shall keep your priest's office for every thing of the altar, and within the veil; and ye shall serve: I have given your priest's office unto you as a serve of gift (a free-will offering): *and the stranger that cometh nigh shall be put to death"* (Numbers 18:7).

Aaron was the only one allowed to go into the Most Holy Place where the Ark was. No one else was allowed to go near it or its furnishings, or they would die. The Levites were to help him with the duties of the Tent of Meeting. The Lord also put Aaron in charge of the offerings that would be presented to Him from the Israelites. From those offerings, the Lord would give to Aaron and his sons their portion and regular share. He also gave Aaron regulations about those offerings he would receive for himself and his family and regulations for using water for cleansing and purification from becoming unclean (see Numbers 18 and 19).

The Sin of Moses and Aaron

While the Israelites were camped at the Desert of Zin at Kadesh, Moses' sister, Miriam, died and they buried her there. There was no water there, and the people started complaining and grumbling at Moses and Aaron again, wishing they had died earlier with those whom the Lord had killed. They complained about no water and no fruit.

> *"And Moses and Aaron went from the presence of the assembly unto the door of the tabernacle of the congregation, and they fell upon their faces: and the glory of the LORD appeared unto them. And the LORD spake unto Moses, saying, Take the rod, and gather thou the assembly together, thou, and Aaron thy brother, and <u>speak</u> ye unto the rock before their eyes; and it shall give forth his water, and thou shalt bring forth to them water out of the rock: so that thou shalt give the congregation and their beasts drink. And Moses took the rod from before the LORD, as he commanded him. And Moses and Aaron gathered the congregation together before the rock, and he said unto them, Hear now, ye rebels; must we fetch you water out of this rock? And Moses lifted up his hand, and with his rod he <u>smote</u> the rock twice: and the water came out abundantly, and the congregation drank, and their beasts also"* (Numbers 20:6-11).

In times past, when there had been no water, the Lord had told Moses to strike the rock; but this time, he told Moses, *"...speak ye unto the rock..."* (Numbers 20:8). Out of Moses' anger, he had struck the rock twice with the rod, instead of holding the rod and speaking to the rock, as the Lord had said. This was a costly error, because the Lord said, *"...Because ye believed me not, to sanctify me in the eyes of the children of Israel, therefore ye shall not bring this congregation into the land which I have given them"* (Numbers 20:12).

Moses and Aaron had forfeited their right to lead the Israelites into the land God had promised to them.

Opposition In the Land

As the Israelites were getting ready to leave Kadesh, which was on the border of Edom, Moses sent a request asking for permission to pass through the land of the Edomites. He told them they would travel along the king's highway only and would pay for any water their livestock drank. Edom refused to let them pass through and warned them they would attack them if they tried. They did come towards them with their army, so Israel went away from them and went to Mount Hor. The Edomites were the descendants of Esau in Seir (see Deuteronomy 2:4).

Earlier, when they were traveling to Kadesh, the Lord had told Moses that it was time for Aaron to die, and his son, Eleazar, would take his place. Now, the Lord told Moses to take Aaron and Eleazar up on Mount Hor and strip Aaron of his clothes and put them on Eleazar in the sight of the Israelites. This would signify to the people that there was a change in the priesthood. Then Aaron died on the mountain.

After Aaron's death, as the Israelites were traveling toward Atharim, the Canaanite king of Arad attacked Israel and took some of them captive. The Israelites made a vow to the Lord that they would destroy them and their cities if the Lord would deliver the people into their hands. The Lord accepted their vow and delivered the Canaanites into their hands, and the Israelites totally destroyed them and their cities.

As they journeyed back toward the Red Sea, the Israelites began to complain about their situation—they complained that they had no bread and water, and they complained that they didn't like the food! So the Lord sent poisonous snakes into their midst and many people were bitten and died. Then the Israelites repented and asked Moses to pray to take away the snakes.

The Lord told Moses, "...*Make thee a fiery serpent, and set it upon a pole: and it shall come to pass, that every one that is bitten, when he looketh upon it, shall live. And Moses made a serpent of brass, and put it upon a pole, and it came to pass, that if a serpent had bitten any man, when he beheld the serpent of brass, he lived*" (Numbers 21:8-9).

In the New Testament Jesus speaks of this Old Testament incident regarding Him, the Son of man:

"And no man hath ascended up to heaven, but he that came down from heaven, even the Son of man (Jesus) which is in heaven. And as Moses lifted up the serpent in the wilderness, even so must the Son of man be lifted up: That whosoever believeth in him should not perish, but have eternal life" (John 3:13-15).

For forty years, the Lord led the Israelites around in the desert until that rebellious generation died off. One day, as they were wandering, they sent a message to king Sihon of the Amorites to ask for passage through his borders by way of the king's highway. King Sihon refused their request and came and fought them. Israel conquered him by the sword and took his land from Arnon to Jabbok and lived in all of his cities. Then they conquered the Amorite villages at Jaazer. When the Israelites went up by Bashan, Bashan's king, Og, came out to fight against them.

The Lord told Moses, *"Fear him not: for I have delivered him into thy hand, all his people, and his land: and thou shalt do to him as thou didst unto Si´-hon king of the Amorites, which dwelt at Hesh´-bon"* (Numbers 21:34).

They obeyed the Lord and possessed king Og's land and sixty of his fortified cities (see Deuteronomy 3:5).

Balaam's Blessings Over Israel

When the Israelites tented in the plains of Moab, the Moabites became afraid of them because they were so large in number. Balak, the Moabite king, hired a man named Balaam from Mesopotamia to come and curse Israel so they could strike them and send them away.

When Balaam arrived, he told king Balak that he would only speak the words that God would give him. Balak took him up to the high places of Baal so he could see the millions of Israelites below the mountain. Three different times Balaam told king Balak to build seven altars and prepare seven oxen and seven rams, and they offered them on each altar. Then Balaam told the king to stand by his burnt offering while he went to inquire of the Lord. Each time Balaam came back with blessings, instead of curses, from the Lord:

> *"How shall I curse, whom God hath not cursed? Or how shall I defy, whom the LORD hath not defied? For from the top of the rocks I see him, and from the hills I behold him: lo, the people shall dwell alone, and shall not be reckoned among the nations. Who can count the dust of Jacob, and the number of the fourth part of Israel? Let me die the death of the righteous, and let my last end be like his!"* (Numbers 23:8-10).

> *"Behold, I have received commandment to bless: and he hath blessed; and I cannot reverse it. He hath not beheld iniquity in Jacob, neither hath he seen perverseness in Israel: the LORD his God is with him, and the shout of a king is among them. God brought them out of Egypt; he hath as it were the strength of a unicorn. Surely there is no enchantment against Jacob, neither is there any divination against Israel: according to this time it shall be said of Jacob and of Israel, What hath God wrought! Behold, the people shall rise up as a great lion, and lift up himself as a young lion: he shall not lie down until he eat of the prey, and drink the blood of the slain"* (Numbers 23:20-24).

So Balak told Balaam to neither curse nor bless them. Balaam said he would speak what the Lord would tell him to speak. Balaam left again, and the Lord gave him a vision:

> *"...Ba´-laam lifted up his eyes, and he saw Israel abiding in his tents according to their tribes; and the spririt of God came upon him. And he took up his parable, and said, Ba´-laam the son of Be´-or hath said, and the man whose eyes are open hath said: he hath said, which heard the words of God, which saw the vision of the Almighty, falling into a trance, but having his eyes open:*

"How goodly are thy tents, O Jacob, and thy tabernacles, O Israel! As the valleys are they spread forth, as gardens by the river's side, as the trees of lign aloes which the LORD hath planted, and as cedar trees beside the waters. He shall pour the water out of his buckets, and his seed shall be in many waters, and his king shall be higher than Agag, and his kingdom shall be exalted. God brought him forth out of Egypt; he hath as it were the strength of a unicorn: he shall eat up the nations his enemies, and shall break their bones, and pierce them through with his arrows. He couched, he lay down as a lion, and as a great lion: who shall stir him up? Blessed is he that blesseth thee, and cursed is he that curseth thee" (Numbers 24:2-9).

Once again, king Balak was angry that Balaam had blessed the Israelites instead of cursing them. Then Balaam gave these prophecies:

"I shall see him, but not now: I shall behold him, but not nigh: there shall come a Star out of Jacob, and a Scepter shall rise out of Israel, and shall smite the corners of Moab, and destroy all the children of Sheth. And Edom shall be a possession, Se´-ir also shall be a possession for his enemies; and Israel shall do valiantly. Out of Jacob shall come he that shall have dominion, and shall destroy him that remaineth of the city.

"And when he looked on Am´-alek, he took up his parable, and said, Am´-alek was the first of the nations; but his latter end shall be that he perish for ever. And he looked up on the Kenites, and took up his parable, and said, Strong is thy dwelling place, and thou puttest thy nest in a rock. Nevertheless the Kenite shall be wasted, until Asshur shall carry thee away captive. And he took up his parable, and said, Alas, who shall live when God doeth this! And ships shall come from the coast of Chittim, and shall afflict Asshur, and shall afflict Eber, and he also shall perish for ever" (Numbers 24:17-24).

More Sin in the Camp

God had chosen the Israelites, and He was faithful to them because of the promises made to their forefathers, but He was also just. While the Israelites were camping at Shittim, the men became sexually involved with some of the Moabite women and began worshiping their gods. They joined themselves to the god, Baal of Peor. This was the very reason the Lord had warned them about intermingling with the ungodly nations. He was very angry and started a plague by commanding them to be put to death.

He said, *"...take all the heads of the people, and hang them up before the LORD against the sun, that the fierce anger of the LORD may be turned away from Israel"* (Numbers 25:4).

So Moses told the judges to carry out God's command. About that time, one of the Israelite men blatantly brought a Midianite woman to his family in front of Moses. Phinehas, son of Eleazar, took a spear and killed both the man and the woman. The plague the Lord had put upon Israel stopped, but still 24,000 of the people died. The Lord made a covenant of peace with Phinehas—a covenant of a lasting priesthood for him and his descendants, *"...because he was zealous for his God, and made an atonement for the children of Israel"* (Numbers 25:13).

The Lord told Moses to fight against the Midianites for the deception they had brought upon the Israelites with their god, Baal of Peor.

He told them to take an army of 1,000 men from each tribe, and Phinehas, the priest, with the holy instruments and the trumpets. With their swords, they killed all the males, the Midianite kings, and even Baalam, who had caused the women to sin against the Lord with Israel. They took the women and children captive, took their animals and goods, and burned their cities and castles.

When they returned to camp, Moses was angry that they had saved the women who had caused Israel to sin. He ordered the deaths of every male child and every woman who was not a virgin. As per the law given to Moses, the men who had gone to war were sent outside the camp for purification. Everything (captives, clothes, metals, wood, and things made from animals) had to be purified with either fire or water.

The booty (persons, cattle, asses, sheep) was then divided up between those who were in the army and the children of Israel. Eleazar, who went to war, gave a portion for sacrifice offerings to the Lord, and the Israelites gave a portion to the Levites who took care of the Tabernacle. The officers brought the jewelry that was taken to make atonement for their souls.

After forty years of wandering through the desert, the last of the older generation was dying off. Now, it was time for the younger generation to prepare for Canaan. To keep from judging the Israelites, we should try and remember that the human heart is prone to sin. By looking at the lives of the Israelites, we can each clearly see our own human condition, with the influence of our sin nature. We can also see why humanity needs a Savior.

In Conclusion

There must have been much excitement in the Hebrew camp knowing they were about to journey to their promised land. They had an army, a new communication system with their trumpets, an orderly camp arrangement by tribes, and God was their leader. However, something was wrong—they had ungrateful hearts, unbelief, and rebellion. They complained about many things. It seemed that when things didn't happen the way they thought they should, they wanted to go back to Egypt—to go back into bondage. How quickly they forgot!

When the spies, who were sent out to explore Canaan came back with a negative report, the Israelites became afraid and began to blame Moses and Aaron for their trouble. That was a costly mistake, which would cause them to forfeit their inheritance in Canaan. In fact, God caused them to wander around in the desert for the next forty years until the older generation died off. Their children would receive their inheritance, instead.

Even after God's anger and His decision to keep the Israelites in the desert for forty years, they continued to complain. Moses became so angry with them over their complaining, that he even disobeyed God by hitting the rock two times to get water out of it, even though God had told him to speak to it. Moses and Aaron, too, would be banned from their promised land because of his disobedience.

God punished the people for their complaining, unbelief, and rebellion, but He still loved them and had mercy upon them. In speaking of Israel, God said, *"...Blessed is he that blesseth thee, and cursed is he that curseth thee"* (Numbers 24:2-9).

It would be through the lineage of the Israelites, that Jesus would be born to save whosoever will choose to come to Him. When God sent the poisonous snakes to bite the Israelites while they were in the desert, He also made a way for them to be saved—all they had to do was look upon the fiery serpent that was up on a pole. We must do the same today. *"...even so must the Son of man be lifted up: That whosoever believeth in him should not perish, but have eternal life"* (John 3:14-15).

As the forty years of wandering is coming to a close, and the older generation has died off, we will now see how God will prepare the younger generation for Canaan. It will be a time of remembering what God has done and a time for renewal as these families prepare to step into the land that their parents were not able to see. Moses will not lead them into Canaan, because of his own disobedience, but God will give them a new leader. Who will this new leader be?

Deeper Insights:

1. The Book of Numbers tells of a time of trouble—a time of unbelief and rebellion. It certainly wasn't the first time those things had reared their ugly heads—we first saw it in the Garden of Eden. Satan was still up to his old evil tricks to turn the hearts of the Israelite men and women away from following God's commands. Read the following scriptures in Numbers and identify what the Israelites did that caused God's

anger: 11:1-6, 10-15; 12:1-2, 10-15; 13:32-33; 14:1-4; 16:1-3, 41; 21:4-5; and 25:1-3.

2. The Israelites were notorious for complaining when things didn't go the way they thought they should. What does the Bible tell us about complaining? Read Philippians 2:14-16.

3. It is easy to pass judgment on the Israelites for acting the way they did after all God had done for them. Before we act too harshly, though, we need to understand that we are all sinners, and we are all prone to unbelief, fear, and rebellion. Even when God does miraculous things in our lives, we have that human tendency to forget what He has done and fall into unbelief the very next time we have a problem. The sins of the Israelites were a good example of the human condition and the need for a Savior.

What does God say about it when we do not trust and obey Him, going our own way to find satisfaction? Read Numbers 15:38-39 and Daniel 9:5.

4. Why should we seek to be content with what God allows for us? James 1:14-17; 1 Timothy 6:6-10; Hebrews 13:5; and Matthew 6:25-34.

What results from discontentment? Read 1 Corinthians 10:10.

What does God say to warn us about unbelief?

Read Hebrews 3:7-19; Romans 11:13-22; and John 3:36; 8:23-24; 12:47-48

What does God call those who are in unbelief? Read Exodus 32:9 and Acts 7:51.

For those who receive Christ as their Lord and Savior, there is hope. We can guard our hearts and choose to resist the devil and His evil ways. Read Ephesians 6:11-18.

What can we do, if we do fall into sin? Read 1 John 1:9.

5. Read Psalm 91. Write down the promises God has for those who put their trust in Him.

6. Why was the Lord so angry when the spies gave the Israelites a negative report about the land He had promised them?

   How did God punish them for their unbelief and fear?

7. Why do you think God included Aaron's budding rod in the Ark of the Covenant? Read Numbers 17:10.

8. Moses and Aaron lost their right to enter into their promise land. Why do you think God's punishment was so harsh for them?

CHAPTER 14

A TIME OF REMEMBRANCE AND RENEWAL

The Lord Chooses Joshua to Replace Moses

After forty years of wandering around in the desert, the older generation, who had left Egypt, had died off, except Moses, Caleb and Joshua (see Numbers 26). Now their children were standing at the borders of Canaan. This was an exciting time for everyone, but Moses would not be the one to lead the tribes into Canaan. In fact, he would die before they crossed over.

> *"And the LORD said unto Moses, Get thee up into this mount Ab´-a-rim, and see the land which I have given unto the children of Israel. And when thou hast seen it, thou also shalt be gathered unto thy people, as Aaron thy brother was gathered. For ye rebelled against my commandment in the desert of Zin, in the strife of the congregation, to sanctify me at the water before their eyes: that is the <u>water of Mer´-i-bah</u> in Ka´-desh in the wilderness of Zin..."* (Numbers 27:12-14).

The *"water of Meribah"* was where Moses, in his anger, had disobeyed the Lord by striking the rock instead of speaking to it.

> *"And the LORD said unto Moses, Take thee Joshua the son of Nun, a man in whom is the Spirit, and lay thine hand upon him"* (Numbers 27:18).

Through the years, it had been obvious that God had been preparing Joshua, Moses' assistant, for this job. Moses laid his hands on Joshua and commissioned him in front of Eleazar and the congregation. After Moses' death, Joshua would have authority to lead the Israelites in and out with the counsel of Eleazar, the priest.

The Lord Designates the Land to the Israelites

The time had come for God to designate the land in Canaan to the twelve tribes of Israel as an inheritance. Each tribe would receive lots, based on their total numbers. All the people who were currently living in the land, must be driven out; "...*those you allow to remain there will become like needles in your eyes. They will become like thorns in your sides. They will give you trouble in the land where you will live. Then I will do to you what I plan to do to them*" (Numbers 33:55-56, NIrV®).

Earlier, the tribes of Reuben and Gad had talked to Moses about living on the land on this side of the Jordan River instead of crossing over with the rest of the tribes, because it was a good place to raise cattle. Moses reminded them of all that they had been through and how the Lord had made their parents wander for forty years in the desert because of their sins against God. He didn't want them to fall into sin again. The Israelites would be going to war in Canaan, and they agreed to cross over and help the rest of the tribes fight for their inherited land before settling in the land they had chosen. Hearing their promise, Moses agreed and gave the Reubenites, Gadites, and the half-tribe of Manasseh the land of Gilead on this side of the Jordan for their inheritance, as they had requested. For those who would be crossing over into Canaan, God made it absolutely clear as to the exact perimeters of the land He was giving to them.

> "*Your southern border will include some of the Desert of Zin. It will be along the border of Edom. On the east, your southern border will start from the end of the Dead Sea. It will cross south of Scorpion Pass. It will continue on to Zin. From there it will go*

south of Kadesh Barnea. Then it will go to Hazar Addar and over to Azmon. There it will turn and join the Wadi of Egypt. It will come to an end at the Mediterranean Sea.

"Your western border will be the coast of the Mediterranean Sea. That will be your border on the west.

"For your northern border, run a line from the Mediterranean Sea to Mount Hor. Continue it from Mounnt Hor to Lebo Hamath. Then the border will go to Zedad. It will continue to Ziphron. It will come to an end at Hazar Enan. That will be your border on the north."

"For your eastern border, run a line from Hazar Enan to Shepham. The border will go down from Shepham to Riblah. Riblah is on the east side of Ain. From there the border will continue along the slopes east of the Sea of Galilee. Then the border will go down along the Jordan River. It will come to an end at the Dead Sea" (Numbers 34:3-12, NIrV®).

The tribes were to give the Levites (priests and families) forty-two cities to live in, including land for their flocks and livestock out of each of their inheritances. They were also to give the Levites six towns (three on one side of the Jericho and three on the other side of the Jericho) as cities of refuge. These cities would be a place where people could go to wait for a trial, if they should accidently kill someone.

Remember What God Has Done

"...watch yourselves very carefully, so that you do not become corrupt and make for yourselves an idol, an image of any shape, whether formed like a man or a woman, or like any animal on earth or any bird that flies in the air, or like any creature that moves along the ground or any fish in the waters below. And

when you look up to the sky and see the sun, the moon and the stars—all the heavenly array—do not be enticed into bowing down to them and worshiping things the LORD your God has apportioned to all the nations under heaven. "But as for you, the LORD took you and brought you out of the iron-smelting furnace, out of Egypt, to be the people of his inheritance, as you now are" (Deuteronomy 4:15-20, NIV®).

"Did ever people hear the voice of God speaking out of the midst of the fire, as thou hast heard, and live? Or hath God assayed to go and take him a nation from the midst of another nation, by <u>temptations</u>, by signs, and by wonders, and by war, and by a mighty hand, and by a stretched out arm, and by great <u>terrors</u>, according to all that the LORD our God did for you in Egypt before your eyes? Unto thee it was showed, that thou mightest know that the LORD he is God there is none else beside him" (Deuteronomy 4:33-35).

The Hebrew word translated *temptations* is "maccâh." The meaning of the word is "…a testing of men (judicial) or of God…trial."[1]

The Hebrew word translated *terrors* is "môrâh." The meaning of the word is "…fearful thing or deed…."[2]

"And because he loved thy fathers, therefore he chose their seed after them, and brought thee out in his sight with his mighty power out of Egypt; To drive out nations from before thee greater and mightier than thou art, to bring thee in, to give thee their land for an inheritance, as it is this day" (Deuteronomy 4:37-38).

"Hear, O Israel: The LORD our God, the LORD is One. And thou shalt love the LORD thy God with all thine heart and with all thy soul, and with all thy might. And these words, which I command thee this day, shall be in thine heart: And thou shalt teach them diligently unto thy children, and shalt talk of them when thou sittest in thine house, and when thou walkest by

the way, and when thou liest down, and when thou risest up. And thou shalt bind them for a sign upon thine hand, and they shall be as frontlets between thine eyes. And thou shalt write them upon the posts of thy house, and on thy gates" (Deuteronomy 6:4-9).

"The LORD did not set his love upon you, nor choose you, because ye were more in number than any people; for ye were the fewest of all people: But because the LORD loved you, and because he would keep the oath which he had sworn unto your fathers, hath the LORD brought you out with a mighty hand, and redeemed you out of the house of bondmen, from the hand of Pharaoh king of Egypt. Know therefore that the LORD thy God, he is God, the faithful God, which keepeth covenant and mercy with them that love him and keep his commandments to a thousand generations" (Deuteronomy 7:7-9).

"And thou shalt remember all the way which the LORD thy God led thee these forty years in the wilderness, to humble thee, and to prove thee, to know what was in thine heart, whether thou wouldest keep his commandments, or no. And he humbled thee, and suffered thee to hunger, and fed thee with man´-na, which thou knewest not, neither did thy fathers know; that he might make thee know that man doth not live by bread only, but by every word that proceedeth out of the mouth of the LORD doth man live" (Deuteronomy 8:2-3).

"Your clothes did not wear out and your feet did not swell during these forty years. Know then in your heart that as a man disciplines his son, so the LORD your God disciplines you" (Deuteronomy 8:4-5, NIV®).

The Lord was bringing them into a good land where they would have need of nothing, but they must remember the Lord and not forget what He had done for them.

"Beware that thou forget not the LORD thy God, in not keeping his commandments, and his judgments, and his statutes, which I command thee this day: Lest when thou hast eaten and art full, and hast built goodly houses, and dwelt therein; And when thy herds and thy flocks multiply, and thy silver and thy gold is multiplied, and all that thou hast is multiplied; Then thine heart be lifted up, and thou forget the LORD thy God, which brought thee forth out of the land of Egypt, from the house of bondage; Who led thee through that great and terrible wilderness, wherein were fiery serpents, and scorpions, and drought, where there was no water; who brought thee forth water out of the rock of flint; Who fed thee in the wilderness with man'-na, which thy fathers knew not, that he might humble thee, and that he might prove thee, to do thee good at thy latter end; And thou say in thine heart, my power and the might of mine hand hath gotten me this wealth. But thou shalt remember the LORD thy God: for it is he that giveth thee power to get wealth, that he may establish his covenant which he sware unto thy fathers, as it is this day" (Deuteronomy 8:11-18).

Why was God blessing the Israelites with this good land?

"After the LORD your God has driven them out before you, do not say to yourself, 'The LORD has brought me here to take possession of this land because of my righteousness.' No, it is <u>on account of the wickedness of these nations</u> that the LORD is going to drive them out before you" (Deuteronomy 9:4, NIV®).

"...it is not because of your righteousness that the LORD your God is giving you this good land to possess, for you are a stiffnecked people" (Deuteronomy 9:6, NIV®).

Moses reminded them of when God had said:

"Ye have been rebellious against the LORD from the day that I knew you" (Deuteronomy 9:24).

"...fear the LORD thy God, to walk in all his ways, and to love him, to serve the LORD your God with all thy heart and with all thy soul" (Deuteronomy 10:12).

"Circumcise therefore the foreskin of your heart, and be no more stiffnecked" (Deuteronomy 10:16).

Blessings and Curses

"But your eyes have seen all the great acts of the LORD which he did. Therefore shall ye keep all the commandments which I command you this day, that ye may be strong, and go in and possess the land, wither ye go to possess it; And that ye may prolong your days in the land, which the LORD sware unto your fathers to give unto them and to their seed, a land that floweth with milk and honey" (Deuteronomy 11:7-9).

Moses told them, *"...the land, whither ye go to possess it, is a land of hills and valleys, and drinketh water of the rain of heaven: A land which the LORD thy God careth for: the eyes of the LORD thy God are always upon it, from the beginning of the year even unto the end of the year. And it shall come to pass, if ye shall hearken diligently unto my commandments which I command you this day, to love the LORD your God, and to serve him with all your heart and with all your soul, That I will give you the rain of your land in his due season, the first rain and the latter rain, that thou mayest gather in thy corn, and thy wine, and thine oil. And I will send grass in thy fields for thy cattle, that thou mayest eat and be full"* (Deuteronomy 11:11-15).

If the Israelites worship other gods, the Lord will *"...shut up the heaven, that there be no rain, and that the land yield not her fruit; and lest ye perish quickly from off the good land which the LORD giveth you"* (Deuteronomy 11:17).

"Behold, I set before you this day a blessing and a curse; A blessing, if ye obey the commandments of the LORD your God, which I command you this day: And a curse, if ye will not obey the commandments of the LORD your God, but turn aside out of the way which I command you this day, to go after other gods, which ye have not known. And it shall come to pass, when the LORD thy God hath brought thee in unto the land whither thou goest to possess it, that thou shalt put the blessing upon mount Ger´-i-zim, and the curse upon mount E´-bal" (Deuteronomy 11:26-29).

Choose Life

"He led you through the desert for 40 years. During that time your clothes didn't wear out. The sandals on your feet didn't wear out either. You didn't eat any bread. You didn't drink any kind of wine. The LORD did all of those things because he wanted you to know that he is the LORD your God" (Deuteronomy 29: 5-6, NIrV®).

"You are standing here in order to enter into a covenant with the LORD your God, a covenant the LORD is making with you this day and sealing with an oath, to confirm you this day as his people, that he may be your God as he promised you and as he swore to your fathers, Abraham, Isaac and Jacob" (Deuteronomy 29:12-13, NIV®).

"Make sure there is no man or woman, clan or tribe among you today whose heart turns away from the LORD our God to go and worship the gods of those nations; make sure there is no root among you that produces such bitter poison" (Deuteronomy 29:18, NIV®).

"The LORD will not spare him, but then the anger of the LORD and his jealousy shall smoke against that man, and all the curses that are written in this book shall lie upon him, and

the LORD shall blot out his name from under heaven. And the
LORD shall separate him unto evil out of all the tribes of Israel,
according to all the curses of the covenant that are written in this
Book of the Law" (Deuteronomy 29:20-21, NIV®).

God was telling them in advance what would happen if they fell
into idolatry. He even prophesied what people would say about them.
People will ask why He did this to them, and this would be the answer
men would give:

"...Because they have forsaken the covenant of the LORD God
of their fathers, which he made with them when he brought them
forth out of the land of Egypt: For they went and served other
gods, and worshiped them, gods whom they knew not, and whom
he had not given unto them" (Deuteronomy 29: 25-26).

God knew Israel was going to fall. Even so, He gave hope to them
so that in the future, after they fell, they would return to Him:

"And it shall come to pass, when all these things are come upon
thee, the blessing and the curse, which I have set before thee, and
thou shalt call them to mind among all the nations, whither the
LORD thy God hath driven thee, And shalt return unto the
LORD thy God, and shalt obey his voice according to all that
I command thee this day, thou and thy children, with all thine
heart, and with all thy soul; That then the LORD thy God will
turn thy captivity, and have compassion upon thee, and will return
and gather thee from all the nations, whither the LORD thy God
hath scattered thee" (Deuteronomy 30:1-3).

"And the LORD thy God will bring thee into the land which
thy fathers possessed, and thou shalt possess it; and he will do
thee good, and multiply thee above thy fathers. And the LORD
thy God will circumcise thine heart, and the heart of thy seed, to
love the LORD thy God with all thine heart, and with all thy

soul, that thou mayest live. And the LORD thy God will put all these curses upon thine enemies, and on them that hate thee, which persecuted thee" (Deuteronomy 30:5-7).

"See, I set before thee this day life and good, and death and evil; In that I command thee this day to love the LORD thy God, to walk in his ways, and to keep his commandments and his statutes and his judgments, that thou mayest live and multiply: and the LORD thy God shall bless thee in the land, whither thou goest to possess it. But if thine heart turn away, so that thou wilt not hear, but shalt be drawn away, and worship other gods, and serve them; I denounce unto you this day, that ye shall surely perish, and that ye shall not prolong your days upon the land, whither thou passest over Jordan to go to possess it…choose life, that both thou and thy seed may live: That thou mayest love the LORD thy God, and that thou mayest obey his voice, and that thou mayest cleave unto him: for he is thy life, and the length of thy days: that thou mayest dwell in the land which the LORD sware unto thy fathers, to Abraham, to Isaac, and to Jacob, to give them" (Deuteronomy 30:15-20).

Joshua Is Commissioned to Succeed Moses

Moses was now 120 years old and the Lord told him, *"…Thou shalt not go over this Jordan. The LORD thy God, he will go over before thee, and he will destroy these nations from before thee, and thou shalt possess them: and Joshua, he shall go over before thee, as the LORD hath said"* (Deuteronomy 31:2-3).

He told the Israelites, *"Be strong and of a good courage, fear not, nor be afraid of them: for the LORD thy God, he it is that doth go with thee; he will not fail thee, nor forsake thee"* (Deuteronomy 31:6).

Then Moses told Joshua, *"Be strong and of good courage: for thou must go with this people unto the land which the LORD hath sworn unto their fathers to give them; and thou shalt cause them to inherit it. And the LORD, he it is that doth go before thee; he will be with thee, he will not fail thee, neither forsake thee: fear not, neither be dismayed* (Deuteronomy 31:7-8).

The Lord Prophesize the Fall of Israel

"And the LORD said unto Moses, Behold, thy days approach that thou must die: call Joshua, and present yourselves in the tabernacle of the congregation, that I may give him a <u>charge</u>. And Moses and Joshua went, and presented themselves in the tabernacle of the congregation. And the LORD appeared in the tabernacle in a pillar of a cloud: and the pillar of the cloud stood over the door of the tabernacle.

"And the LORD said unto Moses, Behold, thou shalt sleep with thy fathers; and this people will rise up, and go a whoring after the gods of the strangers of the land, whither they go to be among them, and will forsake me, and break my covenant which I have made with them. Then my anger shall be kindled against them in that day, and I will forsake them, and I will hide my face from them, and they shall be devoured, and many evils and troubles shall befall them; so that they will say in that day, Are not these evils come upon us, because our God is not among us?" (Deuteronomy 31:14-17).

The Hebrew word translated *charge*, is "tsâvâh." The meaning of the word is "...appoint...send with command...."[3]

God told Moses to write a song so when the Israelites fell away from Him, they would read it and it would testify against them.

"And it shall come to pass, when many evils and troubles are befallen them, that this song shall testify against them as a witness; for it shall not be forgotten out of the mouths of their seed: for I know their imagination which they go about, even now, before I have brought them into the land which I sware" (Deuteronomy 31:21).

Moses' song is recorded in Deuteronomy 32 where he declares his God to be the *"Rock"* in five different verses, most explicitly, *"...the Rock of his salvation;"*

The Book of the Law Was Placed in the Ark

Moses then wrote down everything he had told them, and the law, and gave it to the Levite priests. He told them that at the end of every seven years, they were to assemble all the Israelites and read this law to them so they would *"learn, and fear the LORD your God, and observe to do all the words of this law"* (Deuteronomy 31:12). This new generation would be responsible for keeping and obeying the law the Lord had given them.

> *"And it came to pass, when Moses had made an end of writing the words of this law in a book, until they were finished, That Moses commanded the Levites, which bare the ark of the covenant of the LORD, saying, Take this book of the law, and put it in the side of the ark of the covenant of the LORD your God, that it may be there for a witness against thee"* (Deuteronomy 31:24-26).

> *"For I know that after my death ye will utterly corrupt yourselves, and turn aside from the way which I have commanded you; and evil will befall you in the latter days; because ye will do evil in the sight of the LORD..."* (Deuteronomy 31:29).

Deuteronomy 18:18-19 records a prophecy given by Moses about Jesus, the Christ, who was coming in the future: *"The LORD thy God will raise up unto thee a Prophet from the midst of thee, of thy brethren, like unto me; unto him ye shall hearken...."* The Lord loved these people He had set aside for Himself. It was to be through them that this prophecy would come to pass through the lineage of the Israelites, bringing salvation to the entire world.

The Death of Moses

Then Moses did as the Lord had told him and once again climbed Mount Nebo to see the land the Israelites were preparing to enter in to—the land that God had given them. Deuteronomy 33 records the last words of Moses bestowing blessings upon each tribe of Israel. After Moses saw the land from Mount Nebo, he died, and the Israelites grieved over him for a month.

> *"And Joshua the son of Nun was full of the spirit of wisdom; for Moses had laid his hands upon him: and the children of Israel hearkened unto him, and did as the LORD commanded Moses"* (Deuteronomy 34:9).

Deuteronomy 34:10 says this of Moses: *"And there arose not a prophet since in Israel like unto Moses, whom the LORD knew face to face."*

This was a sad story for Moses, but the story did not end here. Later, Christ did become the real sacrificial Lamb, making atonement once and for all for the sins of humanity. This, of course included the sins of Moses and Aaron. They, along with the other men and women of the Old Testament, who believed in the promises of God, will join the believers in Christ in the eternal Promised Land in heaven. God is faithful!

In Conclusion

The Israelites had literally been wandering around in the desert, led by God's hand, until the unbelieving generation, who had left Egypt, had died off. He did it to humble them and to test them to see what was in their hearts—to see if they would love and obey Him. He disciplined them when they disobeyed Him, because He loved them. He had clothed them, fed them, provided water for them, and protected them all those years. Even their shoes and their clothes did not wear out. How can there be any doubt that God loves Israel? Now God was preparing this generation of children to enter into Canaan, the land that was promised to Abraham.

God set the exact perimeters of the land He was giving to them, so there was, and still should not be, any question as to the borders of the land that belongs to the Israelites. With that land, came responsibilities—they must drive out all occupants of the land and destroy everything that belonged to their enemies. They must not intermingle with them by making treaties or intermarrying with them or the people of the land "...*will become pricks in their eyes and thorns in their sides, and shall vex you in the land wherein ye dwell*" (Numbers 33:55). They were not to practice idolatry in any shape or form on earth or worship anything that God had made in the heavens.

Moses reviewed the Ten Commandments and all the laws and ordinances God had given to their parents on Mount Sinai and the Great Commandment to love the Lord with all their hearts, minds, and souls. God told them that someday they would be wealthy and satisfied. He wanted them to remember all that He had done for them so they would not try and take credit for their own gain and forget about God. He urged them to teach all these things to their children. If they would fear God and love and serve Him, they would receive blessings (life) for obedience and curses (death) for disobedience. They belonged to God.

Moses prophesied of a Prophet (Christ), Who would be coming to them in the future, and God had entered into a renewed covenant relationship with them, which He sealed with an oath—they would be His people, and He would be their God.

God prophesied that they would reject Him, and He would send them into captivity. He even gave Moses the words to a song so when it happened, they would remember their God and return to Him. Then He would have compassion on them and bring them out of their captivity.

God showed Moses the new land from the top of the mountain but was not allowed to enter. After his death, the Israelites mourned for a month over the death of their godly leader. God appointed Joshua to take Moses' place in leading them into Canaan.

"And Joshua the son of Nun was full of the spirit of wisdom; for Moses had laid his hands upon him: and the children of Israel hearkened unto him, and did as the LORD commanded Moses" (Deuteronomy 34:9).

God had made promises to their forefathers, and no matter what the Israelites may, or may not, do, God would keep those promises. The salvation of the souls of the whole world was hanging on His faithfulness. He had chosen this people, entered into covenant with them, and He would never let them go. It would be through them, whether they were wrong, right, or indifferent, that God would bless all nations through the death and life of His Son, Jesus Christ. We are now going to join the Israelites as they cross over into Canaan. What will they do with all that God has given them? Will they obey His commands and receive His blessings of life, or will they fall back into rebellion and unbelief and receive His curses?

Deeper Insights:

1. Read Psalm 1:1-3; 119:9-16, 33-40, 65-72, 86-88, 97-104, 105-112, and 169-176.

   God gave His word to us through the law, the Ten Commandments, but we find in the Psalms above that there is something deeper than legalistically obeying the commandments. What does the Psalmist express about the law in each of the Psalms above?

   The word of God sustains us spiritually, just as the spiritual food of manna sustained the Israelites. Read John 6:35.

2. *"When ye are passed over Jordan into the land of Canaan; Then ye shall drive out all the inhabitants of the land from before you, and destroy all their pictures, and destroy all their molten images, and quite pluck down* (demolish) *all their high places"* (Numbers 33:51-52).

Why do you think God required these radical steps? What do you think might happen if they left some of the pagan people or their idol paraphernalia?

Read Numbers 33:55. What do you think God meant by this Scripture?

3. God was deadly serious about the sin of idolatry. Read Deuteronomy 4:15-28 and 12:29-31.

What did Moses prophesy would happen if they fell into idolatry? Read Deuteronomy 4:26-28 and Deuteronomy 8:19-20; 13:1-10.

4. List the ways that God said the Israelites were they to remember His commands and promises and teach them to their children? Read Deuteronomy 6:5-9.

5. Why did God want them to remember all his commands? Read Deuteronomy 6:20-25 and 8:11-18.

6. God gave the Israelites the specific boundaries of the land He was giving to them, which is found in Numbers 34:1-12, 14-15. There can be no doubt where He drew the lines of the homeland for the Israelites. God was bringing them into a beautiful land. List some of the blessings God was giving them in this new land they were inheriting from Him. Read Deuteronomy 8:7-10 and 11:11-15.

7. God would give them blessings and curses—life and death.

Read Deuteronomy 11:29. Now read Deuteronomy 27:1-13. What were they supposed to do with the blessings? Read Deuteronomy 27:11-12 and 28:1-14.

What shall they do that with the curses? Read Deuteronomy 27:13-26; 28:15-19. Verses 20-68 describe the consequences for their disobedience.

8. What did Moses prophesy God would do if they returned to Him after they had fallen away from Him? Read Deuteronomy 4:29-31; 30:1-9.

9. Today, we can still choose to receive blessings or curses. If we choose Christ as our Lord and Savior, we receive blessings because of God's grace.

   Read the following scriptures and identify the blessings we receive as believers in Christ:

   Matthew 6:25-26, 30-33; John 3:16, 5:24, 10:27-29; Acts 1:8, 13:38, 39; Romans 8:1, 3-11, 15-17, 30, 34; 2 Corinthians 5:17; Ephesians 1:3-5; Colossians 1:14.

10. The Bible says Jesus became a curse for us when He died on the cross, taking all of our sins upon him. If we reject Him, the One Who can forgive us and save us because of the sacrifice of His own life, we take on the curse of spiritual death because we have no other sacrifice to take the curse from us. Jesus paid the price for our souls—we have been bought with the price of His own life. Without Him, we have no hope and cannot save ourselves, so eternal death becomes our curse.

    Read the following scriptures and identify the curses that will befall everyone who ignores Jesus Christ's grace, love, mercy, grace and forgiveness.

    Matthew 25:41, 13:40-42, 10:28; John 5:29; 2 Thessalonians 1:7-9; Revelations 20:11-15

CHAPTER 15

CROSSING OVER

God Affirms Joshua As Leader

The Lord told Joshua, son of Nun, *"...go over this Jordan, thou, and all this people, unto the land which I do give to them, even to the children of Israel. Every place that the sole of your foot shall tread upon, that have I given unto you, as I said unto Moses... There shall not any man be able to stand before thee all the days of thy life: as I was with Moses, so I will be with thee: I will not fail thee, nor forsake thee. Be strong and of a good courage: for unto this people shalt thou divide for an inheritance the land, which I sware unto their fathers to give them"* (Joshua 1:2-6).

So Joshua told the Israelites in Shittim, to prepare their food as they would be crossing over the Jordan River to their promised land in three days. The families of the Reubenites, Gadites, and the half-tribe of Manasseh would stay on their land and wait for them to return. Joshua told the people: *"Remember the word which Moses the servant of the LORD commanded you, saying, The LORD your God hath given you rest, and hath given you this land"* (Joshua 1:13).

Rahab, the Prostitute

Meanwhile, Joshua sent two spies out to take a look at the land, particularly Jericho. When the spies forded the river and arrived at the city of Jericho, they found lodging in the house of Rahab, a prostitute. She lived in a house that was located on the city wall, and the Israelite spies were seen in or about her house. The king was told that spies had come to spy on his land, so he sent a message to Rahab to bring the men out of her house, but she hid them and lied, saying the men had left the city.

Rahab believed in her heart that the Lord had given all the land to the Israelites, including Jericho, and she told the spies that the people in Jericho were afraid of the Israelites because they had heard the Lord had done so much for them and had helped them conquer kings. She told them, "...*the LORD your God, he is God in heaven above, and in earth beneath*" (Joshua 2:11). Rahab asked the spies to spare her life and the lives of her family in return for her helping them. The spies told her, "... *Our life for yours, if ye utter not this our business. And it shall be, when the LORD hath given us the land, that we will deal kindly and truly with thee*" (Joshua 2:14).

Obeying the spies, Rahab took a rope and hung it out of her window to let them down to the ground, telling them to go and hide in the hills for three days until the men who were looking for them had returned to the city. Then they would be safe to leave. The spies told Rahab that when the Israelites come into the city, hang a scarlet cord through the same window from which she was helping them escape. She and her family must all stay inside the house at that time, and must not to tell anyone what the spies were doing, or the deal would be off. Rahab agreed, and the spies left and hid for three days before returning to their camp across the Jordan River. When they returned to their camp, they told Joshua all that had happened and how the people of Jericho were afraid of the Israelites because of the things God had done for them.

God Parts the Jordan River

The Israelites left Shittim and camped at the Jordan River for three days. Joshua sent out these orders for the Israelites:

> "...*When you see the ark of the covenant of the LORD your God, and the priests the Levites bearing it, then ye shall remove*

from your place, and go after it. Yet there shall be a space between you and it, about two thousand cubits by measure: come not near unto it, that ye may know the way by which ye must go: for ye have not passed this way heretofore" (Joshua 3:3-4).

He also told the people to consecrate themselves, because the next day the Lord was going to do wonders among them. God was with Joshua, and He would confirm that to the Israelites.

"And the LORD said unto Joshua, this day will I begin to magnify thee in the sight of all Israel, that they may know that, as I was with Moses, so I will be with thee. And thou shalt command the priests that bear the ark of the covenant, saying, When ye are come to the brink of the water of Jordan, ye shall stand still in Jordan" (Joshua 3:7-8).

Joshua assured the Israelites that the Lord was with them and He would drive out their enemies from the land:

"...it shall come to pass, as soon as the soles of the feet of the priests that bear the ark of the LORD, the Lord of all the earth, shall rest in the waters of Jordan, that the waters of Jordan shall be cut off from the waters that come down from above; and they shall stand upon a heap" (Joshua 3:13).

It was harvest time, and the Jordan River was at flood stage. As soon as the priests' feet touched the edge of the water, the river stopped flowing downstream and piled up in the town of Adam, which was a town far upstream. Even the water that flowed into the Dead Sea stopped.

"And the priests that bare the ark of the covenant of the LORD stood firm on dry ground in the midst of Jordan, and all the Israelites passed over on dry ground, until all the people were passed clean over Jordan" (Joshua 3:17).

The first to cross over were 40,000 men, who were armed and prepared for war. They were from the tribes of Reuben, Gad, and the half tribe of Manasseh. The Lord told Joshua to pick twelve men, one man from each tribe. Tell each one to pick up a stone from the middle of the river where the priests had stood and carry the stones to the other side where they would be spending the night. They were to do this for a sign to their children.

> "...that when your children ask their fathers in time to come, saying, What mean ye by these stones? Then ye shall answer them, That the waters of Jordan were cut off before the ark of the covenant of the LORD; when it passed over Jordan, the waters of Jordan were cut off: and these stones shall be for a memorial unto the children of Israel for ever" (Joshua 4:6-7).

After all the people had crossed over Jordan, the men gathered the stones from where the priests were standing in the Jordan and carried them to the other side where they were preparing to camp. The priests stayed in the middle of the river until Joshua took the stones and set them up for a memorial.

> "On that day the LORD magnified Joshua in the sight of all Israel; and they feared him, as they feared Moses, all the days of his life" (Joshua 4:14).

> "Joshua therefore commanded the priests, saying, Come ye up out of Jordan. And it came to pass, when the priests that bare the ark of the covenant of the LORD were come up out of the midst of Jordan, and the soles of the priests' feet were lifted up unto the dry land, that the waters of Jordan returned unto their place, and flowed over all his banks, as they did before" (Joshua 4:17-18).

> "For the LORD your God dried up the waters of Jordan from before you, until ye were passed over, as the LORD your God did to the Red Sea, which he dried up from before us, until we were

gone over: That all the people of the earth might know the hand of the LORD, that it is mighty: that ye might fear the LORD your God for ever" (Joshua 4:23).

Joshua Circumcises the Israelites

"The Israelites had moved about in the desert forty years until all the men who were of military age when they left Egypt died, since they had not obeyed the LORD...So he raised up their sons in their place..." (Joshua 5:6-7, NIV®).

These sons needed to be circumcised to be included in the covenant with God. So Joshua made sharp knives, probably out of stone, as Moses had, and circumcised all the males.

"And the LORD said unto Joshua, This day have I rolled away the reproach of Egypt from off you. Wherefore the name of the place is called Gil'-gal unto this day" (Joshua 5:9).

The Israelites camped there at Gilgal until they were healed. They also celebrated the Passover and took their first bite of corn from the land. The next day the Lord stopped providing manna for them.

The Lord Appears To Joshua

"And it came to pass, when Joshua was by Jericho, that he lifted up his eyes and looked, and, behold there stood a man over against him with his sword drawn in his hand: and Joshua went unto him, and said unto him, Art thou for us, or for our adversaries? And he said, Nay; but as captain of the host of the LORD am I now come. And Joshua fell on his face to the earth, and did worship, and said unto him, What saith my lord unto his servant? And the captain of the LORD'S host said unto Joshua, Loose thy shoe

from off thy foot; for the place whereon thou standest is holy. And Joshua did so" (Joshua 5:13-15).

The Lord made Himself known to Joshua in much the same way He had made Himself known to Moses. If this had been an angel, he would not have allowed Joshua to worship him.

The Lord Gives Jericho To the Israelites

"The gates of Jericho were shut tight and guarded closely because of the people of Israel. No one went out. No one came in. Then the LORD spoke to Joshua. He said, 'I have handed Jericho over to you. I have also handed its king and its fighting men over to you.

"March around the city once with all of your fighting men. In fact, do it for six days. Have seven priests get trumpets that are made out of rams' horns. They must carry them in front of the ark. On the seventh day, march around the city seven times. Have the priests blow the trumpets as you march. You will hear them blow a long blast on the trumpets. When you do, have all of the men give a loud shout. The wall of the city will fall down. Then the whole army will go up to the city. Every man will go straight in. So Joshua, the son of Nun, called for the priests. He said to them, 'Go and get the ark of the covenant of the LORD. I want seven of you to carry trumpets in front of it.' He gave an order to the men. He said, 'Move out! March around the city. Some of the fighting men must march in front of the ark of the LORD.'" (Joshua 6:1-6, NIrV®).

Joshua also told the fighting men to not give out a war cry or raise their voices until the day he gave the command. After they marched around the city once, they went back to their camp and spent the night. They did this for six days, and on the seventh day, they went around the city seven times.

"...And it came to pass at the seventh time, when the priests blew with the trumpets, Joshua said unto the people, Shout; for the LORD hath given you the city. And the city shall be accursed, even it, and all that are therein, to the LORD: only Rahab the harlot shall live, she and all that are with her in the house, because she hid the messengers that we sent" (Joshua 6:16-17).

Joshua made it perfectly clear that nothing was to be brought out of the city, except Rahab and her family. Everything else was set aside for destruction.

"So the people shouted when the priests blew with the trumpets: and it came to pass, when the people heard the sound of the trumpet, and the people shouted with a great shout, that the wall fell down flat, so that the people went up into the city, every man straight before him, and they took the city. And they utterly destroyed all that was in the city, both man and woman, young and old, and ox, and sheep, and ass, with the edge of the sword" (Joshua 6:20-21).

After taking the precious metals—silver, gold, bronze, and iron for the Lord's house, they burned the city.

"And Joshua saved Rahab the harlot alive, and her father's household, and all that she had; and she dwelleth in Israel even unto this day; because she hid the messengers, which Joshua sent to spy out Jericho" (Joshua 6:25)

"By faith the walls of Jericho fell down, after they were compassed about seven days. By faith the harlot Rahab perished not with them that believed not, when she had received the spies with peace" (Hebrews 11:30-31).

The Sin of the Accursed Things

God had promised that He would be with the Israelites and drive out the enemies of their land; and He had started with Jericho. However, since God sees and knows everything, He knew that Achan, a man from the tribe of Judah, had disobeyed His command and had taken an *"accursed thing"* ("...usually a doomed object...things which should have been utterly destroyed...")[1]. When it came time to conquer the next town of Ai, a smaller town than Jericho, the Israelites began to suffer loss. Joshua could not understand why the Lord had allowed this defeat and the possibility of being overtaken by other armies that would hear about it. He went before the Lord, tearing his clothes and *"...fell to the earth upon his face before the ark of the LORD until the eventide, he and the elders of Israel, and put dust upon their heads"* (Joshua 7:6).

The Lord told Joshua, *"... Israel hath sinned, and they have also transgressed my covenant which I commanded them: for they have even taken of the* <u>*accursed thing*</u>*, and have also stolen, and dissembled also, and they have put it even among their own stuff. Therefore the children of Israel could not stand before their enemies, but turned their backs before their enemies, because they were accursed: neither will I be with you any more, except ye destroy the accursed from among you"* (Joshua 7:11-12).

Joshua called the tribes forward, and God selected Achan from the tribe of Judah.

> *"...Joshua said to Achan, 'My son, give glory to the LORD, the God of Israel, and honor him. Tell me what you have done; do not hide it from me'"* (Joshua 7:19, NIV®).

Achan told Joshua that he had taken a *"...Babylonish garment, two hundred shek´-els of silver and a wedge of gold..."* (Joshua 7:21), because he coveted them and hid them in his tent. Then all Israel stoned Achan, his family, and all of his animals and burned all of them. They made a heap of stones there, which they called the *"Valley of Achor"* to remember what had taken place.

After Israel had rid their camp of evil, *"...the LORD said unto Joshua, Fear not, neither be thou dismayed: take all the people of war with thee, and arise, go up to A´-i-: see, I have given into thy hand the king of A´-i, and his people, and his city, and his land: And thou shalt do to A´-i and her king as thou didst unto Jericho and her king: only the spoil thereof, and the cattle thereof, shall ye take for a prey unto yourselves: lay thee an ambush for the city behind it"* (Joshua 8:1-2).

Joshua took 30,000 of his best soldiers to Ai, set an ambush and killed 12,000 men and women of Ai that day. Joshua hung the king and buried him under a pile of rocks in front of the destroyed city. After the battle with Ai, Joshua went up on Mount Ebal and built an altar to the Lord, using no tools, as Moses had instructed him earlier; and he offered burnt offerings and fellowship offerings to the Lord.

"Joshua copied the written law of Moses on stones. He did it while all of the people of Israel were watching...including outsiders and citizens...Israel's elders, officials and judges were also there. All of them faced the priests, who were Levites. They were carrying the ark. Half of the people stood in front of Mount Gerizim. The other half stood in front of Mount Ebal. Moses, the servant of the LORD, had earlier told them to do it..." (Joshua 8:32-33, NIrV®).

When Joshua finished writing the law on the stones, he read all the words he had written, including the blessings and curses, to everyone who was there. These were the words that God had given Moses.

More Victories

The Gibeonites had heard about Israel, and they deceived Israel into believing they had come from a very long way to be their servants so they would not be killed. Joshua made a treaty of peace with them, but three days later, they found out the Gibeonites had lied to them.

They were not from far away, but neighbors who lived close by. Joshua confronted them about their deception, and because of the treaty he had made with them, he did not kill them, but he did make them to be woodcutters and water carriers for Israel.

Adoni-Zedek, king of Jerusalem, heard about all the victories of Israel and its peace treaty with the Gibeonites and became afraid, so he joined with four other Amorite kings and attacked Gibeon. Even though Gibeon was a great city, they called Joshua for help. The Lord told Joshua he would be victorious in this battle, too. Joshua led Israel in a march, which lasted all night, to prepare for a surprise attack against the armies of the five kings of Jerusalem, Hebron, Jarmuth, Lachish, and Eglon. After the LORD brought them into confusion, the Israelites killed many, and the LORD showered the kings and their men with huge hailstones, killing more men than the Israelites had. That day, in front of the Israelites, Joshua said:

> "...Sun, stand thou still upon Gibeon; and thou, Moon, in the valley of Aj´-alon. And the sun stood still, and the moon stayed, until the people had avenged themselves upon their enemies...So the sun stood still in the midst of heaven, and hasted not to go down about a whole day. And there was no day like that before it or after it, that the LORD hearkened unto the voice of a man: for the LORD fought for Israel" (Joshua 10:12-14).

Joshua heard that the five kings had ran away and hid at Makkedah in a cave, so he led Israel to surround the cave. He closed it off with large rocks and placed men to guard the mouth of it. The rest of the men were told to go and pursue the enemy that was trying to get back to their cities from the battle, and they destroyed them all. Meantime, Joshua's soldiers brought the five kings out of the cave, and he hung them and buried them in the cave. Then Joshua destroyed Makkedah and everyone in it. After that battle, the Lord delivered the five kings into Joshua's hands.

> "So Joshua smote all the country of the hills, and of the south, and of the vale, and of the springs, and all their kings: he left none

remaining, but utterly destroyed all that breathed, as the LORD God of Israel commanded. And Joshua smote them from Ka´-desh-bar´-ne-a even unto Ga´-za, and all the country of Go´-shen, even unto Gib´-eon. And all these kings and their land did Joshua take at one time, because the LORD God of Israel fought for Israel. And Joshua returned, and all Israel with him, unto the camp to Gil´-gal" (Joshua 10:40-43).

News of Israel's victories was spreading quickly. When the king of Hazor heard about Israel's victories, he united with other kings forming a large army to make war with Israel.

"And the LORD said unto Joshua, Be not afraid because of them: for tomorrow about this time will I deliver them up all slain before Israel…" (Joshua 11:6).

Joshua and the Israelites went to the Waters of Merom, attacked them, and totally defeated them with no survivors remaining. He even hamstrung all their horses and burned their chariots. Joshua also went to Hazor and killed everyone there, including the king, and entirely burned Hazor. He took all the royal cities and killed all the people and their kings, and they plundered everything for themselves.

"So Joshua took all that land, the hills, and all the south country, and all the land of Go´-shen, and the valley, and the plain, and the mountain of Israel, and the valley of the same; Even from the mount Ha´-lak, that goeth up to Se´-ir, even unto Ba´-al-gad in the valley of Leb´-a-non under mount Herman: and all their kings he took and smote them, and slew them. Joshua made war a long time with all those kings. There was not a city that made peace with the children of Israel, save the Hi´-vites the inhabitants of Gib´-eon: all other they took in battle. For it was of the LORD to harden their hearts, that they should come against Israel in battle, that he might destroy them utterly, and that they might have no favor, but that he might destroy them, as the LORD commanded Moses" (Joshua 11:16-20).

Joshua also defeated all the Anakites in the hills, although there were some left in Gaza, Gath, and Ashdod.

> *"So Joshua took the whole land, according to all that the LORD said unto Moses; and Joshua gave it for an inheritance unto Israel according to their divisions by their tribes. And the land rested from war"* (Joshua 11:23).

Division of Their Promised Land

> *"When Joshua had grown old, the LORD said to him, 'You are now very old, and there are still very large areas of land to be taken over. This is the land that remains: all the regions of the Philistines and Geshurites: from the Shihor River on the east of Egypt to the territory of Ekron on the north, all of it counted as Canaanite though held by the five Philistine rulers in Gaza, Ashdod, Ashkelon, Gath and Ekron; the territory of the Avvites on the south, all the land of the Canaanites, from Arah of the Sidonians as far as Aphek, and the border of the Amorites, the area of the Byblos; and all Lebanon to the east, from Baal Gad below Mount Hermon to Lebo Hamath.*

> *"As for all the inhabitants of the mountain regions from Lebanon to Misrephoth, Maim, that is, all the Sidonians, I myself will drive them out before the Israelites. Be sure to allocate this land to Israel for an inheritance, as I have instructed you, and divide it as an inheritance among the nine tribes and half of the tribe of Manasseh"* (Joshua 13:1-7, NIV®).

Joshua 13 records the divisions of land east of the Jordan, for half of Manasseh, the Reubenites, and the Gadites. Joshua 14-17 records the allotments given to Caleb, Judah, Ephraim, and half of Manasseh. Forty-five years prior, when Caleb had come back from Canaan as a spy with a good report and followed after the Lord, Moses had promised him some land. So he was given Hebron, a part of Judah. Judah was unable to drive out the Jebusites from their allotment. Manasseh and Ephraim had become two tribes and they received Joseph's share, but like Judah, they did not drive out the Canaanites from their share either. They allowed them to stay and work for them as slaves.

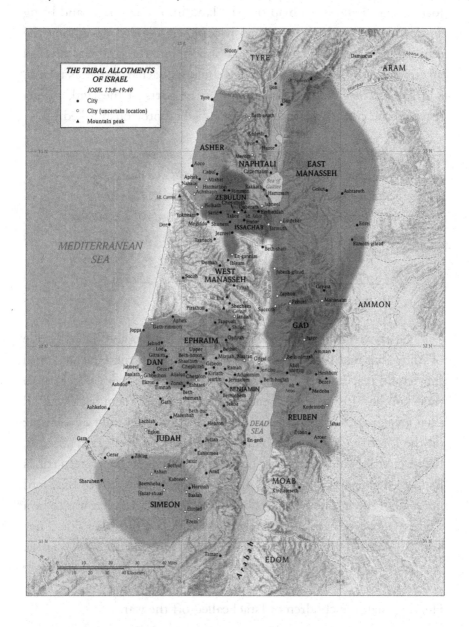

All the Israelites came together at Shiloh, set up the *"...tabernacle of the congregation there. And the land was subdued before them"* (Joshua 18:1). Everyone would worship and bring their sacrifices to the Tabernacle at Shiloh.

There were still seven tribes who were waiting for their inheritance. Joshua sent men out to map out the land into seven parts and bring its description back to Joseph so it could be divided up among the remaining tribes. Joshua cast lots at Shiloh, and the land was divided up and given to Benjamin, Simeon, Zebulun, Issachar, Asher, Naphtali, and Dan. When they had divided up their parts of the land, Joshua received the city, Timnathserah, which he had previously asked for.

> *"And the LORD gave unto Israel all the land which he sware to give unto their fathers; and they possessed it, and dwelt therein. And the LORD gave them rest round about, according to all that he sware unto their fathers: and there stood not a man of all their enemies before them; the LORD delivered all their enemies into their hand. There failed not aught of any good thing which the LORD had spoken unto the house of Israel; all came to pass"* (Joshua 21:43-45).

The eastern tribes—the Reubenites, the Gadites and the half-tribe of Manasseh had kept their promise to fight with the Israelites until they could rest from war, and it was now time for them to return to their families. Joshua gave them blessings and sent them back with all their great wealth of plunder. On their way home, they built a great altar on the forefront of Israel. When the children of Israel heard about it, they went to them to make war because they thought the eastern tribes had rebelled against the Lord, and they feared the wrath of the Lord upon all of them. The eastern tribes explained that the altar was to be a witness between them and the rest of the tribes on the other side. They said, *"...we will worship the LORD at his sanctuary with our burnt offerings, sacrifices and fellowship offerings. Then in the future your descendants will not be able to say to ours, 'You have no share in the LORD'"* (Joshua 22:27, NIV®). Hearing that, the children of Israel called off the war.

Joshua's Farewell to the Leaders

Joshua called all the leaders of Israel to come to him. He said, *"...I am old and stricken in age: And ye have seen all that the LORD your God hath done unto all these nations because of you; for the LORD your God is he that hath fought for you. Behold, I have divided unto you by lot these nations that remain, to be an inheritance for your tribes, from Jordan, with all the nations that I have cut off, even unto the Great Sea westward. And the LORD your God, he shall expel them from before you, and drive them from out of your sight; and ye shall possess their land, as the LORD your God hath promised unto you. Be ye therefore very courageous to keep and to do all that is written in the book of the law of Moses, that ye turn not aside therefrom to the right hand or to the left..."* (Joshua 23:2-6).

The Canaanites were the descendants of Ham. Their religion was idolatrous, wicked, and profane, and God, being perfectly holy and just, was destroying them because of their wickedness. Joshua told the Israelites to follow his instructions: drive the Canaanite nations from their sight; obey all that is written in the book of the law of Moses; do not associate with these nations that remain among them; do not invoke the names of their gods or swear by them; do not serve them or bow down to them; hold fast to the Lord their God; and love the Lord their God.

> *"For the LORD hath driven out from before you great nations and strong: but as for you, no man hath been able to stand before you unto this day. One man of you shall chase a thousand: for the LORD your God, he it is that fighteth for you, as he hath promised you. Take good heed therefore unto yourselves, that ye love the LORD your God"* (Joshua 23:9-11).

> *"But if you turn away and ally yourselves with the survivors of these nations that remain among you and if you intermarry with them and associate with them, then you may be sure that the LORD your God will no longer drive out these nations before you. Instead, they will become snares and traps for you, whips on*

your backs and thorns in your eyes, until you perish from this good land, which the LORD your God has given you" (Joshua 23:12-13, NIV®).

Joshua Renews the Covenant At Shechem

Joshua told the people what the Lord said.

> *"...I have given you a land for which ye did not labor, and cities which ye built not, and ye dwell in them; of the vineyards and oliveyards which ye planted not do ye eat. Now therefore fear the LORD, and serve him in sincerity and in truth: and put away the gods which your fathers served on the other side of the flood, and in Egypt; and serve ye the LORD. And if it seem evil unto you to serve the LORD, choose you this day whom ye will serve; whether the gods which your fathers served that were on the other side of the flood, or the gods of the Am'-orites, in whose land ye dwell: but as for me and my house, we will serve the LORD. And the people answered and said, God forbid that we should forsake the LORD, to serve other gods..."* (Joshua 24:13-16).

> *"If ye forsake the LORD, and serve strange gods, then he will turn and do you hurt, and consume you, after that he hath done you good"* (Joshua 24:20).

After the people heard this, they said once again that they would serve the Lord. Joshua told them:

> *"Ye are witnesses against yourselves that ye have chosen you the LORD, to serve him. And they said, We are witnesses"* (Joshua 24:22).

Joshua drew up an agreement (covenant) that day, based on the decrees and laws of God and wrote them in the Book of the Law. He set up a large stone by the Sanctuary to be a witness unto them, because it had heard the words of the Lord. Then Joshua died at 110 years old.

"...they buried him in the border of his inheritance in Tim´-nath-se´-rah, which is in mount E´-phra-im, on the north side of the hill of Ga´-ash. And Israel served the LORD all the days of Joshua, and all the days of the elders that overlived Joshua, and which had known all the works of the LORD, that He had done for Israel. And the bones of Joseph, which the children of Israel brought up out of Egypt, buried they in She´-chem, in a parcel of ground which Jacob bought of the sons of Ha´-mor the father of She´-chem for a hundred pieces of silver: and it became the inheritance of the children of Joseph. And El-e-a´-zar the son of Aaron died; and they buried him in a hill that pertained to Phin´-e-has his son, which was given him in mount E´-phra-im" (Joshua 24:30-33).

In Conclusion

At last, after forty years, God gave the commands for the Israelites to cross over into Canaan, the very land God had promised to give to Abraham's descendants. Early on Moses had sent out spies to check out the land, but they could not enter because of unbelief. Now Joshua had sent spies out into the land, but this time, the outcome was much different.

God was faithful in keeping His promise that the Israelites would inherit the new land of Canaan, and the Israelites did cross over the flooding Jordan River to their new land. God held back the raging river, in much the same way as He held back the raging Red Sea so their fathers could cross over.

God led them on in one war victory over another, defeating the enemies of Canaan, and then He gave them rest. Even after Joshua's death, God would continue to fight for them, if they would continue to love and obey Him. Even though they had God, would they be able to sustain their faith without a human leader to guide them?

Deeper Insights:

1. Why did He select Joshua to replace Moses?

   Read the following scriptures and try to determine what characteristics Joshua had that would give God reason to select him for the job:

   Exodus 17:8-14; 24:12-13; 33:11

   Numbers 13:3, 8, 16-17; 14:1-9, 36-38; 27:18-23; 32:11-12

2. Besides God verbally speaking with Joshua, as he had done with Moses, we find that Joshua and Moses had other similarities, as well. Read the following scriptures to see if you can remember what some of those similarities were:

   Joshua 3:7-8; 4:14, 23; 5:5-7, 13-15; 7:5-9; 8:30-34

3. Why did the Lord tell Joshua to tell the Israelites to gather stones from the riverbed and take them to where they were going to spend the night? Read Joshua 4:1-7.

   Today how can we leave "*stones*" for our own children or family that will answer their questions about who Christ is?

4. Joshua sent out two men from Gilgal to check out the walled city of Jericho in Canaan. At first, we may be a little startled to find they spent the night at a prostitute's house. The Bible doesn't tell us why or how they knew to stay there, but we do know that God was in it, because Rahab was a woman of faith in a pagan city. What did Rahab believe? Read Joshua 2:8-14.

   How did Rahab act on what she believed. Read Joshua 2:2-7, 15-16, 15-16, 18-21, and James 2:25.

   Apparently, Rahab was the only person in the city, except her own family, who did have faith, and God spared her. Read Joshua 6:24-25 and Hebrews 11:31.

   Rahab is listed as an ancestress of Jesus. Read Matthew 1:5

5. In the battle of Ai, Achan stole an accursed thing—a *"Babylonish garment"* and some silver and gold. God said the men were to take vessels made of silver, gold, brass, and iron to put in the Lord's treasury, but nothing else. Why did God not want them to take anything else? Read Joshua 6:17-18.

    What was the outcome of that disobedience?

    Read Joshua 7:19-26.

6. The people that had come out of bondage in Egypt were not able to enter into their promised land because of unbelief. What promise had God given them in Deuteronomy 12:9-10?

    The Lord fulfilled His promise to the tribes that chose to remain on the east side of the Jordan and to the tribes that crossed over. Read Joshua 1:12-16; 21:43-45 and 22:1-9.

    He also gave the children of Israel on the other side of the Jordan peace and rest. Read Joshua 21:43-44.

    Today there is also a rest for the believers of Christ. Read Mark 6:31; Hebrews 4:1-11; Revelation 6:11; 14:13. What kind of rest are these scriptures talking about?

CHAPTER 16

THE TIME OF THE JUDGES

God Tests the Israelites

Even though the tribes were divided into their inherited lots, they still had a centralized place in Shiloh where the tribes came together to offer sacrifices and to worship. However, with Joshua gone, they did not have a leader to intercede for them and guide them. They did not have a leader to lead them into battle with their enemies that were still left in their land. The Israelites asked the Lord who would be leading them against the Canaanites?

> *"And the LORD said, Judah shall go up: behold, I have delivered the land into his hand"* (Judges1:2).

Why did God want the tribe of Judah to go up first? The man, Judah, was born to Jacob (Israel) and his wife, Leah. He was the one who had convinced his brothers to sell Joseph to the Ishmaelites instead of killing him. He was the one who offered himself as a ransom for his brother, Benjamin. He was the one who led is father, Jacob (Israel), into Goshen to live near Joseph in Egypt. Judah also fathered a son, Perez, from whose lineage Christ would come. Before Israel's death, he had bestowed Judah's birthright upon him and prophesied over him about the coming Messiah:

> *"Judah, thou art he whom thy brethren shall praise: thy hand shall be in the neck of thine enemies; thy father's children shall*

*bow down before thee. Judah is a lion's whelp: from the prey, my
son, thou art gone up: he stooped down, he couched as a lion, and
as an old lion; who shall rouse him up? The <u>scepter</u> shall not
depart from Judah, nor a <u>lawgiver</u> from between his feet, until
<u>Shi'-loh</u> come; and unto him shall the gathering of the people be.
Binding his foal unto the vine, and his ass's colt unto the choice
vine; he washed his garments in wine, and his clothes in the blood
of grapes: his eyes shall be red with wine, and his teeth white with
milk."* –Genesis 49:8-12*

The Hebrew word translated *Judah* is "Yᵉhûwdâh." The meaning
of the word is "...celebrated." The descendants of Judah would later
be called Jews.[1]

The Hebrew word translated *sceptre* is "shêbet." The meaning of
the word is "...to branch off...a stick (for punishing, writing, fighting,
ruling, walking, etc.)...a clan...correction, dart, rod...staff, tribe."[2]

The Hebrew word translated *lawgiver,* is "châqaq." The meaning of
the word is "...to hack, i.e. engrave...to enact laws being cut in stone
or metal tablets in primitive times...appoint, decree, governor...."[3]

The Hebrew word translated *Shiloh* is "Shîylôh." The meaning of
the word is "tranquil...an epithet of the Messiah...."[4]

The Lord was with them and would show himself through Judah.
So Judah, assisted by the Simeonites, went to war and conquered the
Canaanites and Perizzites and attacked and burned Jersualem. Then they
went down and fought *"...against the Ca'-naanites, that dwelt in the mountain,
and in the south, and in the valley"* (Judges1:9). They continued forward and
conquered the Canaanites in Hebron, Sheshai, Ahiman, Talmai, and
Debir. Judah joined the Simeonites to conquer the Canaanites living
in Zephath; Gaza, Ashkelon, Ekron; and the hill country. However,
the men of Judah could not defeat the people who lived in the plains,
because they had iron chariots. "This was the beginning of the Iron
Age. The Philistines introduced and controlled the iron industry in
Palestine and guarded it jealously."[5] The Israelites could not compete
with their power. Earlier on, Caleb had run the people of Anak out of
the land of Hebron, and the house of Joseph had conquered Bethel.

Even though the Lord had told the Israelites to drive the enemies from their land, the tribes of Manasseh, Ephraim, Zebulun, Asher, Naphtali, and Benjamin did not drive the Canaanites from their land. They allowed the Canaanites to live among them, and some used them as slaves, which was a direct disobedience to the Lord. This disobedience was the beginning of defeat. Living, mingling, and intermarrying with the idolatrous Canaanites would bring temptations to the Israelites that would take them away from the Lord their God.

The Caananites were Baal worshipers, and the Israelites were in covenant with the one true living God of their forefathers. Both religions had some similar rituals and traditions, which made it easy for the Israelites to become deceived and forget about their covenant with the Lord. As they became familiar with the Canaanites, some of the Israelites began to join with them in their religion of Baalism, while others combined parts of both religions. The Israelites had been given specific holy standards to live by to honor their Lord, and they were not to compromise with any other religion. When united in faith and obedience to the Lord their God, they stood strong, but living among the Canaanites and indulging in their idolatrous practices caused them to forget they had been set apart as God's holy nation, and they fell into sin, and God kept His promise:

> *"And an angel of the LORD came up from Gil´-gal to Bo´-chim, and said, I made you to go up out of Egypt, and I have brought you unto the land which I sware unto your fathers; and I said, I will never break my covenant with you. And ye shall make no league with the inhabitants of this land; ye shall throw down their altars: but ye have not obeyed my voice: why have ye done this? Wherefore I also said, I will not drive them out from before you; but they shall be as thorns in your sides, and their gods shall be a snare unto you"* (Judges 2:1-3).

The Israelites were brokenhearted and repentant, and they gave offerings unto the Lord. After some time, however, as that generation of people who had been with Joshua began to die off, a new generation rose up who no longer knew the Lord. They had no remembrance of what God had done for their ancestors in Egypt, in the desert, and in Canaan after they first arrived there. They began to worship Baal, whom they believed would bring good crops, and the Ashtoreth and Astartes, "local male and female gods of fertility and a fruitful land."[6] The Lord's anger kindled against them, and he sold them to their enemies, and he was no longer with them when they went to war. It became a time of great anguish. God would use these enemies to prove Israel.

> *"And the anger of the LORD was hot against Israel; and he said, Because that this people hath transgressed my covenant which I commanded their fathers, and have not hearkened unto my voice; I also will not henceforth drive out any from before them of the nations which Joshua left when he died: that through them, I may prove Israel, whether they will keep the way of the LORD to walk therein, as their fathers did keep it, or not"* (Judges 2:20-22).

The Lord had left these enemies in the land *"...to test all those Israelites who had not experienced any of the wars in Canaan (he did this only to teach warfare to the descendants of the Israelites who had not had previous battle experience): the five rulers of the Philistines, all the Canaanites, the Sidonians, and the Hivites...They were left to test the Israelites to see whether they would obey the LORD's commands, which he had given their forefathers through Moses"* (Judges 3:1-4, NIV®).

God Raises Up Judges

Even though the Israelites were unfaithful to the Lord, He was still faithful to them because of the covenant and promises He had made with their forefathers. He still had great love and compassion for them. Whenever the Israelites turned away from God and fell into idolatrous sin, God would bring them into oppression, using the enemies that He had purposefully left in the land. He did this so they would turn back to

Him. When the oppression became unbearable, the Israelites would cry out to God, and God would raise up judges to save and deliver them. God picked the judges to deliver them from those who mistreated them (Judges 2:16), but God would still be their King. The concept of a judge was not new to the Israelites. Moses had been their first judge back at Mount Sinai, and he had appointed other judges to help him with minor disputes, but he had handled the more complex disputes.

"The difference between a judge and a king is this: a king gives to his son in succession his throne, but a judge is raised up according to a crisis and endowed with special gifts from God for that one period of time."[7]

These judges were not perfect. Some were even violent and ruthless, but they were appointed, anointed, and empowered by God because of the faith they had in Him. When God placed His Spirit upon them, they were bold, courageous, and loyal to His cause.

There were twelve noteworthy judges the Lord raised up for His purposes. God was in charge of what happened to them, and He guided them. All dates listed below were taken from the Zondervan Handbook to the Bible.[8]

Othniel of Judah: In about 1200 BC the Israelites sinned against the Lord and served the Baals and the Asherahs, "sacred poles, symbol of the Canaanite mother-goddess."[9]

"...*The LORD*... *sold them into the hand of Chu´-shan-rish-a-tha´-im king of Mes-o-po-ta´mi´a*" (Judges 3:8), whom they served for eight years. When the people cried out to the Lord, He put His Spirit upon Othniel, and he became judge. After going to war, the Lord gave Chushanrishathaim into Othniel's hands, and there was rest for forty years (found in Judges 3:8-11).

Ehud of Benjamin: In about 1170 BC "...*the children of Israel did evil again in the sight of the LORD: and the LORD strengthened Eg´-lon the king of Moab against Israel, because they had done evil in the sight of the LORD. And he gathered unto him the children of Ammon and Am´-a-lek, and went and smote Israel, and possessed the city of palm trees* (Jericho).[10] *So the children of Israel served Eg´-lon the king of Moab eighteen years*" (Judges 3:12-14).

When the people cried out to the Lord, He raised Ehud up as a deliverer, and Ehud killed king Eglon. Ehud and the Israelites killed 10,000 Moabite men and subdued Moab. The land rested for eighty years.

Shamgar: In about 1150 BC Shamgar brought victory against the Philistines and saved Israel by striking down 600 Philistines with an oxgoad (see Judges 3:31).

Deborah of Ephraim and **Barak** of Naphthali (counts as one judge): In about 1125 BC *"…the children of Israel again did evil in the sight of the LORD…And the LORD sold them into the hand of Ja´-bin king of Canaan, that reigned in Ha´-zor; the captain of whose host was Sis´-e-ra, which dwelt in Ha-ro´-sheth of the Gentiles. And the children of Israel cried unto the LORD: for he had nine hundred chariots of iron; and twenty years he mightily oppressed the children of Israel"* (Judges 4:1-3).

This was the second king of Hazor whose name was Jabin. The first Jabin had been killed in a battle with Joshua.

Deborah was a prophetess who was already judging the Israelites. She commanded Barak of Naphtali to gather 10,000 men of Naphtali and Zebulun and meet her at Mount Tabor, where she would lure Sisera, Jabin's army commander. Barak refused to go unless Deborah accompanied him, so she let him know that the Lord would hand over the honor of the victory to a woman. The battle took place as planned and all of Sisera's troops were killed, but Sisera had fled on foot to the tent of Jael. Jael was the wife of Hebor the Kenite, who was a friend of Sisera's. After she invited him into her tent and gave him some milk to drink, he fell asleep, and she drove a peg into his head with a hammer.

"So God subdued on that day Ja´-bin the king of Canaan before the children of Israel. And the hand of the children of Israel prospered, and prevailed against Ja´-bin the king of Canaan, until they had destroyed Ja´-bin king of Canaan" (Judges 4:23-24).

Judges 5 records the song Deborah wrote, which she and Barak sang on that day of victory.

Gideon of Manasseh: In about 1100 BC the Israelites sinned against the Lord, and He gave them over to the Midianites for seven years. Their oppression was so great that the Israelites found places to hide in the mountains and caves. The Midianites, Amalekites, and others would come on their camels and destroy the Israelites' land. They would come and steal their animals and their crops at harvest time, completely ruining the land for the people. When the Israelites cried to the Lord, He reminded them of their disobedience.

> "...I brought you up from Egypt, and brought you forth out of the house of bondage; And I delivered you out of the hand of the Egyptians, and out of the hand of all that oppressed you, and drove them out from before you, and gave you their land; And I said unto you, I am the LORD your God; fear not the gods of the Am´-orites, in whose land ye dwell: but ye have not obeyed my voice" (Judges 6:8-10).

The Lord sent his angel to Gideon, a "*mighty warrior*" and assigned him the task of saving Israel. The Lord reduced Gideon's army from 22,000 down to 300 men to keep Israel from trying to take credit for saving themselves, and He gave victory to Gideon and his army. During that time, Gideon also attacked the towns of Succoth and Peniel for not supplying he and his troops food to eat when they had asked for it.

The Israelites asked Gideon and his son, Abimelech, to rule over them, but he refused, telling them that the Lord would rule over them. Gideon requested that each one give him a share of the plunder from the war—one gold earring from each one, and then Gideon made a gold ephod, probably "an image of God, which the law forbade,"[11] and set it up in his home town of Ophrah. So Israel once again became ensnared with idol worship, worshiping Gideon's ephod, which was also a snare for Gideon's family, but Gideon did bring peace to Israel for forty years.

Tola of Issachar in Ephraim: God raised Tola up as a military leader to save Israel, and he led them for twenty-three years (see Judges 10:1-2).

Jair, a military leader, of Gilead: Jair led Israel for twenty-two years. He had thirty sons who rode their donkeys to controll thirty cities (see Judges 10:3-5).

Jephthah of Gilead: In about 1070 BC the Israelites served the Baals and the Ashtoreths, and the gods of Aram, Sidon, Moab, Ammonites, and the gods of the Philistines.

> *"And the anger of the LORD was hot against Israel, and he sold them into the hands of the Philis'-tines, and into the hands of the children of Ammon. And that year they vexed and oppressed the children of Israel: eighteen years, all the children of Israel that were on the other side Jordan in the land of the Am'-orites, which is in Gil'-e-ad. Moreover the children of Ammon passed over Jordan to fight also against Judah, and against Benjamin, and against the house of E'-phra-im; so that Israel was sore distressed"* (Judges 10:7-9).

When the Israelites cried out to God, He told them to go and cry out to their gods. The Israelites acknowledged their sins to God and got rid of their foreign gods, and the Lord once again showed compassion on them. Then the Ammonites encamped in Gilead and the Israelites encamped in Mizpah.

Jephthah was a powerful warrior. When the Ammonites made war on Israel, the elders of Gilead asked Jephthah to accompany them in battle with the promise that he would be in charge of all the people in Gilead. Jephthah sent a message to the Ammonite king to find out why he had made war on Gilead and received this response:

> *"...Because Israel took away my land, when they came up out of Egypt, from Arnon even unto the Jab'-bok, and unto Jordan: now therefore restore those lands again peaceably"* (Judges 11:13).

Jephthah wrote the king a response about what had really happened with the land., which is found in Deuteronomy 2:26-28. This had happened when Moses was trying to lead Israel through Edom and Moab and had asked permission to pass through on their lands, but permission was not granted. The Israelites then bypassed their land and traveled through the desert on the eastern side of Moab, the other side of Arnon. Later, when Israel had asked permission of king Sihon of the Amorites to pass through Heshbon, he fought with Israel, and the Lord caused Israel to defeat Sihon and capture the land from the Arnon to the Jabbok and from the desert to the Jordan. He explained that the Lord had given the land to Israel, and they had occupied it for 300 years since.

The king of Ammon ignored Jephthah. The Spirit of the Lord came upon Jephthah, and he advanced against the Ammonites. Jephthah vowed to the Lord, *"...If thou shalt without fail deliver the children of Ammon into mine hands, Then it shall be, that whatsoever cometh forth of the doors of my house to meet me, when I return in peace from the children of Ammon, shall surely be the LORD'S, and I will offer it up for a burnt offering"* (Judges 11:30-31).

Jephthah won the war, and the first thing that came out of the door of his house was his only child, his daughter! Jephthah kept his vow to the Lord, and His daughter gave him this response:

> *"...let this thing be done for me: let me alone two months, that I may go up and down upon the mountains, and bewail my virginity, I and my fellows. And he said, Go. And he sent her away for two months: and she went with her companions, and bewailed her virginity upon the mountains. And it came to pass at the end of two months, that she returned unto her father, who did with her according to his vow which he had vowed..."* (Judges 11:37-39).

This is a hard thing to understand, but it does paint a picture of the hard times of that day. It illustrates the "gut" faith of the mighty judges of God and the blind faith and trust of all others who followed the Lord their God. Jephthah went on to lead a battle between Gilead and Ephraim, where 42,000 Ephraimites were killed. Jephthah was Israel's judge for six years and died.

Ibzan of Bethlehem; **Elon** of Zebulun; and **Abdon** of Ephraim (Judges 12:8-15): Ibzan led Israel for seven years and died. He gave away his children in marriage with those outside their clan. Elon led Israel for ten years and died. Abdon led Israel for eight years and died.

Samson of Dan: (Judges 13:1-16:31): In about 1070 BC the Philistines were living along the southern coast of Canaan. They were expanding their territory into "Gaza, Ashdod, Ashkelon, Ekron...and Gath... and on the edge of Shephelah. Other smaller towns and villages of the southern coastal plain came under Philistine rule...now they threatened the tribal allotments of Judah and Dan."[12]

> *"And the children of Israel did evil again in the sight of the LORD; and the LORD delivered them into the hand of the Philis'-tines for forty years. And there was a certain man of Zor'-ah, of the family of the Danites, whose name was Mano'-ah; and his wife was barren and bare not. And the angel of the LORD appeared unto the woman, and said unto her, Behold, now, thou art barren, and bearest not: but thou shalt conceive, and bear a son. Now therefore beware, I pray thee, and drink not wine nor strong drink, and eat not any unclean thing: For, lo, thou shalt conceive, and bear a son; and no razor shall come on his head: for the child shall be a Nazarite unto God from the womb: and he shall begin to deliver Israel out of the hand of the Philis'-tines"* (Judges 13:1-5).

As he grew, *"...the Spirit of the LORD began to move him at times in the camp of Dan..."* (Judges 13:25).

When Samson became a man, he saw a daughter of the Philistines who he wanted to have as his wife. His parents tried to talk him into finding a wife out of the Hebrew tribes, but to no avail. Samson and his parents went to meet the Philistine woman at Timnah. God would use this situation to bring trouble with the Philistines who were controlling the Israelites.

While they were there, *"a young lion roared against him. And the Spirit of the LORD came mightily upon him, and he rent him as he would have rent a kid* (baby goat), *and he had nothing in his hand: but he told not his father or his mother what he had done. And he went down, and talked with the woman; and she pleased Samson well. And after a time he returned to take her, and he turned aside to see the carcase of the lion: and, behold, there was a swarm of bees and honey in the carcase of the lion. And he took thereof in his hands, and went on eating, and came to his father and mother, and he gave them, and they did eat: but he told not them that he had taken the honey out of the carcase of the lion"* (Judges 14:5-9).

Here we see that Samson deceived his Hebrew parents into eating honey from a dead animal, which was against God's law. Samson didn't seem to respect his parents or their religious beliefs, which became apparent when he chose to marry a wife from a pagan nation. Later, we find that he even spent the night with a harlot. However, God still had a plan, and he had picked Samson for the job of judge.

Samson's father went to see the Philistine woman, and Samson prepared a customary bridegroom feast. Samson was given thirty companions, and he gave them all a riddle to solve within seven days.

"Out of the eater came forth meat, and out of the strong came forth sweetness" (Judges 14:14).

No one could guess the riddle, and on the seventh day, Samson's companions coerced Samson's wife into enticing Samson to tell her the answer to the riddle, and she gave the answer to them. When Samson found out what they had done, he was very angry; and the Spirit of the Lord came upon him with great power. He went to Ashkelon and killed thirty of their men and robbed them of their clothes to give to those who had coerced his wife for the answer to the riddle. Samson lost his wife, for she was given to a friend who had attended the wedding.

Later, at wheat harvest, Samson took a young goat and went to see her, but when he tried to enter her room, her father refused him entrance and tried to give him his younger daughter for a wife. Samson was determined to get even with the Philistines. He went out and caught 300 foxes and tied each pair tail to tail. He attached a torch to each pair of tails, lit the torches and turned the foxes loose in the Philistine's field of grain, and everything burned up. When the Philistines found out what Samson had done, they burned the woman and her father to death. Samson decided to take revenge on them and killed many of them and hid in a cave. When the Philistines found out where Samson was hiding, they went to him and bound him with cords. On the way to the Philistines, the Spirit of the Lord came upon him in power, and the bindings dropped off from him. He found a new jawbone of a donkey and slew a thousand men. After that, Samson judged Israel for twenty years.

The Philistines tried to kill Samson again when he went to spend the night with a harlot in Gaza. They surrounded her house and waited for him at the city gate until morning. At midnight, Samson got up *"and took the doors of the gate of the city, and the two posts, and went away with them, bar and all, and put them upon his shoulders, and carried them up to the top of an hill that is before He´-bron"* (Judges 16:3).

Eventually, Samson fell in love with a woman named Delilah, who lived in the Valley of Sorek in Gaza. The Philistine rulers told Delilah to entice Samson to tell her where he was getting his great strength. Three different times Delilah tried to trick Samson into telling her what the source of his strength was, but each time she asked, he would make up untrue stories. With each answer, while the Philistines laid in wait to capture him, she would tie him up while he slept. Then she would say, *"The Philistines be upon thee, Samson,"* so he would jump up quickly from his sleep and pretend to not be able to set himself free.

Delilah kept telling Samson that he was making a fool out of her, and that if he loved her, he would confide in her, so the third time she asked him, Samson told her the truth.

> *"...No razor has ever been used on my head,"* he said, *"because I have been a Nazarite dedicated to God from my mother's womb. If my head were shaved, my strength would leave me, and I would become as weak as any other man"* (Judges 16:17, NIV®).

> *"And she made him sleep upon her knees; and she called for a man, and she caused him to shave off the seven locks of his head;*

and she began to afflict him, and his strength went from him. And she said, The Philis'-tines be upon thee, Samson. And he awoke out of his sleep, and said, I will go out as at other times before, and shake myself. And he wist not that the LORD was departed from him. But the Philistines took him, and put out his eyes, and brought him down to Ga'-za, and bound him with fetters of brass; and he did grind in the prison house. Howbeit the hair of his head began to grow again after he was shaven" (Judges 16:19-22).

The Philistine rulers began to rejoice and offer a great sacrifice to their god, Dagon, saying, *"...Our god has delivered Samson our enemy, into our hand"* (Judges 16:23). When they called Samson out to entertain them, he told the servant, *"...Suffer me that I may feel the pillars whereupon the house standeth, that I may lean upon them. Now the house was full of men and women; and all the lords of the Philis'-tines were there; and there were upon the roof about three thousand men and women, that beheld while Samson made sport"* (Judges 16:26-27).

Then he prayed, *"...O Lord God, remember me, I pray thee, and strengthen me, I pray thee, only this once, O God, that I may be at once avenged of the Philis'-tines for my two eyes"* (Judges 16:28). *"...Let me die with the Philistines..."* (Judges 16:30).

God granted Samson his last request. Samson pushed with all his might, and the temple fell down on the rulers killing the 3,000 men and women who fell with it. Samson died after judging Israel for twenty years, and the Philistines continued to oppress the Israelites.

During that time, worship and sacrifice was still taking place at God's house in Shiloh, but much corruption had leaked into the lives of the Israelites. The sacrificial system and priesthood that God had set up with Moses had become distorted, and there was great confusion and chaos.

The Story of Ruth

This story has been included here to show the ancestry of king David and Jesus, the Messiah, which can be found in Matthew 1:5-6. Sometime during the time of the judges, there was a famine, and a man from Bethlehem-Judah took his wife and two sons to Moab to live for a period of time. While there, he died, and both of his sons married Moabite women—Orpah and Ruth. Then the sons also passed away.

Naomi, the man's wife, heard that there was now food in Bethlehem and made a decision to go back there and live. Naomi felt that her daughters-in-law should stay in Moab to try and build a life for themselves. Orpah chose to stay, but Ruth chose to go with her mother-in-law. She told Naomi:

> "...whither thou goest, I will go; and where thou lodgest, I will lodge: thy people shall be my people, and thy God my God: Where thou diest, will I die, and there will I be buried: the LORD do so to me, and more also, if aught but death part thee and me" (Ruth 1:16-17).

They returned to Bethlehem during the barley harvest. Naomi's husband had a wealthy kinsman named Boaz, who owned part of the barley field. Ruth asked Naomi to go and glean in his field after the reapers to try and find grace in the eyes of Boaz. When Boaz came to the field, he inquired about Ruth, and his servant told him she had come to town with Naomi. Boaz told Ruth to stay and work his field with his maidens and to drink water whenever she was thirsty. He also provided protection for her, telling the young men not to touch her.

> "Then she fell on her face, and bowed herself to the ground, and said unto him, Why have I found grace in thine eyes, that thou shouldest take knowledge of me, seeing I am a stranger? And Bo´-az answered and said unto her, It hath fully been showed me, all that thou hast done unto thy mother-in-law since the death of thine husband: and how thou hast left thy father and thy mother, and the land of thy nativity, and art come unto a people which thou knewest not heretofore. The LORD recompense thy work, and full reward be given thee of the LORD God of Israel, under whose wings thou art come to trust" (Ruth 2:10-12).

Boaz told the young men to let Ruth glean among the sheaves and to leave some for her to glean. So Ruth gleaned from Boaz's field during both the barley and wheat harvest, taking the gleanings home to Naomi each day.

Naomi came up with a plan for Ruth. She told Ruth to go to the threshing floor, where Boaz would go to lay down to sleep after he had finished eating and drinking. She told her to uncover his feet and lay down at them. Ruth did as Naomi told her, and when Boaz awoke and discovered Ruth at his feet, he asked her who she was. She told him that he was a *"near kinsman."*

> *"And he said, Blessed be thou of the LORD, my daughter: for thou hast showed more kindness in the latter end than at the beginning, inasmuch as thou followedst not young men, whether poor or rich. And now, my daughter, fear not; I will do to thee all that thou requirest: for all the city of my people doth know that thou art a virtuous woman. And now it is true that I am thy near kinsman: howbeit there is a kinsman nearer than I. Tarry this night, and it shall be in the morning, that if he will perform unto thee the part of a kinsman, well; let him do the kinsman's part; but if he will not do the part of a kinsman to thee, then will I do the part of a kinsman to thee, as the LORD liveth: lie down until the morning"* (Ruth 3:9-13).

The next day Boaz went to the city gate, taking along ten elders, and met with Naomi's other kinsman.

> *"...Na-o´-mi, that is come again out of the country of Moab, selleth a parcel of land, which was our brother E-lim´-e-lech's...If thou wilt redeem it, redeem it: but if thou wilt not redeem it, then tell me, that I may know: for there is none to redeem it beside thee; and I am after thee. And he said, I will redeem it.*

When the kinsman realized that he must also buy it from Ruth, the wife of the dead, he refused to redeem it and he released it to Boaz.

> *"And Bo´-az said unto the elders, and unto all the people, Ye are witnesses this day, that I have bought all that was E-lim´-e-lech's,*

and all that was Chil´-i-on's and Mah´-lon's, of the hand of Na-o´-mi. Moreover Ruth the Mo´-abitess, the wife of Mah´-lon, have I purchased to be my wife, to raise up the name of the dead upon his inheritance, that the name of the dead be not cut off from among his brethren, and from the gate of his place: ye are witnesses this day" (Ruth 4:9-10).

"So Bo´-az took Ruth, and she was his wife: and when he went in unto her, the LORD gave her conception, and she bare a son. And the women said unto Na-o´-mi, Blessed be the LORD, which hath not left thee this day without a kinsman, that his name may be famous in Israel. And he shall be unto thee a restorer of thy life, and a nourisher of thine old age: for thy daughter-in-law, which loveth thee, which is better to thee than seven sons, hath born him. And Na-o´-mi took the child, and laid it in her bosom, and became nurse unto it. And the women her neighbors gave it a name, saying, There is a son born to Na-o´-mi; and they called his name O´-bed: he is the father of Jesse, the father of David" (Ruth 4:13-17). Verses 18-22 record the lineage from Pharez to David.

In Conclusion

Without a leader, the clans were no longer unified. as one nation, falling to the influence of the cultures and gods of the land in which they lived. Each period of sin brought oppression. Oppression caused them to cry out to God for help, and God would rise up a judge to save them.

Even though the men God chose to be judges could be ruthless and sinful, God saw something in each one that qualified them for the position. They were ready to do what God told them to do to judge the Israelites. Sometimes the actions of the judges led to gruesome violence to cleanse the land from those who were trying to pollute Israel, God's firstborn son. The judges did not operate under their own power, but were empowered by the Spirit of God to do what would normally be impossible. Gideon, Barak, Jephthah, and Samson are acknowledged in the New Testament in Hebrews 11:32-33 for their faith in God.

While the Israelites were under the leadership of the judges, they obeyed God; but every time a judge died, the people would sin even more, basing their faith on their immediate circumstances. Then they would go back to worshipping other gods.

It seemed that everything concerning the Lord had become perverted. Even though God's house was in Shiloh, and the Israelites clans would come together for centralized worship, shrines began to be set up in individual homes, and people appointed themselves and other people to become priests. Some priests even hired out for money, not regarding the standard the Lord had set up within the Levitical priesthood. When things became difficult they fell into idolatry in order to seek help. God had foretold to Moses that they would do this. When they sinned, God would lead them into oppression by their enemies, but He was still faithful to them, as He had promised. He always delivered them when they would cry out to Him with repentance. This repetitive behavior pattern lasted for about 200 years after they entered their promised land. *"In those days there was no king in Israel: every man did that which was right in his own eyes"* (Judges 21:25).

The time of the judges helps us begin to understand the cost of our salvation. Many hardships were experienced, and many sacrifices were made by the Israelites on this journey to the Cross.

Eventually, Israel reached a point where they forgot that God was their King. It wouldn't be long before they would be crying out for a king to lead them like the other nations had, and God would give them what they asked for.

Deeper Insights:

1. When the Israelites asked God who would lead them against the Canaanites, He told them, *"...Judah shall go up..."* (Judges 1:2), but why? We have already established that Jacob's son, Judah, was a leader who thought more of others than his own self,

especially those he loved. He was willing to sacrifice himself for others and for God. Read Psalm 60:7, a Psalm David wrote about Judah.

Now read Genesis 49:8-10, the prophecy given by Jacob (Israel) about his son, Judah.

After reading the prophecy in Genesis 49:8-10 about Judah, and looking at the word definitions of Judah on the first page of this chapter, what do you think the prophecy means?

2. An angel of the Lord had warned the Israelites. Read Judges 2:1-3. After the Israelites began to conquer their land, some of the tribes disobeyed God's commands about driving the enemies out of their land. They allowed the Canaanites to stay in and live among them.

    What were some of the problems that began to occur? Read Judges 2:11-13. What did God do about their sin? Read Judges 2:14-15.

3. Why did God raise up judges for the Israelites? Read Judges 2:16-18. What would happen to the people when the judges would die? Read Judges 2:19.

4. This new generation of Israelites were the descendants of those who were delivered out of bondage in Egypt. Their grandparents had died in the desert because of unbelief and disobedience. Why did God leave enemies in the land to test them? Read Judges 2:20-23 and 3:1-4. What happened to the Israelites when they lived among their enemies? Read Judges 3:5-7.

5. When Israel had no human leader, their tribes became divided and isolated. They weren't strong enough to stand against the influences of the pagan cultures, and neither are we. We, too, have the same enemy as the one who afflicted the Israelites—*"... the devil, as a roaring lion, walketh about, seeking whom he may devour"* (I Peter 5:8).

By joining ourselves with other believers in Christ, in what ways can we support each other and show love to each other to urge each other on in our faith?

6. Even though our nation is filled with Christian churches, it is also filled with moral depravity and lawlessness. What are some of the signs that indicate this is happening to our nation?

What does the Bible give warning about? Read 2 Corinthians 6:14-18.

In what ways have Christians become responsible for the moral decay in our nation?

How have Christians become unequally yoked with unbelievers?

In what ways have we, as Christians, given in to pagan cultures and forms of worship?

In what areas do you see oppression showing itself in our nation?

For individuals and for nations, there is only one hope: Read 2 Chronicles 7:14.

CHAPTER 17

SAMUEL, SAUL, AND DAVID

Samuel, the Last Judge

Samuel was the last judge that God would give to Israel, and from the beginning, it is clear that He had set him apart for a special purpose.

Elkanah was a Zuphite from Ephraim, who had two wives—Peninnah, who had children; and Hannah, his favorite, who had none, *"...the LORD had shut up her womb"* (I Samuel 1:5). Peninnah constantly chided Hannah about her barrenness, and one day, while at the Temple in Shiloh, Hannah prayed:

> *"...O LORD of hosts, if thou wilt indeed look on the affliction*
> *of thine handmaid, and remember me, and not forget thine*
> *handmaid, but wilt give unto thine handmaid a man child, then*
> *I will give him unto the LORD all the days of his life, and there*
> *shall no razor come upon his head"* (1 Samuel 1:11).

Throughout the pages of the Bible, we have been seeing that God has orchestrated the births of His great men, and so it was with Samuel. God chose the day and the hour to open Hannah's womb to bring about the life of her son, Samuel. She stayed at home with Samuel, and did not take him to the Tabernacle when the family went to offer their annual sacrifices. She told her husband, *"...I will not go up until the child be weaned, and then I will bring him, that he may appear before the LORD, and there abide for ever"* (1 Samuel 1:22).

When Samuel was weaned, at the age between "2-3,"[1] Hannah took him to the Temple in Shiloh, along with her sacrifices, flour, and wine. She told the priest, Eli, about the vow she had made to the Lord and how He had granted her petition. She told him, "...*Therefore also I have lent him to the LORD; as long as he liveth he shall be lent to the LORD. And he worshiped the LORD there*" (1 Samuel 1:26-28).

1 Samuel 2:2 records the song of Hannah's prayer, where she says, "*There is none holy as the LORD: for there is none besides thee: neither is there any rock like our God.*"

The Lord Prophesize About Eli

Eli was a priest who served in the Tabernacle sanctuary at Shiloh, which Joshua had set up. He had two sons, Hophni and Phinehas, who were also serving there. The Lord would soon put them to death because they were sinning against Him by being greedy and taking the best pieces of the offering (fat offerings) for themselves before giving the sacrifices to God (see 1 Samuel 2:29). They were also having sex with the women who gathered at the Tabernacle door. Eli knew about their sins, and he had confronted them, but he didn't do anything to correct them. One day the Lord sent a man of God to Eli to prophesy to him about the upcoming death of he and his family:

> "...*thou shalt see an enemy in my habitation, in all the wealth which God shall give Israel: and there shall not be an old man in thine house for ever... and all the increase of thine house shall die in the flower of their age. And this shall be a sign unto thee, that shall come upon thy two sons, on Hoph´-ni and Phin´-e-has; in one day they shall die both of them. And I will raise me up a faithful priest, that shall do according to that which is in mine heart and in my mind: and I will build him a sure house; and he shall walk before mine anointed for ever*"
> (1 Samuel 2:32-35).

The faithful priest God was talking about would be Samuel. In I Samuel 2, we see the relationship between Samuel and the Lord: (Verse 18) *"…Samuel ministered before the LORD, being a child, girded with a linen e´-phod* (he wore priests' clothes)." (Verse 26) *"And the child Samuel grew on, and was in favor both with the LORD, and also with men."*. (3:1) *"And the child Samuel ministered unto the LORD before E´-li. And the word of the Lord was precious* (not given often) *in those days; there was no open vision."*

Even so, the Lord had not yet revealed Himself to Samuel, and Samuel did not know God in a personal way.

One night when Samuel and Eli had lain down to go to sleep in the Tabernacle, the LORD stood by Samuel and called to him:

> *"Behold, I will do a thing in Israel, at which both the ears of every one that heareth it shall tingle. In that day I will perform against E´-li all things which I have spoken concerning his house: when I begin, I will also make an end. For I have told him that I will judge his house for ever for the iniquity which he knoweth; because his sons made themselves vile, and he restrained them not. And therefore I have sworn unto the house of E´-li, that the iniquity of E´-li's house shall not be purged with sacrifice nor offering for ever"* (1 Samuel 3:11-14).

The next morning Samuel told Eli everything the Lord had prophesied to him. As Samuel grew up, the Lord was with him, and Israel knew that he was a prophet of the Lord, *"And the LORD appeared again in Shi´-loh: for the LORD revealed himself to Samuel in Shi´-loh by the word of the LORD"* (1 Samuel 3:21).

The Philistines Steal the Ark of the Covenant

There was a battle between the Philistines and the Israelites, and the Israelites lost 4,000 men. They went to the sanctuary at Shiloh and brought the Ark of the Covenant out to their battlefield to save them from the Philistines. It was a serious mistake to use the Ark as protection against the Philistines without conferring with the Lord, but the people rejoiced with great shouting when the Ark was brought to them. The Philistines heard the shouting, and when they realized the Ark was in the Israelite camp, they became afraid because they had heard of the power of the Israelite God. Still, they attacked Israel, killing 30,000 Israelite footmen, including Eli's sons, and took the Ark with them when they left.

When ninety-eight year old Eli, the priest, heard the Ark had been captured, he fell over backward and broke his neck and died. His daughter-in-law also died giving birth to her son, Ichabod. The woman that was with her declared, *"The glory is departed from Israel; for the ark of God is taken..."* (1 Samuel 4:22). Eli's family was cut off, just as the Lord had prophesied.

> *"And the Philis'-tines took the ark of God, and brought it into the house of Da'-gon, and set it by Da'-gon.* (Dagon was the "fish-god...a Philistine deity....")[2] *And when they of Ash'-dod arose early on the morrow, behold, Da'-gon was fallen upon his face to the earth before the ark of the LORD. And they took Da'-gon, and set him in his place again. And when they arose early on the morrow morning, behold, Da'-gon was fallen upon his face to the ground before the ark of the LORD; and the head of Da'-gon and both the palms of his hands were cut off upon the threshold; only the stump of Da'-gon was left to him"* (1 Samuel 5:2-4).

The Lord's hand became very heavy upon the people who lived in Ashdod. He brought destruction and afflicted the people with tumors, which were caused by the "Bubonic plague carried by the rat-flea."[3] The Philistines needed to get rid of the Ark and moved it to Gath, and the same thing happened to the people of Gath. They moved it to Ekron, and the same thing happened to them. Finally, after seven months, they decided to send it back to Israel, and they asked the Israelite priests how they should go about sending the Ark back.

The priests told them, *"...get a new cart ready, with two cows that have calved and have never been yoked. Hitch the cows to the cart, but take their calves away and pen them up. Take the ark of the LORD and put it on the cart, and in a chest beside it put the gold objects you are sending back to him as a guilt offering...*" (1 Samuel 6:7-8, NIV®).

The "*gold objects*" were gold tumors, which represented the cities that had housed the Ark and the gold rats, which represented "*...the number of Philistine towns belonging to the fortified towns with their country villages*" (1 Samuel 6:4, NIV®).

> *"And he smote the men of Beth-she´-mesh, because they had looked into the ark of the LORD, even he smote of the people fifty thousand and threescore and ten men: and the people lamented, because the LORD had smitten many of the people with a great slaughter*" (1 Samuel 6:19).

> *"And the men of Kir´-jath-je´-a-rim came, and fetched up the ark of the LORD, and brought it into the house of A-bin´-a-dab in the hill, and sanctified El-e-a´-zar his son to keep the ark of the LORD*" (1 Samuel 7:1).

The Ark stayed there for twenty years and never returned to Shiloh. The Israelites had lost the Ark, and the glory of the Lord was gone from them. Even though they kept falling into idolatry, they still mourned after the Lord.

Samuel said to them, "*...If ye do return unto the LORD with all your hearts, then put away the strange gods and Ash´-ta-roth from among you, and prepare your hearts unto the LORD, and serve him only: and he will deliver you out of the hand of the Philis´-tines*" (1 Samuel 7:3).

Samuel assembled the Israelites together at Mizpeh, and he interceded for them. They poured water out before the Lord, and fasted. The Philistines heard that they were all assembled together and came to attack them. Samuel began sacrificing a burnt offering and praying out to the Lord.

> *"And as Samuel was offering up the burnt offering, the Philis´-tines drew near to battle against Israel: but the LORD thundered*

with a great thunder on that day upon the Philis´-tines, and discomfited them: and they were smitten before Israel. And the men of Israel went out of Miz´-peh and pursued the Philis´-tines, and smote them..." (1 Samuel 7:10-11).

With God's help, Israel subdued the Philistines that day.

The First King of Israel

"*...Samuel judged Israel all the days of his life. And he went from year to year in circuit to Beth-el, and Gil´-gal, and Miz´-peh, and judged Israel in all those places. And his return was to Ra´-mah; for there was his house; and there he judged Israel; and there he built an altar unto the LORD*" (1 Samuel 7:15-17).

When Samuel became old, he appointed his two sons, Joel and Abiah, as judges in Beersheba. They did not walk in God's ways, "*...but turned aside after lucre and took bribes, and perverted judgment*" (I Samuel 8:3). This gave the Israelite elders an excuse to ask Samuel for a king to judge them in the same way kings judged other nations. Samuel wasn't comfortable with their request and asked the Lord what to do.

"*And the LORD said unto Samuel, Hearken unto the voice of the people in all that they say unto thee: for they have not rejected thee, but they have rejected me, that I should not reign over them*" (1 Samuel 8:7).

Samuel went and explained to the Israelites what it would be like to live under a human king, instead of God, Who had been their King.

"*...He will take your sons, and appoint them for himself, for his chariots, and to be his horsemen; and some shall run before his chariots. And he will appoint him captains over thousands, and captains over fifties; and will set them to ear* (to plow) *his* *ground, and to reap his harvest, and to make his instruments of war, and instruments of his chariots. And he will take your daughters to be confectionaries* (perfumers) *and to be cooks, and to be bakers. And he will take your fields, and your vineyards, and your olive yards, even the best of them, and give them to his servants. And he will take the tenth of your seed, and of your vineyards, and give to his officers, and to his servants. And he will take your menservants, and your maidservants, and your goodliest young men, and your asses, and put them to his work. He will take the tenth of your sheep: and ye shall be his servants. And ye shall cry out in that day because of your king which ye shall have chosen you; and the LORD will not hear you in that day"* (1 Samuel 8:11-18).

The people listened to what Samuel said, but they still wanted a king so they could be like other nations who had kings to lead them into battle. The Lord told Samuel, *"Tomorrow about this time I will send thee a man out of the land of Benjamin, and thou shalt anoint him to be captain over my people Israel, that he may save my people out of the hand of the Philis'-tines: for I have looked upon my people, because their cry is come unto me. And when Samuel saw Saul, the LORD said unto him, Behold the man whom I spake to thee of! This same shall reign over my people"* (1 Samuel 9:16-17).

At the proper time, *"...Samuel took a vial of oil, and poured it upon his head, and kissed him, and said, Is it not because the LORD hath anointed thee to be captain over his inheritance?"* (1 Samuel 10:1).

In Samuel 10, we find that Samuel sent Saul out from him with prophetic instructions to go from place to place where he would find certain signs to look for along the way. The first sign would be two men that would tell him his father's Asses had been found; the second sign would be three men carrying kids, bread, and wine; and the third sign would be that he would meet a group of prophets carrying musical instruments, and prophesying. At that time, the Spirit of the Lord would come upon Saul, and he would also prophesy. Then Samuel instructed him to go to Gilgal to the *"hill of God,"* where the Philistine garrison was located and wait seven days for Samuel to come to him to offer burnt offerings and peace offerings to the Lord.

> *"And it was so, that when he had turned his back to go from Samuel, God gave him another heart: and all those signs came to pass that day. And when they came thither to the hill, behold, a company of prophets met him; and the spirit of God came upon him, and he prophesied among them"* (1 Samuel 10:9-10).

Samuel called all the people together in Mizpeh and told them,*"...Thus saith the LORD God of Israel...ye have this day rejected your God, who himself saved you out of all your adversities and your tribulations; and ye have said unto him, Nay, but set a king over us. Now therefore present yourselves before the LORD by your tribes, and by your thousands"* (1 Samuel 10:18-19). Then Samuel installed Saul as king and talked to them about kingdom living, writing the regulations down for them in a book. He also offered up burnt offerings and peace offerings unto the Lord.

Samuel told the people, *"Now therefore behold the king whom ye have chosen, and whom ye have desired! And, behold, the LORD hath set a king over you. If ye will fear the LORD, and serve him, and obey his voice, and not rebel against the commandment of the LORD, then shall both ye and also the king that reigneth over you continue following the LORD your God: But if ye will not obey the voice of the LORD, but rebel against the commandment of the LORD, then shall the hand of the LORD be against you, as it was against your fathers"* (1 Samuel 12:13-14)

> *"Is it not wheat harvest today? I will call unto the LORD, and he shall send thunder and rain; that ye may perceive and see that your wickedness is great, which ye have done in the sight of the LORD, in asking you a king. So Samuel called unto the LORD; and the LORD sent thunder and rain that day: and all the people greatly feared the LORD and Samuel. And all the people said unto Samuel, Pray for thy servants unto the LORD thy God, that we die not: for we have added unto all our sins this evil, to ask us a king"* (1 Samuel 12:17-19).

Saul Disobeys the Lord

King Saul was rebellious and liked doing things his own way, even if it meant disobeying God's commands. We see this pattern beginning to develop after he had been king for only two years. The Philistines came with 36,000 chariots and horsemen and an army too numerous to count. The Israelites were so afraid that they hid in every place they could find—caves and pits, and some even crossed the Jordan to seek refuge.

Saul waited seven days in Gilgal for Samuel to return, as Samuel had earlier instructed him to do, but Samuel was late. After some of the Hebrews had deserted Saul, he took things into his own hands, and offered the Lord's burnt offering to try and win God's favor against the Philistines. However, Saul was not a priest, and he was not authorized to make offerings. When Samuel arrived, and saw what Saul had done, he told him he had disobeyed the Lord's command, and now his kingdom would not last.

> *"...the Lord hath sought him a man after his own heart, and the LORD hath commanded him to be captain over his people, because thou hast not kept that which the LORD commanded thee"* (1 Samuel 13:14).

On another occasion, Samuel told Saul to attack and destroy the Amalekites. Saul was told that he and his soldiers were not to take any plunder, but they were to destroy everything and everybody—leaving no survivors, which would fulfill God's prophecy He had given to Moses in Exodus 17:14:

> *"...I will utterly put out the remembrance of Am'-a-lek from under heaven."*

After Saul and his army destroyed everything that was weak and kept the strong animals for themselves, Saul captured king Agag. The Lord told Samuel He was grieved over Saul's disobedience and was sorry that He had made Saul king. Samuel cried all night to the Lord about Saul. In the meantime, Saul also went to Carmel to *"...set up a monument in his own honor"* (I Samuel 15:12, NIV®).

When Samuel went to Saul to ask him why he had disobeyed the Lord, Saul lied to him and told him he had done everything the Lord had told him to do. Samuel could hear the noises of the animals that he had taken as plunder, and when he asked Saul about them, Saul cast blame on the people for bringing the best of the animals to sacrifice to the Lord. Samuel told him,*"...to obey is better than sacrifice, and to hearken than the fat of rams. For rebellion is as the sin of witchcraft, and stubbornness is as iniquity and idolatry. Because thou hast rejected the word of the LORD, he hath also rejected thee from being king"* (1 Samuel 15:22-23).

Saul confessed his sins and asked God's forgiveness, but God did not change His mind.

> *"...As Samuel turned to leave, Saul caught hold of the hem of his robe, and it tore. Samuel said to him, The LORD has torn the kingdom of Israel from you today and has given it to one of your neighbors—to one better than you"* (1 Samuel 15:27-28, NIV®).

Saul asked Samuel to stay with him so he could worship the Lord, then Samuel went and cut king Agag in pieces after he told Saul, *"... As thy sword hath made women childless, so shall thy mother be childless among women..."* (1 Samuel 15:33). Samuel and the Lord both grieved over Saul, but Samuel never saw him again.

The Lord Chooses a New King For Israel

One day, the Lord told Samuel to quit grieving over Saul, fill his horn with oil, and go to Bethlehem to see a man named Jesse (Ruth and Boaz's grandson). Samuel didn't want to go, because he was afraid Saul would find out and kill him.

> *"...And the LORD said, Take a heifer with thee, and say, I am come to sacrifice to the LORD. And call Jesse to the sacrifice, and*

I will show thee what thou shalt do: and thou shalt anoint unto
me him whom I name unto thee" (1 Samuel 16:2-3).

When Samuel arrived at Jesse's house, he consecrated Jesse and his sons and invited them to join him at the sacrifice. When Samuel saw Jesse's oldest son, Eliab, he was sure that he would be the one the Lord would choose as the new king; but the Lord told him he was not the one. The Lord said, *"...the LORD seeth not as man seeth; for man looketh on the outward appearance, but the LORD looketh on the heart"* (1 Samuel 16:7).

After Jesse had asked all seven of his sons to pass in front of Samuel, and the Lord had not chosen one as king, Samuel asked Jesse if he had any more sons. Jesse told him there was one more son, a shepherd boy, named David, who was out tending his sheep. Samuel told Jesse to bring him, and when he came, the Lord said, *"...Arise, anoint him: for this is he. Then Samuel took the horn of oil, and anointed him in the midst of his brethren: and the Spirit of the LORD came upon David from that day forward"* (1 Samuel 16:12-13).

The Spirit of the Lord had left Saul, and the Lord sent an evil spirit to torment him. One day, his servants recommended that he allow them to find someone who could play a harp to make him well. When Saul heard about the shepherd boy, David, who could play the harp, he sent for him. As time went on, Saul grew to love David and made him his armor-bearer.

"And it came to pass, when the evil spirit from God was upon
Saul, that David took a harp, and played with his hand: so Saul
was refreshed, and was well, and the evil spirit departed from
him" (I Samuel 16:23).

Saul asked Jesse's permission to allow David to stand before him, so David was allowed to go back and forth in order to continue tending his father's sheep. David was a shepherd over his father's sheep and was able to relate his own relationship with the Lord as his own Shepherd, penning the beautiful 23rd Psalm, *"The Lord is my shepherd...."*

David and the Giant Philistine

The Philistines were a thorn in the Israelites' side. When they were camped at Socoh in Judah with a valley between them and the Israelite army, the Philistines sent a man out from Gath, whose name was Goliath. He would stand in the valley and yell at Israel to come and kill him, with the promise that if they did, then the Philistines would concede and serve the Israelites. He said if they didn't kill him, the Israelites would serve the Philistines. Everyone, including Saul, was terrified of Goliath. Goliath came every day in the morning and then again in the evening for forty days, chiding the Israelites to come and fight with him. Goliath was a big man.

> *"He was more than nine feet tall. He had a bronze helmet on his head. He wore a coat of bronze armor. It weighed 125 pounds. On his legs he wore bronze guards. He carried a bronze javelin on his back. His spear was as big as a weaver's rod. Its iron point weighed 15 pounds. The man who carried his shield walked along in front of him"* (1 Samuel 17:5-7, NIrV®).

Jesse's three oldest sons were in the war camp with Saul, and so was David, when he wasn't tending his father's sheep at Bethlehem. One day, Jesse sent David with food for them and their commander so he could also check on the welfare of his sons. When David arrived, the soldiers on both sides were lined up for battle, and he could hear all the things Goliath was saying to defy Israel. David heard someone say, *"… the man who killeth him, the king will enrich him with great riches, and will give him his daughter, and make his father's house free in Israel"* (I Samuel 17:25).

When David heard this, he told them he would fight Goliath, but Saul tried to discourage him because he was only a boy. David quickly enlightened Saul and told him,

> *"…Thy servant kept his father's sheep, and there came a lion, and a bear, and took a lamb out of the flock: And I went out after him, and smote him, and delivered it out of his mouth: and*

when he arose against me, I caught him by his beard, and smote him, and slew him. Thy servant slew both the lion and the bear: and this uncircumcised Philis´-tine shall be as one of them, seeing he hath defied the armies of the living God. And David said moreover, The LORD that delivered me out of the paw of the lion, and out of the paw of the bear, He will deliver me out of the hand of this Philis´-tine. And Saul said unto David, Go, and the LORD be with thee" (1 Samuel 17:34-37).

Saul dressed David in his own armor and put a brass helmet on his head, but it was heavy and uncomfortable for David. He took off Saul's garments, took his staff, and went and found five smooth stones from the nearby creek. After putting the stones in his pouch, and with his sling in his hand, he approached Goliath. Goliath couldn't believe that there was a boy standing in front of him, who was supposed to kill him. He made fun of David and bragged about his own strength and victory over him.

David said to him, *"...Thou comest to me with a sword, and with a spear, and with a shield: but I come to thee in the name of the LORD of hosts, the God of the armies of Israel, whom thou hast defied. This day will the LORD deliver thee into mine hand; and I will smite thee, and take thine head from thee; and I will give the carcasses of the host of the Philis´-tines this day unto the fowls of the air, and to the wild beasts of the earth; that all the earth may know that there is a God in Israel"* (1 Samuel 17:45-46).

"...David put his hand in his bag, and took thence a stone, and slang it, and smote the Philis´-tine in his forehead, that the stone sunk into his forehead; and he fell upon his face to the earth" (1 Samuel 17:49).

"...David ran, and stood upon the Philis´-tine, and took his sword, and drew it out of the sheath thereof, and slew him, and cut off his head therewith. And when the Philis´-tines saw their champion was dead, they fled" (I Samuel 17:51).

David carried Goliath's head to Jerusalem and put Goliath's weapons in his own tent. When Saul asked to see David, he carried Goliath's head to him, as well. It was at that time, Jonathan, Saul's son, and David became best friends. Jonathan made a covenant with David, giving him some of his clothes and his sword, bow, and belt. At that time, David stopped living in his father's house and stayed with Saul and Jonathan.

Saul's Jealousy

Saul promoted David to a high-ranking position in his army, and David was successful in everything Saul told him to do. In fact, David was so successful that the Israelites were talking about it. One day Saul heard some Israelite women singing, *"...Saul hath slain his thousands, and David his ten thousands"* (1 Samuel 18:7). This made Saul jealous of David, fearing that David might eventually take his kingdom. He was so jealous that one day, while David was playing his harp for Saul, God sent an evil spirit that forced Saul to throw his javelin at David, but David managed to escape.

The Lord was no longer with Saul, but He was with David, and Saul became afraid of David. He sent him away to be in charge of over 1,000 of his men in some of his war campaigns, but David continued to be successful. *"...all Israel and Judah loved David..."* (1 Samuel 18:16). This bothered Saul even more, because he was afraid that Israel would love David more than him.

Saul made a deal with David that if David would serve him in battle, he would give him his daughter, Merab; but after David had obeyed Saul, he gave his daughter to Adriel, the Meholathite, instead. When Saul found out that another of his daughters, Michal, was in love with David, Saul devised a plan. He told David to bring him 100 Philistine foreskins, then after that he would give him Michal. The king was hoping the Philistines would kill David. David rose to the challenge, killed 200 Philistines and brought their foreskins to Saul. He married Saul's daughter, Michal, and became more successful in battle and more well known to Israel.

This enraged Saul even more, and he told Jonathan and his servants to kill David. Jonathan warned David of his father's plan and David went into hiding. Jonathan convinced his father not to kill David, because David had brought him so many benefits, and he was an innocent man. David came back and went to war again with the Philistines and slaughtered many. One day, while David was playing his harp for Saul, the Lord sent the evil spirit upon Saul again. The evil spirit forced Saul to try and kill David with his javelin, but he missed, and David escaped again. From that time on, Saul was out to kill David, and David began a life as a fugitive, with Saul and his men hot on his heels.

Saul told his son, Jonathan, *"For as long as the son of Jesse liveth upon the ground, thou shalt not be established, nor thy kingdom. Wherefore now send and fetch him unto me, for he shall surely die. And Jonathan answered Saul his father, and said unto him, Wherefore shall he be slain? What hath he done? And Saul cast a javelin at him to smite him: whereby Jonathan knew that it was determined of his father to slay David"* (1 Samuel 20:31-33).

Jonathan went to David and told him what Saul had said. The two of them wept, and made a covenant with each other, *"And Jonathan said to David, Go in peace, forasmuch as we have sworn both of us in the name of the LORD, saying, The LORD be between me and thee, and between my seed and thy seed for ever. And he arose and departed: and Jonathan went into the city"* (1 Samuel 20:42).

God had chosen Saul as king to fight Israel's enemies, the Philistine armies, and he did. When he wasn't busy doing that, he and his men would search for David to try to capture him and kill him. In fact, David literally spent about twenty years as a refugee, running for his life.

Saul was ruthless, and he hated David. One example of his ruthlessness was when Saul commanded his servant, Doeg, to go to Nob and kill eighty-five priests, men, women, children, and animals because Ahimelech, the priest, had helped David. David had not been completely honest with the priest and told him he was on king's business, and Ahimelech gave him the bread that was used for worship and Goliath's sword.

It just so happened that Doeg was also there that day and went and told king Saul what the priest had done to help David, and king Saul took revenge. David had seen Doeg, too, and he knew he had been recognized by him. He fled to king Achish of Gath and was recognized there, too. Out of fear, he portrayed himself as a mad man, and the king wanted nothing to do with him.

David escaped and hid away in the cave of Adullam, where about 400 men, who were outcasts, were there, too, and joined up with him. He became their captain, and they would join him in battles against the Philistines. The prophet, Gad, told David to leave and go to to Judah. While in Judah, the priest's son, Abiathar, who had escaped Saul's massacre at Nob, came and told David that Saul had killed the Lord's priests. David worried that Abiathar would now be sought out by Saul, too, and told him to stay with him where he would be protected. From then on, David was either hiding from Saul or he and his men were fighting the Philistines, and God gave them victories.

Saul and his men were always one step behind David, but God continuously protected David and his men from him. They went out into the wilderness in a mountain in Ziph where Saul looked for him everyday. Saul was always one step behind them. During that time, Saul's son, Jonathan, came to him and told him, *"...Fear not: for the hand of Saul my father shall not find thee; and thou shalt be king over Israel, and I shall be next unto thee; and that also Saul my father knoweth. And they two made a covenant before the LORD: and David abode in the wood, and Jonathan went to his house"* (I Samuel 23:17-18). Jonathan knew he would not become Israel's next king and that David would. He was not jealous or envious like his father, but he had love and respect for David.

David Protects the Lord's Anointed

During one of Saul's pursuits, he heard David was in the wilderness in Engedi. So he brought 3,000 men from Israel to pursue David. David and his men were hiding in a cave *"...upon the rocks of the wild goats"* (1 Samuel 24:2). It just so happened to be the same cave where Saul had stopped to go to the bathroom. David quietly came upon Saul and cut off the skirt of Saul's robe without him knowing it. David felt bad after that because he knew God had anointed Saul. He followed after Saul out of the cave and spoke to him:

> *"Behold, this day thine eyes have seen how that the LORD had delivered thee today into mine hand in the cave: and some bade me kill thee: but mine eye spared thee; and I said, I will not put forth mine hand against my lord; for he is the LORD'S anointed. Moreover, my father, see, yea, see the skirt of thy robe in my hand: for in that I cut off the skirt of thy robe, and killed thee not, know thou and see that there is neither evil nor transgression in mine hand, and I have not sinned against thee; yet thou huntest my soul to take it"* (1 Samuel 24:10-11).

Saul told David, *"...Thou art more righteous than I: for thou hast rewarded me good, whereas I have rewarded thee evil. And thou hast showed this day how that thou hast dealt well with me: forasmuch as when the LORD had delivered me into thine hand, thou killedst me not. For if a man find his enemy, will he let him go well away? Wherefore the LORD reward thee good for that thou hast done unto me this day. And now, behold, I know well that thou shalt surely be king, and that the kingdom of Israel shall be established in thine hand. Swear now therefore unto me by the LORD, that thou wilt not cut off my seed after me, and that thou wilt not destroy my name out of my father's house. And David sware unto Saul. And Saul went home; but David and his men gat them up unto the hold"* (1 Samuel 24:17-22).

Around that same time, Samuel died, and the Israelites mourned over his death and buried him at Ramah. David moved on to Maon, where he married two wives. (Saul had taken David's wife, Michal, and had given her to Phalti, the son of Lachish.)

David realized that Saul would probably seek him out again to try and kill him, so he and his, now 600, men and their families went to Gath in the land of the Philistines. One day, David heard Saul was close by, so he sent spies to overlook Saul's camp, and the Lord caused a deep sleep to fall upon Saul and his men. David and Abishai went down into the camp, and Abishai wanted to kill Saul. David would not let him bring harm to Saul, because he was the Lord's anointed. David took Saul's spear and his container of water and left his camp without anyone knowing he was there.

> *"Then David went over to the other side, and stood on the top of a hill afar off; a great space being between them: And David cried to the people, and to Abner the son of Ner, saying, Answerest thou not, Abner? Then Abner answered and said, Who art thou that criest to the king? And David said to Abner, Art not thou a valiant man? And who is like to thee in Israel? Wherefore then hast thou not kept thy lord the king? For there came one of the people in to destroy the king thy lord. This thing is not good that thou hast done. As the LORD liveth, ye are worthy to die, because ye have not kept your master, the LORD'S anointed. And now see where the king's spear is, and the cruse of water that was at his bolster"* (1 Samuel 26:13-16).

David also asked Saul who it was that stirred him up against him, causing him to want to kill him—was it the Lord or people? When Saul heard David, he once again confessed his sin:

> *"...I have sinned: return, my son David: for I will no more do thee harm, because my soul was precious in thine eyes this day: behold, I have played the fool, and have erred exceedingly"* (1 Samuel 26:21).

David loved Saul and had always recognized that Saul was the Lord's anointed, and he had respected that. Now, finally, David was free of Saul, and Saul never bothered him again. After the Lord delivered David from Saul and his other enemies, he wrote Psalm 18, a song to the Lord. Here are a few excerpts from that song that show the very heart of David:

> (Verses 1-3) *"I WILL love thee, O LORD, my strength. The LORD is my rock, and my fortress, and my deliverer; my God, my strength, in whom I will trust; my buckler, and the horn of my salvation, and my high tower. I will call upon the LORD, who is worthy to be praised: so shall I be saved from mine enemies.*

(Verses 31-35) *"For who is God, save the LORD? And who is a rock, save our God? God is my strength and power; and he maketh my way perfect. He maketh my feet like hinds' feet: and setteth me upon my high places. He teacheth my hands to war; so that a bow of steel is broken by mine arms. Thou hast also given me the shield of thy salvation: and thy gentleness hath made me great."*

(Verses 48-50) *"He delivereth me from mine enemies: yea, thou liftest me up above those that rise up against me: thou hast delivered me from the violent man. Therefore will I give thanks unto thee, O LORD, among the heathen, and sing praises unto thy name. Great deliverance giveth he to his king; and showeth mercy to his anointed, to David, and to his seed for evermore."*

The Demise of Saul

Later on, king Achish and the Philistines decided to go to war with Israel again, and the two armies camped where they could see each other. When Saul saw how large the Philistine army was, he consulted a witch for advice instead of going to the Lord. Earlier, Saul had expelled all the mediums and spiritists from his land, but now he sought one for himself. He told the woman to bring up Samuel, and the woman said she saw spirits coming up out of the earth. She told Saul, *"...An old man cometh up; and he is covered with a mantle. And Saul perceived that it was Samuel, and he stooped with his face to the ground, and bowed himself"* (1 Samuel 28:14). Samuel spoke to Saul:

"...the LORD hath rent the kingdom out of thine hand, and given it to thy neighbor, even to David: Because thou obeyedst not the voice of the LORD, nor executedst his fierce wrath upon Am'-a-lek, therefore hath the LORD done this thing unto this day. Moreover the LORD will also deliver Israel with thee into the hand of the Philis'-tines: and tomorrow shalt thou and thy sons be with me: the LORD also shall deliver the host of Israel into the hand of the Philis'-tines" (1 Samuel 28:17-19).

When the Philistines were preparing to war with Israel at Jezreel, the Philistine lords were not comfortable with David, Saul's servant, and his men accompanying them. So the king ordered David to take his men and go home, even though he had found no fault with David. When David and his men arrived at his home in Ziklag, everything had been burned up, and the Amalekites had taken all the people captive, even David's two wives. The Lord told David to go and fight and that he would succeed. David and 400 of his men and pursued the Amalekites. They came across an Egyptian, who was an abandoned slave to the Amalekites, and David asked him to help them find the Amalekites. When they found them, David and his men attacked and defeated them, except for some who escaped on camels, and they recovered all their people, flocks, and herds. David shared the plunder he obtained from the Amalekites with the Israelite tribes and each man received his own wife and children back, including David.

Just as had been prophesied to Saul, the Philistines went to war with the Israelites, and many Israelites were killed, including Saul, who had reigned over Israel for forty-two years, and his sons, Jonathan, Abindab, and Malki-Shua. Saul became seriously wounded.

"Then said Saul to his armor-bearer, Draw thy sword, and thrust me through therewith; lest these uncircumcised come and abuse me. But his armor-bearer would not; for he was sore afraid. So Saul took a sword, and fell upon it. And when his armor-bearer saw that Saul was dead, he fell likewise on the sword, and died. So Saul died, and his three sons, and all his house died together" (1 Chronicles 10:4-6).

After his death, the Philistines cut off Saul's head and took his armor, broadcasting the news of his death all through the land of the Philistines. They pinned Saul and his sons' bodies to the wall of Beth Shan, after putting his armor in their temple of idol worship. The people of Jabesh-Gilead went to Beth Shan and took their bodies down, burned them, and buried their bones at Jabesh.

Later, an Amalekite man who had been in Saul's camp, came and told David that Saul and Jonathan had died. When David asked him how he knew, he told him that he happened to come upon Saul who was being chased by the Philistines, and Saul spoke to him:

> "...*Stand, I pray thee, upon me, and slay me: for anguish is come upon me, because my life is yet whole in me. So I stood upon him, and slew him, because I was sure that he could not live after that he was fallen: and I took the crown that was upon his head, and the bracelet that was on his arm, and brought them hither unto my lord*" (2 Samuel 1:9-10).

> "*So Saul died for his transgression which he committed against the LORD, even against the word of the LORD, which he kept not, and also for asking counsel of one that had a familiar spirit, to inquire of it; And inquired not of the LORD...*" (1 Chronicles 10:13-14).

David asked the Amalekite, "*...How wast thou not afraid to stretch forth thine hand to destroy the LORD'S anointed? And David called one of the young men, and said, Go near, and fall upon him. And he smote him that he died. And David said unto him, Thy blood be upon thy head; for thy mouth hath testified against thee, saying, I have slain the LORD'S anointed*" (2 Samuel 1:14-16).

David was deeply grieved over the deaths of Saul and Jonathan and wrote a lament about them, which is recorded in 2 Samuel 1:19-25.

In Conclusion

The Lord appointed Samuel, a young man whose mother had dedicated him to the Lord even before his conception, to become Israel's last judge. Samuel would also be Israel's prophet and priest, anointing Israel's first two kings.

The Israelites had been not been satisfied with God as their King, and they had rejected Him. They wanted a king to lead them into battle like the other nations had. God gave them king Saul, who He had chosen to defeat Israel's enemies, the Philistines. Saul, however, was not to be the king God had in mind to be Israel's royal leader. David, a shepherd boy, who was *"a man after God's own heart,"* was the one God was preparing for the royal position.

Saul's jealousy over David caused David great agony and anxiety as he spent about twenty years of his life living as a refugee, running from one place to another to escape the murderous hands of Saul. These years brought fear, loneliness, and hunger. They also brought him closer to the Lord with each day as he saw the hand of God protecting and leading him. His close friendship with Saul's son, Jonathan, was also a constant encouragement.

Those years of hardship tested and proved the very heart of David. He wasn't perfect, and at times, he fell into fear, deception, and faithlessness; but he loved and obeyed the Lord. The suffering he endured prepared him for the important task that lie ahead—David, the prophesied, iconic Christ, will be Israel's next beloved king.

Deeper Insights:

1. Hannah was a sorrowful, barren woman who asked God for a child. Read the vow she made to God in 1 Samuel 1:11. How did Hannah keep her word to the Lord? Read 1 Samuel 1:28.

   Read Hannah's Song about the Lord. Read 1 Samuel 2:1-10.

2. The Lord had stopped appearing at His house in Shiloh because of the spiritual corruption of the Israelites. What happened when Samuel was serving in the Temple? Read 1 Samuel 3:21.

3. The Lord had been the Israelites' King from the beginning, and He had led them in victorious battles, but now they wanted a human king, but why? Read 1 Samuel 8:20.

   Read 1 Samuel 9:16. Why did God choose Saul from the tribe of Benjamin to be their new king?

4. When Samuel anointed David, what happened to David? Read 1 Samuel 16:13.

5. God gave Saul a new heart, and the Spirit of God came upon him. Yet, we find Saul rebelled against God's commands, exalted himself, and lied to Samuel. What did Samuel say to Saul? Read 1 Samuel 15:22-23.

   How do you think rebellion can be compared to witchcraft and stubbornness be compared to iniquity and idolatry?

   What did God do to Saul? Read 1 Samuel 16:14. Why do you think the evil spirit would depart when David played the harp?

6. In the beginning of their relationship, Saul loved David.

   Read 1 Samuel 18:5-9. What changed their relationship?

   Saul spent about twenty years chasing David down to kill him. David had opportunities to kill Saul, but why did he choose not to? Read 1 Samuel 24:4-7.

7. Read Psalm 52, David's prophesy of the demise of Doeg, Saul's servant, who had gone to the Tabernacle and killed eighty-five priests, men, women, children, and animals.

8. Read Psalm 54, where David asked God to save him from his enemies.

9. When Saul became afraid of the Philistines, he inquired of the Lord, but the Lord would not answer him. So he went to seek counsel from the witch of Endor. Read 1 Chronicles 10:13-14 to see why Saul died.

   God had given the Hebrews laws about the magic arts. Read the following scriptures to try and determine why God did not want them to become involved with the magic arts:

   Leviticus 19:31; 20:6, 27; Deuteronomy 18:9-14; Micah 5:12

   What does the New Testament say about the magic arts and those who practice them? Read

   Acts 13:6-12 and Galatians 5:19-20

CHAPTER 18

KING DAVID

David Becomes King of Judah

> *"He* (God) *chose David also his servant, and took him from the sheepfolds: from following the ewes great with young he brought him to feed Jacob his people, and Israel his inheritance. So he fed them according to the integrity of his heart; and guided them by the skillfulness of his hands"* (Psalm 78:70-72).

David relied on the Lord for everything in his life and upon His guidance in everything he did, and he was not afraid to do whatever the Lord told him to do. After Saul's death, David asked the Lord where he should go to live, and the Lord told him to go to Hebron in Judah, so David took his wives, and his men and went. The men of Judah anointed David as king over the house of Judah. At about the same time, Abner, Saul's army commander, took Saul's son, Ishbosheth, to Mahanaim *"...and made him king over Gilead, and over the Ash´-u-rites, and over Jez´-reel, and over E´-phra-im, and over Benjamin, and over all Israel"* (2 Samuel 2:9), where he reigned for two years. *"...But the house of Judah followed David"* (2 Samuel 2:10).

A long war broke out between the house of Saul and the house of David, and David became stronger, and the house of Saul grew weaker. Finally, Abner agreed to bring Israel into David's kingdom, and David asked him to bring Saul's daughter, Michal to him, as well. She was the wife Saul had promised to David, but gave to another man. Abner told the elders of Israel and those in Benjamin, *"...Ye sought for David in times past to be king over you: Now then do it: for the LORD hath spoken of David, saying, By the hand of my servant David I will save my people Israel out of the hand of the Philistines, and out of the hand of all their enemies"* (2 Samuel 3:17-18).

David's army commander, Joab, who had been out on raiding parties, returned to find that Abner had met with David, and David had sent him away in peace. Joab told David that Abner had only come to deceive him. Without David's knowledge, Joab overtook Abner and killed him, because earlier Abner had killed his brother at Gibeon. When David heard that Joab had killed Abner, he pronounced curses on Joab's house, and mourned over Abner. He said, *"the LORD shall reward the doer of evil according to his wickedness"* (2 Samuel 3:39).

Saul's son, Ishbosheth, who was reigning over Israel, became afraid when he heard that Abner had died in Hebron, and the news also troubled Israel. Two of Ishbosheth's men, who led bands of raiders, were Baanah and Rechab. They went into Ishbosheth's house and killed him and proudly took his head to David, saying, *"...Behold the head of Ish-bosh´-eth the son of Saul thine enemy, which sought thy life, and the LORD has avenged my lord the king this day of Saul and of his seed"* (2 Samuel 4:8). David was so angry he ordered their deaths and buried Ishbosheth's head in Abner's tomb.

David Is Anointed King of Israel

When David was about thirty years old, every tribe in Israel came to him saying, *"...we are thy bone and thy flesh. Also in time past, when Saul was king over us, thou wast he that leddest out and broughtest in Israel: and the LORD said to thee, Thou shalt feed my people Israel, and thou shalt be a captain over Israel"* (2 Samuel 5:1-2).

King David made a compact with the elders at Hebron, and they anointed him to be the king of Israel. He would be their king for forty years, reigning over Judah from Hebron for seven and a half years and over Israel and Judah from Jerusalem for thirty-three years. During these years, David had thirty-seven mighty men who were valiant and loyal to him and who fought fiercely and bravely in his battles. (2 Samuel 23:8-39 gives a list of these mighty men and acknowledges their honor and bravery.) King David and his men attacked the fort of the Jebusites, which was located high on a hill. *"...David took the stronghold of Zion: the same is the City of David"* (2 Samuel 5:7). This Jebusite city was a city the Benjamites had earlier failed to conquer. The Jebusites were descendants of Canaan, Noah's son (see Genesis 10:16).

> *"So David dwelt in the fort, and called it the city of David. And David built round about from Mil'-lo and inward. And David went on, and grew great, and the LORD God of hosts was with him. And Hiram king of Tyre sent messengers to David, and cedar trees, and carpenters, and masons: and they built David a house. And David perceived that the LORD had established him king over Israel, and that he had exalted his kingdom for his people Israel's sake"* (2 Samuel 5:9-12).

During that time, David fathered six sons while in Hebron, all born of different wives (see 2 Samuel 3:2-5). Then he took more wives and concubines and had eleven more sons (their names are recorded in 2 Samuel 5:14-15).

David Brings the Ark to Jerusalem

One day David consulted with the captains, the leaders, and the Israelites:

> *"...If it seem good unto you, and that it be of the LORD our God, let us send abroad unto our brethren everywhere, that are left in all the land of Israel, and with them also to the priests and Levites which are in their cities and suburbs, that they may gather themselves unto us: And let us bring again the ark of our God to us: for we inquired not at it in the days of Saul. And all the congregation said that they would do so: for the thing was right in the eyes of all the people"* (1 Chronicles 13:2-4). *"And David*

made him houses in the city of David, and prepared a place for
the ark of God, and pitched for it a tent" (1 Chronicles 15:1).

The Ark of God was carried on a new cart and brought from the house of Abinadab, where it had remained for twenty years in Gibeah. Uzzah and Ahio, sons of Abinadab, were guiding the new cart with the Ark of God on it, and Ahio was walking in front of it. David and the whole house of Israel were celebrating with all their might before the Lord, with songs and with all their instruments. When they reached the place of the threshing floor, the oxen shook the cart, and Uzzah put his hand on the Ark to keep it from falling. God killed him for touching the Ark, and he died. The wrath of God made David afraid to bring the Ark to the city of David, and he left it at the house of Obededom the Gittite for three months, where the Lord blessed the entire family. When David went to bring the Ark of God to the city of David again, he went about it differently than before. This time he told the Levites, *"... None ought to carry the ark of God but the Levites: for them hath the LORD chosen to carry the ark of God, and to minister unto him for ever"* (1 Chronicles 15:2).

> *"Then David summoned the priests...and the Levite leaders.... He said to them, 'You are the leaders of the Levite families. You must purify yourselves and all your fellow Levites, so you can bring the ark of the LORD, the God of Israel, to the place I have prepared for it. Because you Levites did not carry the ark the first time, the anger of the LORD our God burst out against us. We failed to ask God how to move it in the proper way'"* (1 Chronicles 15:11-13, NLT).

After purifying themselves, *"...the Levites carried the ark of God on their shoulders with its carrying poles, just as the LORD had instructed Moses. David also ordered the Levite leaders to appoint a choir of Levites who were singers and musicians to sing joyful songs to the accompaniment of lyres, harps, and cymbals"* (1 Chronicles 15:15-16, NLT).

> *"...So David went and brought up the ark of God from the house of O´-bed-e´-dom into the city of David with gladness. And it was*

so, that when they that bare the ark of the LORD had gone six paces, he sacrificed oxen and fatlings. And David danced before the LORD with all his might; and David was girded with a linen e´-phod. So David and all the house of Israel brought up the ark of the LORD with shouting, and with the sound of the trumpet" (2 Samuel 6:12-15).

Michal, David's wife, looked out her window, and when she saw David dancing with celebration, she hated him. When the Ark of the Lord reached the city, it was placed on Mount Zion in the tent that king David had prepared for it. He made burnt offerings and peace offerings to the Lord, and the Levites led the people in worship and in giving thanks to the Lord. Afterwards David gave bread, meat, and wine to every man and woman. David re-established the Levitical priestly order and sacrificial system in the Tabernacle, according to Moses. When David arrived at home to bless his household, his wife, Michal said hateful words to him:

> *"...How glorious was the king of Israel today, who uncovered himself today in the eyes of the handmaids of his servants, as one of the vain fellows shamelessly uncovereth himself! And David said unto Michal, It was before the LORD, which chose me before thy father, and before all his house, to appoint me ruler over the people of the LORD, over Israel: therefore will I play before the LORD. And I will yet be more vile than thus, and will be base in mine own sight: and of the maidservants which thou hast spoken of, of them shall I be had in honor. Therefore Michal the daughter of Saul had no child unto the day of her death"* (2 Samuel 6:20-23).

God Established David's Family Forever

After David had been living peacefully in his palace for a while, he began to feel bad that he had a beautiful palace made of cedar wood, and the Lord was living in a tent. David talked to Nathan, the prophet, about it, and Nathan told him to go and do what he wanted, but that night the Lord spoke to Nathan about His own plan for the future:

> *"Go and tell my servant David...I have not dwelt in any house since the time that I brought up the children of Israel out of Egypt, even to this day, but have walked in a tent and in a tabernacle. In all the places wherein I have walked with all the children of Israel spake I a word with any of the tribes of Israel, whom I commanded to feed my people Israel, saying, Why build ye not me a house of cedar?*

> *"...I took thee from the sheepcote from following the sheep, to be ruler over my people, over Israel: And I was with thee whithersoever thou wentest, and have cut off all thine enemies out of thy sight, and have made thee a great name, like unto the name of the great men that are in the earth. Moreover I will appoint a place for my people Israel, and will plant them, they may dwell in a place of their own, and move no more; neither shall the children of wickedness afflict them any more, as beforetime. And as since the time that I commanded judges to be over my people Israel, and have caused thee to rest from all thine enemies. Also the LORD telleth thee that he will make thee a house.* (The Lord is talking about David's family line to Jesus.)

> *"And when thy days be fulfilled, and thou shalt sleep with thy fathers, I will set up thy seed* (David's son)*after thee, which shall proceed out of thy bowels, and I will establish his kingdom. He shall build a house for my name, and I will stablish the throne of his kingdom for ever. I will be his father, and he shall be my son. If he commit iniquity, I will chasten him with the rod of men, and with the stripes of the children of men: But my mercy shall not depart away from him, as I took it from Saul, whom I put away before thee. And thine house and thy kingdom shall be established for ever before thee: thy throne shall be established for ever"* (2 Samuel 7:5-16).

This seed from David, who would build God's earthly house, would be his son, Solomon; but the throne that would be established forever would be the throne of Jesus Christ. David spoke to the Lord:

> *"And what nation in the earth is like thy people, even like Israel, whom God went to redeem for a people to himself, and to make him a name, and to do for you great things and terrible, for thy land, before thy people, which thou redeemedst to thee from Egypt, from the nations and their gods? For thou hast confirmed to thyself thy people Israel to be a people unto thee for ever: and thou, LORD, art become their God. And now, O LORD God, the word that thou hast spoken concerning thy servant, and concerning his house, establish it for ever, and do as thou hast said"* (2 Samuel 7:23-25).

David Enlarges His Kingdom

David began to enlarge his territory, and he defeated the Philistines and the Moabites, forcing them to become his servants. He defeated king Hadadezer of Zobah and recovered his border along the Euphrates River, gaining much wealth in chariots, horses, and soldiers. When the Syrians came to help Hadadezer, David killed 22,000 of them, and they also became his servants. He took brass and the gold shields that belonged to Hadaezer's servants. King Toi of Hamath sent his son, Joram, to David with items of silver, gold, and brass to congratulate David in his victory over Hadadezer, which David dedicated to the Lord, as he had done with the silver and gold he had plundered from the other nations. Then David also made servants of the Edomites and the Ammonites.

David was a good king to his people, and he loved the Lord. He did everything the Lord told him to do and was fair with all people, and the Lord gave him success in all that he put his hand to. Besides David's *"mighty men,"* he set up righteous leaders around him: a recorder, priests, a scribe, prince guardians, and chief rulers.

Even though David was busy conquering other nations, he could not forget about his love for Jonathan, Saul's son. He asked if there were any living relatives from Saul's household that he could show kindness to honor his beloved Jonathan. Ziba, a servant of Saul's household, told David that Jonathan had a living son named Mephibosheth, who was crippled in his feet. David sent for him and told him, *"...Fear not: for I will surely show thee kindness for Jonathan thy father's sake, and will restore thee all the land of Saul thy father; and thou shalt eat bread at my table continually"* (2 Samuel 9:7). So David gave Mephibosheth *"...all that pertained to Saul and to all his house"* (2 Samuel 9:9).

King David Sins With Bathsheba

David had a heart for God, but, like all humans, he had been born with a sin nature, and Satan, *"...the prince of the power of the air..."* (Ephesians 2:2), would take advantage of this sin nature. He had every reason to want to ruin David. After all, Jesus would be born of his lineage and would be called the *"Son of David"* (Matthew 1:1).

It was in the springtime, *"...when kings go forth to battle..."* (2 Samuel 11:1), that David sent Joab and his army out to fight the Ammonites; but David stayed home and didn't go. One evening, as he arose from his bed and went out on his roof, he noticed a beautiful woman who was bathing. He inquired and found out that Bathsheba was married to Uriah, a Hittite. Lust got the best of him, and he sent for her anyway. He had sex with her, and later she told him she had become pregnant. David sent for her husband to come to him from the battlefield, and he told him to go home to his house and wash his feet. He was hoping that Uriah would have sex with his wife, Bathsheba, to make it seem like the baby was his. However, when Uriah left David, he didn't go home but stayed and slept in the palace with the servants. He was a noble man. When David asked him why he didn't go home, he said, *"...The ark, and Israel, and Judah, abide in tents; and my lord Jo'-ab, and the servants of my lord, are encamped in the open fields; shall I then go into mine house, to eat and to drink, and to lie with my wife? as thou livest, and as thy soul liveth, I will not do this thing"* (2 Samuel 11:11).

David urged Uriah to stay another day with him and made him drunk, but Uriah still slept in the palace with the servants. Out of desperation to conceal his sin, David wrote a letter to Joab, his army commander, and sent it to him with Uriah when he went back to the war. The letter said, *"...Set ye U-ri´-ah in the forefront of the hottest battle, and retire ye from him, that he may be smitten, and die"* (2 Samuel 11:15).

Joab did what the king said, and Uriah was killed. Uriah's wife grieved over her husband, and then David married her, and she gave birth to a son. However, the Lord was not happy about what David had done.

> *"And the LORD sent Nathan unto David. And he came unto him, and said unto him, There were two men in one city; the one rich, and the other poor. The rich man had exceeding many flocks and herds: But the poor man had nothing, save one little ewe lamb, which he had bought and nourished up: and it grew up together with him, and with his children; it did eat of his own meat, and drank of his own cup, and lay in his bosom, and was unto him as a daughter. And there came a traveler unto the rich man, and he spared to take of his own flock and of his own herd, to dress for the wayfaring man that was come unto him; but took the poor man's lamb, and dressed it for the man that was come to him.*

> *"And David's anger was greatly kindled against the man; and he said to Nathan, As the LORD liveth, the man that hath done this thing shall surely die: And he shall restore the lamb fourfold, because he did this thing, and because he had no pity.*

> *"And Nathan said to David, Thou art the man. Thus saith the LORD God of Israel, I anointed thee king over Israel, and I delivered thee out of the hand of Saul; And I gave thee thy master's house, and thy master's wives into thy bosom, and gave thee the house of Israel and of Judah; and if that had been too*

little, I would moreover have given unto thee such and such things. Wherefore hast thou despised the commandment of the LORD, to do evil in his sight? thou hast killed U-ri´-ah the Hit´-tite with the sword, and hast taken his wife to be thy wife, and hast slain him with the sword of the children of Ammon.

"Now therefore the sword shall never depart from thine house; because thou hast despised me, and hast taken the wife of U-ri´-ah the Hit´-tite to be thy wife. Thus saith the LORD, Behold, I will raise up evil against thee out of thine own house, and I will take thy wives before thine eyes, and give them unto they neighbor, and he shall lie with thy wives in the sight of this sun. For thou didst it secretly: but I will do this thing before all Israel, and before the sun."

David's heart was filled with remorse. He told Nathan, *"…I have sinned against the LORD. And Nathan said unto David, The LORD also hath put away thy sin; thou shalt not die. Howbeit, because by this deed thou hast given great occasion to the enemies of the LORD to blaspheme, the child also that is born unto thee shall surely die"* (2 Samuel 12:1-14).

David's heart was broken that he had sinned against the Lord—lust, adultery, deception, and murder. He wrote these Psalms to the Lord regarding his sins.

Psalm 51: (Verses 1-4) *"Have mercy upon me, O God, according to thy loving-kindness: according unto the multitude of thy tender mercies blot out my transgressions. Wash me thoroughly from mine iniquity, and cleanse me from my sin. For I acknowledge my transgressions: and my sin is ever before me. Against thee, thee only, have I sinned, and done this evil in thy sight…"*

(Verses 10-12) *"Create in me a clean heart, O God; and renew a right spirit within me. Cast me not away from thy presence; and take not thy Holy Spirit from me. Restore unto me the joy of thy salvation; and uphold me with thy free Spirit."*

(Verses 16-17) *"For thou desirest not sacrifice; else would I give it: Thou delightest not in burnt offering. The sacrifices of God are a broken spirit: a broken and a contrite heart, O God, thou will not despise."*

Psalm 32:5: *"I acknowledged my sin unto thee, and mine iniquity have I not hid. I said, I will confess my transgressions unto the LORD; and thou forgavest the iniquity of my sin. Selah."*

God's Judgment Upon David's House

David had repented, but God would still bring His judgment upon David's house. After Nathan left, the Lord struck David and Bathsheba's son with an illness, and he died.

"And David comforted Bath-she'-ba his wife, and went in unto her, and lay with her: and she bare a son, and he called his name Solomon: and the LORD loved him. And he sent by the hand of Nathan the prophet; and he called his name Jed-i-di'-ah, because of the LORD" (2 Samuel 12:24).

The Hebrew word translated *Jedidiah* is "Yᵉdîydᵉyâh." The meaning of the word is "...beloved of Jah...".[1] The Hebrew word translated *Jah is* "Yâhh." The meaning of the word is "...the Lord, most vehement....".[3]

Even though God blessed David and Bathsheba with Solomon, the Lord's prophecies of judgment against David's house continued to come to pass. David's son, Absalom, had a virgin sister named Tamar, and David's other son, Amnon, fell in love with her and raped her. When Absalom heard what happened to his sister, he took her into his house and let her live there. David heard about what had happened, and he was angry. Two years after the rape incident, Absalom planned Amnon's murder and ordered his men to kill him. After the murder, he ran away and stayed with Talmai, the son of the king of Geshur, for three years. David mourned for Amnon, his son, for a season and then after three years, he longed to see Absalom. Through Joab's intervention, David allowed Absalom to come back to live in Jerusalem in his own house, but he was not yet ready to see him.

After two years of not seeing his father, Absalom sent for Joab, who arranged a meeting with David. When Absalom came, he bowed down, and his father kissed him. Absalom was next in line to be king, but he was not the one the Lord had in mind. David's other son, Solomon, not Absalom, would be the next king. This led Absalom to form a conspiracy against David.

For four years he played the Israelites into his hand trying to convince them that they needed a judge and that he would be a good judge who could bring justice to them. He would do this when the people were on their way to see king David to ask him for justice.

Then one day he deceptively asked the king for permission to go to Hebron because he had vowed to the Lord he would go there to worship, so David let him go. Absalom took 200 men with him from Jerusalem, but they were unaware of his evil plan.

"...Ab´-sa-lom sent spies throughout all the tribes of Israel, saying, As soon as ye hear the sound of the trumpet, then ye shall say, Ab´-sa-lom reigneth in He´-bron" (2 Samuel 15:10).

He had gathered a large group of people as he was planning his conspiracy, and had gained the love and loyalty of the Israelites. When king David heard what was happening, he gathered his household, his servants, and all his men, leaving ten concubines to take care of his house and left the palace in Jerusalem so that Absalom would not come and attack and kill them. All along the way, people cried when they saw the king's procession leaving their kingdom, heading out into the desert and crossing over the brook of Kidron. Zadok, the priest, and the Levites were with David, too, carrying the Ark of the Covenant of God. When the Ark was set down, king David ordered Zadok, Abiathar, and their two sons, to take the Ark of the Covenant back to Jerusalem. David, and the people with him, walked up to the Mount of Olives. Their heads were covered, and David walked in his bare feet.

They were all weeping. David heard that Ahithophel, his advisor, was also a conspirator, alongside Absalom. *"...the counsel of A-hith´-o-phel, which he counseled in those days, was as if a man had inquired at the oracle of God: so was all the counsel of A-hith´-o-phel both with David and with Ab´-sa-lom"* (2 Samuel 16:23). So David prayed that his councel would be turned into foolishness.

After David climbed to the top of the mountain and worshiped God, he met Hushai, his friend, the Archite. David told him to go back to Jerusalem and lie to Absalom, saying that he would be his servant. He told him to go and stay in the palace and report everything he heard to the priests, Zadok and Abiathar. They, in turn, would send their sons to report back to David. After going a little farther, David met Ziba, Mephibosheth's steward, who brought him donkeys, food, and wine for David's household and his men. Earlier, David had given Ziba everything that had belonged to Jonathan's son, Mephibosheth, who was living in Jerusalem. Mephibosheth had been heartsick after David left the kingdom.

The Death of Absalom

Absalom and all those with him went to Jerusalem. As had been prophesied by Nathan, Absalom had sex with his David's concubines on the roof for everyone to see. Ahithophel's councel was turned to foolishness when David's friend, Hushai, foiled his plan to take 12,000 men to pursue and kill David and bring his people back. Instead, Hushai advised Absalom to lead his men in a surprise attack and then he sent a message to David advising him about what was going to take place. (The Lord had planned this so evil would come upon Absalom.) Absalom took Hushai's advice, and he also appointed Amasa to take Joab's place as commander. Ahithophel hung himself because Absalom had taken Hushai's advice instead of his own.

David and his people traveled to the city of Mahanaim, where the people supplied them with food to eat. When Absalom and Israel crossed over the Jordan, the people of Mahanaim told David to wait by the city gate and they would enter into the battle with Absalom instead of him. David told his commanding officers to be careful with his son, Absalom. They defeated Absalom, who lost 20,000 Israelite men in that battle in Ephraim. After the battle, Absalom was riding his mule and met David's servants. His mule ran under some thick boughs of an oak tree, which caught him up in the air away from his mule. The mule ran away, leaving Absalom hanging from the tree. A little later, Joab came by and struck Absalom with darts in his heart, then some of Joab's armor-bearers came along and finished killing him, and they buried him under a pile of stones. When David heard about his son's death, he wept and grieved so much that he discouraged the men who had brought him victory in the battle with Absalom. Joab talked with Davd:

> *"Today you have humiliated all your men, who have just saved your life and the lives of your sons and daughters and the lives of your wives and concubines. You love those who hate you and hate those who love you. You have made it clear today that the commanders and their men mean nothing to you. I see that you would be pleased if Absalom were alive today and all of us were dead. Now go out and encourage your men…if you don't go out, not a man will be left with you by nightfall"* (2 Samuel 19:5-7).

The Israelites had all gone home, thinking that king David had ran away after hearing about his son, Absalom, and they were not interested in bringing him back as king, and David knew it. As he sat in the Gate, king David sent a message to the priests, Zadok and Abiathar, to speak to the elders of Judah: *"Ye are my brethren, ye are my bones and my flesh: wherefore then are ye the last to bring back the king? And say ye to A-ma´-sa, Art thou not of my bone, and of my flesh? God do so to me, and more also, if thou be not captain of the host before me continually in the room of Jo´-ab. And he bowed the heart of all the men of Judah, even as the heart of one man; so that they sent this word unto the king, Return thou, and all thy servants"* (2 Samuel 19:12-14

David Regains His Kingdom

When the king reached the Jordan, the men of Judah, and Shimei, along with over 1,000 other Benjamites from the tribe of Benjamin, met him at Gilgal to bring him across the river and to ferry his household across. Shimei had cursed David the day he was leaving Jerusalem. He now fell down before king David and said, *"...Let not my lord impute iniquity unto me, neither do thou remember that which thy servant did perversely the day that my lord the king went out of Jerusalem, that the king should take it to his heart. For thy servant doth know that I have sinned: therefore, behold, I am come the first this day of all the house of Joseph to go down to meet my lord the king"* (2 Samuel 19:19-20). Now we will, once again, see the heart of David—this could have been a death penalty, but David pardoned him.

Saul's son, Mephibosheth, whom David had fed at his own table, came down to meet David. David asked him why he had not gone with him when David had left Jerusalem. Mephibosheth told him, *"...My lord, O king, my servant deceived me: for thy servant said, I will saddle me an ass, that I may ride thereon, and go to the king; because thy servant is lame. And he hath slandered thy servant unto my lord the king; but my lord the king is as an angel of God: do therefore what is good in thine eyes"* (2 Samuel 19:26-27). David's heart was tender towards him, and he told Mephibosheth that he and Ziba were to divide the land, but he told the king to give it all to Ziba.

Then came Barzillai, the old man who had provided David with food. David asked him to come with him to live in Jerusalem, but he, being old, and not wanting to be a burden to the king, asked that David take his servant, Chimham, in his place, and allow him to go to his own home.

After that, all the people went over the Jordan with the king, including Chimhan, all the people of Judah, and half of Israel.

The men from the ten tribes of Israel questioned the king as to why the men of Judah stole him and took him over the Jordan. The men of Judah responded, *"...the king is near of kin to us: wherefore then be ye angry for this matter? have we eaten at all of the king's cost? Or hath he given us any gift?"* (2 Samuel 19:42).

The men of Israel said, *"...We have ten parts in the king and we have also more right in David than ye: why then did ye despise us, that our advice should not be first had in bringing back our king?"* (2 Samuel 19:43).

Sheba, a man of Belial, who was the son of a Benjamite *"...blew a trumpet, and said, We have no part in David, neither have we inheritance in the son of Jesse: every man to his tents, O Israel"* (2 Samuel 20:1).

The tribes of Israel abandoned king David and followed Sheba, but the tribes of Judah and Benjamin stayed in support of king David. So David returned to Jerusalem as king over Judah and Israel, from the Jordan to Jerusalem. He kept the concubines who had had sex with his son—the women he had left to watch his palace, but he kept them in confinement and never had sex with them again.

One day, David sent Amasa out to assemble the men of Judah, including himself, to come to him in three days, but he did not return in that allotted time. King David was concerned that Sheba might escape and build cities of defense, bringing harm to Judah. So he sent Abishai (who served under Amasa) and his men, including Joab, the Cherethites, the Pelethites, and David's mighty men, out to pursue Sheba. Along the way, Joab killed Amasa with his sword.

When Joab and his men arrived in the town of Abel looking for Sheba, the citizens, who were filled with fear, cut off Sheba's head and threw it to them from over the wall.

God Avenges the Land of Israel

A famine came upon the land that lasted for three years, and David asked the Lord why. The Lord told him, *"...It is for Saul, and for his bloody house, because he slew the Gib´-eonites"* (2 Samuel 21:1).

David asked the Gibeonites, *"What shall I do for you? And wherewith shall I make the atonement, that ye may bless the inheritance of the LORD?"* (2 Samuel 21:3) They asked that seven male descendants of Saul be handed over to them. David gave them seven sons of Saul, and the Gibeonites killed them; but David spared Mephibosheth, Saul's grandson.

*"And he brought up from thence the bones of Saul and the bones
of Jonathan his son; and they gathered the bones of them that were
hanged. And the bones of Saul and Jonathan his son buried they
in the country of Benjamin in Ze´-lah, in the sepulcher of Kish
his father: and they performed all that the king commanded. And
after that God was entreated for the land"* (2 Samuel 21:13-14).

Goliath had defied Israel's army when David was but a shepherd boy,
and now God would avenge Israel for that. As the Israelites continued
to war with the Philistines, one by one, Goliath's four sons fell to their
death. The Bible gives a description of the death of Goliath's last son:

He *"...was a man of great stature, that had on every hand six
fingers, and on every foot six toes, four and twenty in number;
and he also was born to the giant. And when he defied Israel,
Jonathan the son of Shim´-e-a the brother of David slew him.
These four were born to the giant in Gath, and fell by the hand
of David, and by the hand of his servants"* (2 Samuel 20:22).

David's song of deliverance is recorded in 2 Samuel 22. In verses
2 and 3, the king declares this: *"...the LORD is my rock, and my fortress,
and my deliverer; the God of my rock...the horn of my salvation...."* In 2 Samuel
23:3, he calls the God of Israel *"...the Rock of Israel."*

David Sins Again

*"And Satan stood up against Israel, and provoked David to
number Israel"* (1 Chronicles 21:1).

David gave Joab orders to go and enroll the fighting men so he would
know how many there were, but Joab knew this was not of the Lord. He
told David he didn't need to do this, because the Lord could make many
more men for war. The census took nine months and twenty days to
complete. There were 800,000 men in Israel and 500,000 men in Judah

who were able to fight and carry a sword (2 Samuel 24:9), not counting the men of Levi and Benjamin. The Lord was not happy with David. David repented that he had sinned against the Lord, and the Lord sent his seer, Gad, to him to give him three options for punishment for his sin: seven years of famine, running from his enemies for three years, or a plague that would last for three days; but David could not choose—he would leave the decision up to the Lord.

> *"... let us fall now into the hand of the LORD; for his mercies are great: and let me not fall into the hand of man"* (2 Samuel 24:14).

The Hebrew word translated *seer is* "chôzeh." The meaning of the word is "...a beholder in vision...."[3]

So the Lord sent a plague to Israel and killed 70,000 people.

> *"And when the angel stretched out his hand upon Jerusalem to destroy it, the LORD repented him of the evil, and said to the angel that destroyed the people, It is enough...And David spake unto the LORD when he saw the angel that smote the people, and said, Lo, I have sinned, and I have done wickedly: but these sheep, what have they done? Let thine hand, I pray thee, be against me, and against my father's house..."* (2 Samuel 24:16-17).

Gad told David, *"...Go up, rear an altar unto the LORD in the threshing floor of A-rau´-nah the Jeb´-u-site"* (2 Samuel 24:18). When he did, Araunah (Or´-nan) saw the angel, and he and his sons hid. When David approached Araunah to buy the place of the threshing floor to stop the plague, Araunah wanted to give it to him, but David said, *"...Nay; but I will verily buy it for the full price: for I will not take that which is thine for the LORD, nor offer burnt offerings without cost"* (1 Chronicles 21:24).

So David bought the threshing floor and some oxen and built an altar, where he offered a sacrifice to the Lord. When he did, the Lord stopped the plague on Israel, *"...and the Lord was entreated for the land"* (2 Samuel 24:25).

"...the tabernacle of the LORD, which Moses made in the wilderness, and the altar of the burnt offering, were at that season in the high place at Gib´-eon. But David could not go before it to inquire of God: for he was afraid because of the sword of the angel of the LORD" (I Chronicles 21:29-30).

2 Samuel 23:2-5 records a song David sang to the Lord to acknowledge Israel's everlasting covenant with the Lord—the Rock:

> *"The Spirit of the LORD spake by me, and his word was in my tongue. The <u>God of Israel</u> said, the <u>Rock of Israel</u> spake to me, He that ruleth over men must be just, ruling in the fear of God. And he shall be as the light of the morning, when the sun riseth, even a morning without clouds; as the tender grass springing out of the earth by clear shining after rain.*

> *"Although my house be not so with God; yet he hath made with me an <u>everlasting covenant</u>, ordered in all things and sure: for this is all my salvation, and all my desire, although he make it not to grow."*

In Conclusion

The Israelites had not listened to what God had said about clearing their new land of all its enemies, and this disobedience had brought much chaos and sin to their lives. God chose the shepherd boy, David, to lead the Israelites back to His law and commandments. David's own trials, sufferings, and battle victories had prepared him for the position of king. The Bible shows that David had a deep emotional heart for God, and the Psalms that he wrote paint a beautiful picture of his heart. He proved he was capable of sinning just like all of mankind, yet the Bible says he was a man after God's own heart (see I Samuel 13:14). How can that be? David loved God with all of his heart, mind, and soul and longed to be obedient to Him. When he sinned, his heart was filled with godly sorrow and repentance.

After God told David to move to Hebron in Judah, David became the king over Judah and Saul's house of Israel. God also gave him victory over the Jebusites who controlled the fort of Zion, which was located on a high hill. After conquering Zion, David lived in the fort, which he named the *"city of David,"* Jerusalem. David brought the Ark to Jerusalem and re-established the Law of Moses, including the Levitical priesthood and sacrificial system. God would, once again, bring atonement to His people.

Even though God meant everything to David, he allowed his own sin nature to lead him into adultery, deception, and murder. God's mercy rained upon him after he sorrowfully repented, but death, rape, murder, betrayal, and even the temporary loss of his kingdom, would become the consequences of God's judgment upon his family.

After reigning as king for over forty years, David watched as ten tribes deserted him, and he saw the loyalty of Judah and Benjamin, who remained at his side. After regaining control of his kingdom, God avenged the land because of Saul's murders and ended the family line of Goliath, who had defied Israel.

God had denied David the right to build His house because of the blood of war on his hands; but at the same time, He promised David an everlasting covenant through his son, Solomon, and his descendants. Christ would come from the house of David and sit on David's throne.

Deeper Insights:

1. Almost half of the Psalms in the Book of Psalms are attributed to David in some way, but not necessarily by his authorship. He wrote messages of praise and worship, love, trust, repentance, and expressed his total reliance upon his God. He withheld nothing from the Lord—not even his sins. If he felt something, feared something, or even questioned something, he went to the Lord, and he wrote about it. David gives all of us hope as we read about the struggles and sins he experienced, and yet received God's forgiveness, love, and mercy, reminding us that

God looks upon the condition of our hearts toward Him. It is about our relationship with Him. Read Psalm 103 to begin to understand the depth of love and gratefulness in David's heart for the mercy of God.

2. There are a few similarities between David and Christ

    a. David's name points to Christ. The Hebrew word translated *David*, is "daw-veed´." The meaning of the word is "...loving...."[4]

    b. David was a shepherd to his sheep and to his people, and he believed the Lord to be his own Shepherd. The Lord is the Shepherd to everyone who believes in Him and obeys Him. Read: Isaiah 40:9-11; Ezekiel 34:11-16, 22-25; John 10:11, 14; Hebrews 13:20-21; and 1 Peter 2:25, 5:2-4

    c. David suffered a great deal, and Christ is seen as the suffering Servant; but neither one took the road of unforgiveness or revenge. Read Psalm 22 and note the ways that this Psalm says that Christ suffered.

        David and Christ both suffered betrayal. Thinking back on what we have read about David, in what ways was he betrayed?

        Read Matthew 26:14-16, 22-24, and 47-50 to see how Judas betrayed Jesus.

    d. Christ was a descendant of David. Read: Jeremiah 23:5-6, 33:14-16 and Matthew 9:27

    e. David's love for the Lord caused him to bring the Ark (God's house) to Jerusalem to re-establish a central place of worship for the Israelites and re-establish God's laws for holy living. The Israelites were already living idolatrous lives before Saul became king, and he did not lead them back to the Lord. In fact, he did not even inquire of the Ark the whole time he was king. David re-established the sacrificial system and the Levitical priesthood. Why do you think it was important for David to re-establish the Law of Moses and the sacrificial system?

   f. The Davidic covenant was fulfilled in Christ when He was born in Bethlehem, the same town that David had been born in. Read Matthew 1:1-6, 20-23; Luke 1:30-33, 68-79; and 2:4-7.

3. David surrounded Himself with his *"mighty men."* Read 2 Samuel 23:8-39 to learn more about these men.

4. God made a covenant with David. God promised David that an everlasting kingdom and an everlasting throne would be established through his son, Solomon. Read 2 Samuel 7:12-16.

Here are a few scriptures that contain prophetic promises of God's covenant with David, which refer to David as a type of Christ, and at times, even Christ, Himself.

Read: Psalms 78:65-71, 89:3-4, 18-37; Isaiah 55:3-5; Jeremiah 30:8-9; Ezekiel 34:22-24, 37:24-28; and Matthew 22:41-44.

5. David was a man who sinned. Why do you think God would say that David was a man after His own heart? Read Psalm 119:174-175 and Psalm 42:1.

CHAPTER 19

MESSIANIC HOPE

God Is Faithful

As we have witnessed in the Old Testament, sin separates man from God. God has been in faithful pursuit of man's heart ever since we succumbed to sin in the Garden of Eden, and He will until we each take our last breath.

We have just walked through about 1,000 years of history with the Hebrew people, and we have seen the persistence of God in preserving a family line—a remnant of people who would choose to love and obey Him. He chose them, redeemed them from Egypt, guided them, protected them, gave them a specified piece of land to live on, fought their enemies, and He traveled with them.

He gave them boundaries, but He also gave them a free will and a free choice. Just like with all of humanity, they often made choices that led them to their own bed of suffering and bondage—and sometimes to their own demise. However, God had a plan, and His covenant people were to play a major role in bringing it to pass. He would not break His promises He had made with their forefathers, Abraham, Isaac, and Jacob and his descendants. At a time, when needed the most, He took David, a shepherd boy, and made him a king to restore worship and atonement and all that had fallen in shambles through their unbelief and rebellion. Not only that, but we find that He also inspired David and others to write words of Messianic hope for the future about a righteous King who would be coming to rule and reign over them forever.

Messianic Prophesies In the Psalms

"One of the most important factors in the national survival of Israel has been the Messianic hope. This hope centres on the return of the age of David whose reign in the past marked the golden age in Israel's history: and it is against this background that the Messianic hope in the Psalter should be viewed. The picture of the Messiah that emerges from the Psalter is a twofold one. First, since Messiah is to be a scion (implant) of the Davidic dynasty, he is to be the King of the Messianic age... Secondly, the Psalter also prepares men's minds for a suffering Messiah."[1]

Listed below are a few prophetic scriptures about this suffering Messiah—the Christ Who was to come. David wrote all but two of these prophecies. Even though, the words "Christ" and "Messiah" are not actually quoted in these Psalms, there can be no doubt that they are speaking of Him. A few scriptures have also been chosen to confirm the fulfillment of these prophecies, but there are many more recorded in the New Testament.

Prophecies of Christ's Persecution and Crucifixion: (written by David)

Psalms 22:1-31:

(V1) "My God, my God, why hast thou forsaken me? Why art thou so far from helping me, and from the words of my roaring?

V6-8 *"I am a worm, and no man; a reproach of men, and despised of the people. All they that see me laugh me to scorn: they shoot out the lip, they shake the head, saying, He trusted on the LORD that he would deliver him: let him deliver him, seeing he delighted in him.*

V13-18 *"They gaped upon me with their mouths, as a ravening and a roaring lion. I am poured out like water, and all my bones are out of joint: my heart is like wax; it is melted in the midst of my bowels. My strength is dried up like a potsherd; and my tongue cleaveth to my jaws; and thou hast brought me into the dust of death. For dogs have compassed me: the assembly of the wicked have inclosed me: they pierced my hands and my feet. I may tell all my bones: they look and stare upon me. They part my garments among them, and cast lots upon my vesture.*

V29-31 *"All they that be fat upon earth shall eat and worship: all they that go down to the dust shall bow before him: and none can keep him alive his own soul. A seed shall serve him; it shall be accounted to the LORD for a generation. They shall come, and shall declare his righteousness unto a people that shall be born, that he hath done this."*

Psalm 34:20:

"He keepeth all his bones: not one of them is broken."

Psalm 35:11:

"False witnesses did rise up; they laid to my charge things that I knew not."

Psalm 35:19:

"Let not them that are mine enemies wrongfully rejoice over me: neither let them wink with the eye that hate me without a cause."

Psalm 69:18-21:

"Draw nigh unto my soul, and redeem it: deliver me because of mine enemies. Thou hast known my reproach, and my shame, and my dishonor: mine adversaries are all before thee. Reproach hath broken my heart; and I am full of heaviness: and I looked for some to take pity, but there was none; and for comforters, but I found none. They gave me also gall for my meat; and in my thirst they gave me vinegar to drink."

Fulfillment of the above prophecies is found in the following New Testament Scriptures:

John 19:31-37; Matthew 27:26-50; and Luke 23:33-38

Prophecy of Christ's <u>Descension and Resurrection</u>: (written by David)

Psalm 16:8-10 (written by David):

"I have set the LORD always before me: because he is at my right hand, I shall not be moved. Therefore my heart is glad, and my glory rejoiceth: my flesh also shall rest in hope. For thou wilt not leave my soul in hell; neither wilt thou suffer thine Holy One to see corruption."

Psalm 49:14-15 (unknown author):

"Like sheep they are laid in the grave; death shall feed on them; and the upright shall have dominion over them in the morning; and their beauty shall consume in the grave from their dwelling. But God will redeem my soul from the power of the grave; for he shall receive me. Selah."

Fulfillment of the above prophecies is found in the following New Testament Scriptures:

Matthew 28:1-17; Mark 16:1-14; Luke 24:1-12; and Acts 2:30-36

Prophecy of Christ's <u>Ascension:</u> (written by David)

Psalm 68:18:

"Thou hast ascended on high, thou hast led captivity captive: thou hast received gifts for men; yea, for the rebellious also, that the LORD God might dwell among them."

Psalm 110:

(V1) *"The LORD said unto my LORD, Sit thou at my right hand, until I make thine enemies thy footstool.*

(V4) *"The LORD hath sworn, and will not repent, Thou art a priest for ever after the order of Melchiz´-edek."*

(Remember, Melchizedek had no beginning and no ending.)

Fulfillment of the above prophecies is found in the following New Testament Scriptures:

Mark 16:19; Luke 24:50-51; John 20:17; Acts 2:34-36; Ephesians 1:19-23, 4:8-10; and Hebrews 5:5-10, and 10:12-13.

Besides David's writings in the Psalms, there are writings by the sons of Korah, Asaph, Ethan, and Solomon, and Moses. Asaph and Ethan were two of the singers chosen by the Levites to sound the brass cymbals during the second attempt to carry the Ark to Jerusalem. Here are two other Messianic Psalms whose authors are not known:

Prophecy of <u>Christ, God's Son</u>: (unknown author)

Psalm 2:

"Why do the heathen rage, and the people imagine a vain thing? The kings of the earth set themselves, and the rulers take counsel together against the LORD, and against his Anointed, saying, Let us break their bands asunder, and cast away their cords from us. He that sitteth in the heavens shall laugh: the LORD shall have them in derision. Then shall he speak unto them in his wrath, and vex them in his sore displeasure.

"Yet have I set my King upon my holy hill of Zion. I will declare the decree: the LORD hath said unto me, Thou art my Son; this

day have I begotten thee. Ask of me, and I shall give thee the heathen for thine inheritance, and the uttermost parts of the earth for thy possession.

"Thou shalt break them with a rod of iron; thou shalt dash them in pieces like a potter's vessel. Be wise now therefore, O ye kings: be instructed, ye judges of the earth. Serve the LORD with fear, and rejoice with trembling. Kiss the Son, leset he be angry, and ye perish from the way, when his wrath is kindled but a little. Blessed are all they that put their trust in him."

Fulfillment of the above prophecies is found in the following New Testament Scriptures:

Matthew 3:16-17.

The Jews were, and many are still today, looking for the Messiah—the One Who will reign and rule as David did so long ago. They do not believe that the Messiah has come yet and are still looking for Him to come from the seed of David, as promised in this Psalm:

"The LORD hath sworn in truth unto David; he will not turn from it; Of the fruit of thy body will I set upon thy throne. If thy children will keep my covenant and my testimony that I shall teach them, their children shall also sit upon thy throne for evermore. For the LORD hath chosen Zion; he hath desired it for his habitation" (Psalm 132:11-12).

It was through David's seed that Christ, the Messiah, did come in the flesh. History documents that. Matthew 1:1-6 records the genealogy of Jesus Christ, beginning with this scripture: *"THE book of the generation of Jesus Christ, the son of David, the son of Abraham."* Fourteen generations are recorded from Abraham to David: Abraham, Isaac, Jacob, Judas (Judah in Greek), Pharez, Hezron, Ram, Amminadab, Nahshon, Salmon, Boaz, Obed, Jesse, and David the king. Jacob, who was renamed Israel had twelve sons, but the family line to Jesus begins with Judah, the third son, positioning Jesus in the royal line of kings from the tribe of Judah. Listen to the prophesy written in Micah 5:2:

> *"But thou <u>Beth-lehem</u> Eph´-ra-tah, though thou be little among the thousands <u>of Judah</u>, yet out of thee shall he come forth unto me that is to be ruler in Israel; whose goings forth have been from old, from everlasting."*

The Rock and the Stone

The Psalmists declare in at least fourteen verses that God is their *"Rock,"* and most profoundly, that He is the *"<u>Rock of Israel</u>"* and the *"<u>Rock of Salvation</u>."* The Apostle Paul, a Jew who was visited by Christ after His Ascension, converted to Christianity. He makes this surprising announcement in 1 Corinthians 10:1-4:

> *"...our fathers were under the cloud, and all passed through the sea; And were all baptized unto Moses in the cloud and in the sea; And did all eat the same spiritual meat; And did all drink the same spiritual drink: for they drank of that spiritual Rock that followed them* (went with them): *and <u>that Rock was Christ</u>."*

> In 2 Samuel 22:47, David says, *"The LORD liveth; and blessed be my rock; and exalted be the <u>God of the rock</u> of my salvation."*

If we believe that Christ is God, the Son, within the Trinity, then we know that Christ was with the Jews through their entire journey.

EPILOGUE

Psalm 118:21-23 looks forward to <u>Jesus Christ</u>, Who had not yet come. The prophet who wrote this Psalm referred to Him as the *"<u>Stone</u>"* and his *"<u>salvation</u>:"* *"I will praise thee: for thou hast heard me, and art become my <u>salvation</u>. The <u>stone</u> which the builders refused is become the <u>head stone</u> of the corner. This is the LORD'S doing; it is marvelous in our eyes."*

If you have been blessed by the things you have read in this book, you won't want to miss Book 2 in this series. We will, once again, join the Israelites and their new king, Solomon, who will build God's cedar house. We will finish our journey with them all the way to the cross where the redemption for all mankind will take place. We will discover how the actions of the wicked kings who reign after king Solomon will determine the fate of the people in both Israel and Judah. We will hear the cries of the prophets of God as they give to them warnings and prophecies about the future in an attempt to turn them back to God; and we will plunge with them into exile and experience their suffering for not doing so. Even then, God will not forget His covenant with their forefathers and will extend His hand of mercy and grace to them.

We will be there when Jesus arrives on the scene to bring a new covenant to fulfill the promises given to Abraham and his descendants; and we will find that He will be rejected by many of those descendants.

Through God's covenant of law, He established His holiness. Through the new covenant of grace through Christ, He gave His righteousness and eternal life to all who believe and accept what He has done for them.

Christ, the Rock, who traveled with the Israelites in the Old Testament, has already become the head Cornerstone. He has united those who had faith in the promises of the Messiah, Who was to come, with those who have faith through the Christ Who did come. That same Christ is coming back again to be our Judge and our King. In Book 2, we will be catching a few glimpses of the events leading up to His return. We will read about "the day of the Lord" and learn about the future that awaits for those who have been cleansed by His blood and for those who have not.

May God bless your hearts and your minds as you continue to search for the truth of the living God.

RESOURCES

Chapter 1

1. James Strong, S.T.D., LL.D., A CONCISE DICTIONARY OF THE WORDS IN THE HEBREW BIBLE IN *STRONG'S EXHAUSTIVE CONCORDANCE OF THE BIBLE* (Nashville: Royal Publishers, Inc.), p. 12, #430
2. Ibid p. 12, #433
3. James Strong, S.T.D., LL.D., A CONCISE DICTIONARY OF THE WORDS IN THE GREEK TESTAMENT in *STRONG'S EXHAUSTIVE CONCORDANCE OF THE BIBLE* (Nashville: Royal Publishers, Inc.), p. 35, #2307
4. James Strong, S.T.D., LL.D., A CONCISE DICTIONARY OF THE WORDS IN THE HEBREW BIBLE IN *STRONG'S EXHAUSTIVE CONCORDANCE OF THE BIBLE* (Nashville: Royal Publishers, Inc.), p. 102, #6942
5. Ibid, p. 47, #3068
6. J.I. Packer and D.J. Wiseman, *NEW BIBLE DICTIONARY, THIRD* EDITION (Leicester, England and Downers Grove: Inter-varsity Press, Reprinted 2006) p. 290
7. Ibid p 753
8. James Strong, S.T.D., LL.D., A CONCISE DICTIONARY OF THE WORDS IN THE HEBREW BIBLE IN *STRONG'S EXHAUSTIVE CONCORDANCE OF THE BIBLE* (Nashville: Royal Publishers, Inc.), p. 85, #5729
9. James Strong, S.T.D., LL.D., A CONCISE DICTIONARY OF THE WORDS IN THE HEBREW BIBLE IN STRONG'S EXHAUSTIVE CONCORDANCE OF THE BIBLE (Nashville: Royal Publishers, Inc.), p. 8, #121
10. J.I. Packer and D.J. Wiseman, NEW BIBLE DICTIONARY, THIRD EDITION (Leicester, England and Downers Grove, Illinois: Inter-varsity Press, Reprinted 2006) p. 239

Chapter 2

1. James Strong, S.T.D., LL.D., A CONCISE DICTIONARY OF THE WORDS IN THE HEBREW BIBLE in *STRONG'S EXHAUSTIVE CONCORDANCE OF THE BIBLE* (Nashville: Royal Publishers, Inc.), p. 80, #5377

2. Ibid p. 11, #2233
3. Ibid p.111, #7611
4. R. Laird Harris, Gleason L. Archer, Jr., Bruce K. Waltke, *Theological Wordbook of the Old Testament*, (Chicago: Moody Publishers, 1980), p. 253

Chapter 3

1. R. Laird Harris, Gleason L. Archer, Jr., Bruce K. Waltke, *Theological Wordbook of the Old Testament*, (Chicago: Moody Publishers, 1980), p. 114
2. James Strong, S.T.D., LL.D., A CONCISE DICTIONARY OF THE WORDS IN THE HEBREW BIBLE in *STRONG'S EXHAUSTIVE CONCORDANCE OF THE BIBLE* (Nashville: Royal Publishers, Inc.), p. 28, #1613
3. Ibid p. 24, #1285
4. *LUTHER'S small Catechism*, (Saint Louis: Concordia Publishing House, 1943), p. 178
5. Ibid p. 97

Chapter 4

1. Pat and David Alexander, *ZONDERVAN HANDBOOK TO THE BIBLE,* (Grand Rapids: Zondervan Publishing House, 1999), p. 134
2. THE GREATEST ARCHAELOLOGICAL DISCOVERIES *in the HOLY BIBLE, KING JAMES VERSION, PTL COUNSELLORS EDITION,* (Nashville: Thomas Nelson, Inc., Publishers, 1975), p. 1230
3. Pat and David Alexander, ZONDERVAN HANDBOOK TO THE BIBLE, (Grand Rapids: Zondervan Publishing House, 1999), pp. 132, 133
4. J.I. Packer and D.J. Wiseman, NEW BIBLE DICTIONARY, THIRD EDITION (Leicester, England and Downers Grove: Inter-varsity Press, Reprinted 2006) p. 444 and 1219
5. James Strong, S.T.D., LL.D., A CONCISE DICTIONARY OF THE WORDS IN THE GREEK TESTAMENT in *STRONG'S EXHAUSTIVE CONCORDANCE OF THE BIBLE* (Nashville: Royal Publishers, Inc.). p. 25, #1482

Chapter 5

1. James Strong, S.T.D., LL.D., A CONCISE DICTIONARY OF THE WORDS IN THE HEBREW BIBLE in *STRONG'S EXHAUSTIVE CONCORDANCE OF THE BIBLE* (Nashville: Royal Publishers, Inc.), p. 125, #8549
2. Ibid p. 8, #87
3. Ibid p. 8, #85
4. Ibid p. 79, #5243

5. Ibid p. 24, #1285
6. Ibid p. 121, #8297
7. Ibid p. 121, #8282, 8283
8. Ibid p. 51, #3327
9. Ibid p. 47, #3068
10. Ibid p. 99, #6711
11. Ibid p. 12, #410
12. Ibid p. 47, #3070
13. Pat and David Alexander, *ZONDERVAN HANDBOOK TO THE BIBLE* (Grand Rapids. Zondervan Publishing House, 1999), p. 139
14. J.I. Packer and D.J. Wiseman, *NEW BIBLE DICTIONARY, THIRD* EDITION (Leicester, England and Downers Grove: Inter-varsity Press, Reprinted 2006) p. 783
15. James Strong, S.T.D., LL.D., A CONCISE DICTIONARY OF THE WORDS IN THE GREEK TESTAMENT in *STRONG'S EXHAUSTIVE CONCORDANCE OF THE BIBLE* (Nashville: Royal Publishers, Inc.). p. 40, #2675
16. Ibid p. 71, #5048
17. Ibid p. 32, #2005
18. Ibid p. 16, #739
19. Ibid p. 71, #5048

Chapter 6

1. Pat and David Alexander, *ZONDERVAN HANDBOOK TO THE BIBLE* (Grand Rapids: Zondervan Publishing House, 1999), p. 139
2. James Strong, S.T.D., LL.D., A CONCISE DICTIONARY OF THE WORDS IN THE HEBREW BIBLE in *STRONG'S EXHAUSTIVE CONCORDANCE OF THE BIBLE* (Nashville: Royal Publishers, Inc.), p. 51, #3290
3. Pat and David Alexander, *ZONDERVAN HANDBOOK TO THE BIBLE* (Grand Rapids: Zondervan Publishing House, 1999), p. 140
4. James Strong, S.T.D., LL.D., A CONCISE DICTIONARY OF THE WORDS IN THE HEBREW BIBLE in *STRONG'S EXHAUSTIVE CONCORDANCE OF THE BIBLE* (Nashville: Royal Publishers, Inc.), p. 65, #4266
5. Ibid p.1437, #4724

Chapter 7

1. James Strong, S.T.D., LL.D., A CONCISE DICTIONARY OF THE WORDS IN THE HEBREW BIBLE in *STRONG'S EXHAUSTIVE CONCORDANCE OF THE BIBLE* (Nashville: Royal Publishers, Inc.), p. 111, #7611
2. Ibid p. 115, #7886
3. Merriam-Webster's Collegiate ®Dictionary, 11th Edition ©2012 by Merriam-Webster, Incorporated (www.Merriam-Webster.com), p. 421

Chapter 8

1. Thomas V. Brisco, *HOLMAN BIBLE ATLAS*, a Complete guide to the Expansive Geography of Biblical History (Nashville: Broadman & Holman Publishers, 1998), p. 52
2. Pat and David Alexander, *ZONDERVAN HANDBOOK TO THE BIBLE* (Grand Rapids: Zondervan Publishing House, 1999), p. 159
3. James Strong, S.T.D., LL.D., A CONCISE DICTIONARY OF THE WORDS IN THE HEBREW BIBLE in *STRONG'S EXHAUSTIVE CONCORDANCE OF THE BIBLE* (Nashville: Royal Publishers, Inc.), p. 47, #3045
4. Ibid p. 43, #2722
5. Ibid p. 52, #3372
6. Ibid p. 32, #1961
7. Ibid p. 47, #3068
8. Ibid p. 25, #1350
9. Pat and David Alexander, *ZONDERVAN HANDBOOK TO THE BIBLE* (Grand Rapids: Zondervan Publishing House, 1999), p. 164
10. Ibid p. 164
11. Pat and David Alexander, *ZONDERVAN HANDBOOK TO THE BIBLE* (Grand Rapids: Zondervan Publishing House, 1999), p. 164
12. Ibid p. 164
13. J.I. Packer and D.J. Wiseman, *NEW BIBLE DICTIONARY, THIRD* EDITION (Leicester, England and Downers Grove: Inter-varsity Press, Reprinted 2006) p. 465
14. Pat and David Alexander, *ZONDERVAN HANDBOOK TO THE BIBLE* (Grand Rapids: Zondervan Publishing House, 1999), p. 164
15. James Strong, S.T.D., LL.D., A CONCISE DICTIONARY OF THE WORDS IN THE HEBREW BIBLE in *STRONG'S EXHAUSTIVE CONCORDANCE OF THE BIBLE* (Nashville: Royal Publishers, Inc.), p. 10, #226
16. James Strong, S.T.D., LL.D., A CONCISE DICTIONARY OF THE WORDS IN THE GREEK TESTAMENT in *STRONG'S EXHAUSTIVE CONCORDANCE OF THE BIBLE* (Nashville: Royal Publishers, Inc.). p. 45, #3083

Chapter 9

1. Pat and David Alexander, *ZONDERVAN HANDBOOK TO THE BIBLE* (Grand Rapids: Zondervan Publishing House, 1999), p. 165
2. James Strong, S.T.D., LL.D., A CONCISE DICTIONARY OF THE WORDS IN THE HEBREW BIBLE in *STRONG'S EXHAUSTIVE CONCORDANCE OF THE BIBLE* (Nashville: Royal Publishers, Inc.), p. 102, #6942
3. Ibid p. 93, #6299
4. Ibid p. 79, #5254
5. Ibid p. 124, #8482
6. Ibid p. 54, #3548
7. Ibid p. 54, #3519
8. Pat and David Alexander, *ZONDERVAN HANDBOOK TO THE BIBLE* (Grand Rapids: Zondervan Publishing House, 1999), p.179

Chapter 10

1. J.I. Packer and D.J. Wiseman, *NEW BIBLE DICTIONARY, THIRD* EDITION (Leicester, England and Downers Grove: Inter-varsity Press, Reprinted 2006) p. 1145
2. James Strong, S.T.D., LL.D., A CONCISE DICTIONARY OF THE WORDS IN THE HEBREW BIBLE in *STRONG'S EXHAUSTIVE CONCORDANCE OF THE BIBLE* (Nashville: Royal Publishers, Inc.), p.120, #8245
3. J.I. Packer and D.J. Wiseman, *NEW BIBLE DICTIONARY, THIRD* EDITION (Leicester, England and Downers Grove: Inter-varsity Press, Reprinted 2006) p. 504
4. James Strong, S.T.D., LL.D., A CONCISE DICTIONARY OF THE WORDS IN THE HEBREW BIBLE in *STRONG'S EXHAUSTIVE CONCORDANCE OF THE BIBLE* (Nashville: Royal Publishers, Inc.), p. 115, #7848
5. Biblical Cyclopedic Index, Tabernacle *HOLY BIBLE, KING JAMES VERSION, PTL COUNSELLORS EDITION,* (Nashville: Thomas Nelson, Inc., Publishers, 1975), p. 285
6. James Strong, S.T.D., LL.D., A CONCISE DICTIONARY OF THE WORDS IN THE HEBREW BIBLE in *STRONG'S EXHAUSTIVE CONCORDANCE OF THE BIBLE* (Nashville: Royal Publishers, Inc.), p. 57, #3742
7. James Strong, S.T.D., LL.D., A CONCISE DICTIONARY OF THE WORDS IN THE GREEK TESTAMENT in *STRONG'S EXHAUSTIVE CONCORDANCE OF THE BIBLE* (Nashville: Royal Publishers, Inc.). p. 37, #2435
8. J.I. Packer and D.J. Wiseman, *NEW BIBLE DICTIONARY, THIRD* EDITION (Leicester, England and Downers Grove: Inter-varsity Press, Reprinted 2006) p. 1148

9. James Strong, S.T.D., LL.D., A CONCISE DICTIONARY OF THE WORDS IN THE HEBREW BIBLE in *STRONG'S EXHAUSTIVE CONCORDANCE OF THE BIBLE* (Nashville: Royal Publishers, Inc.), p. 54, #3519

10. Ibid p. 115, #7848

11. Ibid p. 58, #3828

Chapter 11

1. James Strong, S.T.D., LL.D., A CONCISE DICTIONARY OF THE WORDS IN THE GREEK TESTAMENT in *STRONG'S EXHAUSTIVE CONCORDANCE OF THE BIBLE* (Nashville: Royal Publishers, Inc.). p. 17, #859

2. James Strong, S.T.D., LL.D., A CONCISE DICTIONARY OF THE WORDS IN THE HEBREW BIBLE in *STRONG'S EXHAUSTIVE CONCORDANCE OF THE BIBLE* (Nashville: Royal Publishers, Inc.), p. 57, #3722

3. Ibid p. 80, #5315

4. Merriam-Webster's Collegiate ®Dictionary, 11th Edition ©2012 by Merriam-Webster, Incorporated (www.Merriam-Webster.com), p. 1094

5. R. Laird Harris, Gleason L. Archer, Jr., Bruce K. Waltke, *Theological Wordbook of the Old Testament*, (Chicago: Moody Publishers, 1980), p. 77

6. Pat and David Alexander, *ZONDERVAN HANDBOOK TO THE BIBLE* (Grand Rapids: Zondervan Publishing House, 1999), p. 180

7. James Strong, S.T.D., LL.D., A CONCISE DICTIONARY OF THE WORDS IN THE HEBREW BIBLE in *STRONG'S EXHAUSTIVE CONCORDANCE OF THE BIBLE* (Nashville: Royal Publishers, Inc.), p. 108, #7381

8. Pat and David Alexander, *ZONDERVAN HANDBOOK TO THE BIBLE* (Grand Rapids: Zondervan Publishing House, 1999), p. 180

9. Biblical Cyclopedic Index, Tabernacle *HOLY BIBLE, KING JAMES VERSION, PTL COUNSELLORS EDITION*, (Nashville: Thomas Nelson, Inc., Publishers, 1975), p. 238

10. Pat and David Alexander, *ZONDERVAN HANDBOOK TO THE BIBLE* (Grand Rapids: Zondervan Publishing House, 1999), p. 185

Chapter 12

1. J.I. Packer and D.J. Wiseman, *NEW BIBLE DICTIONARY, THIRD* EDITION (Leicester, England and Downers Grove: Inter-varsity Press, Reprinted 2006) p. 164

2. Pat and David Alexander, *ZONDERVAN HANDBOOK TO THE BIBLE* (Grand Rapids: Zondervan Publishing House, 1999), p. 187

3. Ibid p. 184

4. Ibid p. 184

5. Ibid p. 189
6. James Strong, S.T.D., LL.D., A CONCISE DICTIONARY OF THE WORDS IN THE HEBREW BIBLE in *STRONG'S EXHAUSTIVE CONCORDANCE OF THE BIBLE* (Nashville: Royal Publishers, Inc.), p. 43, #2763
7. Ibid p. 43, #2764
8. Ibid p. 102, #6918

Chapter 13 N/A

Chapter 14

1. James Strong, S.T.D., LL.D., A CONCISE DICTIONARY OF THE WORDS IN THE HEBREW BIBLE in *STRONG'S EXHAUSTIVE CONCORDANCE OF THE BIBLE* (Nashville: Royal Publishers, Inc.), p. 68, #4531
2. Ibid p. 63, #4172
3. Ibid p. 98, #6680

Chapter 15

1. James Strong, S.T.D., LL.D., A CONCISE DICTIONARY OF THE WORDS IN THE HEBREW BIBLE in *STRONG'S EXHAUSTIVE CONCORDANCE OF THE BIBLE* (Nashville: Royal Publishers, Inc.), p. 43, #2764

Chapter 16

1. James Strong, S.T.D., LL.D., A CONCISE DICTIONARY OF THE WORDS IN THE HEBREW BIBLE in *STRONG'S EXHAUSTIVE CONCORDANCE OF THE BIBLE* (Nashville: Royal Publishers, Inc.), p. 47, #3063
2. Ibid p. 111, #7626
3. Ibid p. 43, #2710
4. Ibid p. 115, #7886
5. Pat and David Alexander, *ZONDERVAN HANDBOOK TO THE BIBLE* (Grand Rapids: Zondervan Publishing House, 1999), p. 239
6. Ibid p. 240
7. THE SCARLET THREAD OF REDEMPTION, *HOLY BIBLE, KING JAMES VERSION, PTL COUNSELLORS EDITION*, (Nashville: Thomas Nelson, Inc., Publishers, 1975), p. 1250
8. Pat and David Alexander, *ZONDERVAN HANDBOOK TO THE BIBLE* (Grand Rapids: Zondervan Publishing House, 1999), p. 239

9. Ibid p. 244
10. Biblical Cyclopedic Index, Tabernacle *HOLY BIBLE, KING JAMES VERSION, PTL COUNSELLORS EDITION*, (Nashville: Thomas Nelson, Inc., Publishers, 1975), p. 166
11. Pat and David Alexander, *ZONDERVAN HANDBOOK TO THE BIBLE* (Grand Rapids: Zondervan Publishing House, 1999), p. 256
12. Thomas V. Brisco, *HOLMAN BIBLE ATLAS*, a Complete guide to the Expansive Geography of Biblical History (Nashville: Broadman & Holman Publishers, 1998), p. 94-95

Chapter 17

1. Pat and David Alexander, *ZONDERVAN HANDBOOK TO THE BIBLE* (Grand Rapids: Zondervan Publishing House, 1999), p. 256
2. James Strong, S.T.D., LL.D., A CONCISE DICTIONARY OF THE WORDS IN THE HEBREW BIBLE in *STRONG'S EXHAUSTIVE CONCORDANCE OF THE BIBLE* (Nashville: Royal Publishers, Inc.), p. 29, #1712
3. Pat and David Alexander, *ZONDERVAN HANDBOOK TO THE BIBLE* (Grand Rapids: Zondervan Publishing House, 1999), p. 258

Chapter 18

1. James Strong, S.T.D., LL.D., A CONCISE DICTIONARY OF THE WORDS IN THE HEBREW BIBLE in *STRONG'S EXHAUSTIVE CONCORDANCE OF THE BIBLE* (Nashville: Royal Publishers, Inc.), p. 47, #3041
2. Ibid p. 47, #3050
3. Ibid p. 38, #2374
4. James Strong, S.T.D., LL.D., A CONCISE DICTIONARY OF THE WORDS IN THE HEBREW BIBLE in *STRONG'S EXHAUSTIVE CONCORDANCE OF THE BIBLE* (Nashville: Royal Publishers, Inc.), p. 30, #1732

Chapter 19

1. J.I. Packer and D.J. Wiseman, *NEW BIBLE DICTIONARY, THIRD EDITION* (Leicester, England and Downers Grove: Inter-varsity Press, Reprinted 2006) p. 984

BIBLIOGRAPHY

1. Biblical Cyclopedic Index, Tabernacle *HOLY BIBLE, KING JAMES VERSION, PTL COUNSELLORS EDITION*, (Nashville: Thomas Nelson, Inc., Publishers, 1975)

2. HOLY BIBLE, KINGS JAMES VERSION, PTL COUNSELLORS EDITION (Nashville: Thomas Nelson, Inc., Publishers, 1975)

3. James Strong, S.T.D., LL.D., A CONCISE DICTIONARY OF THE WORDS IN THE GREEK TESTAMENT in *STRONG'S EXHAUSTIVE CONCORDANCE OF THE BIBLE* (Nashville: Royal Publishers, Inc.)

4. James Strong, S.T.D., LL.D., A CONCISE DICTIONARY OF THE WORDS IN THE HEBREW BIBLE in *STRONG'S EXHAUSTIVE CONCORDANCE OF THE BIBLE* (Nashville: Royal Publishers, Inc.)

5. J.I. Packer and D. J. Wiseman, *NEW BIBLE DICTIONARY, THIRD* EDITION (Leicester, England and Downers Grove: Inter-varsity Press, Reprinted 2006)

6. *LUTHER'S Small Catechism*, (Saint Louis: Concordia Publishing House, 1943)

7. Merriam-Webster's Collegiate ®Dictionary, 11ᵗʰ Edition ©2012 by Merriam-Webster, Incorporated (www.Merriam-Webster.com)

8. Pat and David Alexander, Rapid Factfinder in *ZONDERVAN HANDBOOK TO THE BIBLE* (Grand Rapids: Zondervan Publishing House, 1999)

9. R. Laird Harris, Gleason L. Archer, Jr., Bruce K. Waltke, *Theological Wordbook of the Old Testament*, (Chicago: Moody Publishers, 1980)

10. THE GREATEST ARCHAELOLOGICAL DISCOVERIES *in the HOLY BIBLE, KING JAMES VERSION, PTL COUNSELLORS EDITION*, (Nashville: Thomas Nelson, Inc., Publishers, 1975)

11. *The Holy Bible, New International Version* (Grand Rapids: Zondervan Publishing House, 2011)

12. THE SCARLET THREAD OF REDEMPTION, *HOLY BIBLE, KING JAMES VERSION, PTL COUNSELLORS EDITION*, (Nashville: Thomas Nelson, Inc., Publishers, 1975)

13. Thomas V. Brisco, *HOLMAN BIBLE ATLAS*, a Complete guide to the Expansive Geography of Biblical History (Nashville: Broadman & Holman Publishers, 1998)

ILLUSTRATIONS

Illustrations by Joe Olivio + Carol Olivio + Joshua N. Crosby, The Tabernacle Tour, (Powell, TN, 1992), pp. 10-65:

Map by Thomas V. Brisco, *HOLMAN BIBLE ATLAS,* a Complete guide to the Expansive Geography of Biblical History (Nashville: Broadman & Holman Publishers, 1998) p. 84: